THE

# ILIAD OF HOMER

*TRANSLATED INTO ENGLISH BLANK VERSE*

BY

WILLIAM CULLEN BRYANT

VOLUME II.

BOSTON
FIELDS, OSGOOD, & CO.
1871

University Press: Welch, Bigelow, & Co.,
Cambridge.

# CONTENTS

## OF VOL. II.

---

## BOOK XVI.

### THE SIXTH BATTLE.—DEATH OF PATROCLUS.



## BOOK XVII.

### THE SEVENTH BATTLE.



## BOOK XVIII.

### THE GRIEF OF ACHILLES FOR THE DEATH OF PATROCLUS.

## BOOK XIX.

### THE RECONCILIATION OF ACHILLES AND AGAMEMNON.



## BOOK XX.

### THE BATTLE OF THE GODS.



## BOOK XXI.

### THE BATTLE IN THE RIVER SCAMANDER.

# *Contents.*

## BOOK XXII.

### THE DEATH OF HECTOR.



## BOOK XXIII.

### THE FUNERAL OF PATROCLUS.



## BOOK XXIV.

### THE BODY OF HECTOR RECOVERED.

# THE ILIAD.

# THE ILIAD.

## *BOOK XIII.*

WHEN Jove had brought the Trojans and their chief,
Hector, beside the ships, he left them there
To toil and struggle and endure, while he
Turned his resplendent eyes upon the land
Of Thracian horsemen, and the Mysians, skilled
To combat hand to hand, and the famed tribe
Of long-lived Hippomulgi, reared on milk,
And the most just of men. On Troy no more
He turned those glorious eyes, for now he deemed
That none of all the gods would seek to aid
Either the Greeks or Trojans in the strife.
The monarch Neptune kept no idle watch;
For he in Thracian Samos, dark with woods,
Aloft upon the highest summit sat,
O'erlooking thence the tumult of the war;

For thence could he behold the Idæan mount,
And Priam's city, and the Grecian fleet.
There, coming from the ocean-deeps, he sat,
And pitied the Greek warriors put to rout
Before the Trojans, and was wroth with Jove.
Soon he descended from those rugged steeps,
And trod the earth with rapid strides; the hills
And forests quaked beneath the immortal feet
Of Neptune as he walked. Three strides he took,
And at the fourth reached Ægæ, where he stopped,
And where his sumptuous palace-halls were built,
Deep down in ocean, golden, glittering, proof
Against decay of time. These when he reached,
He yoked his swift and brazen-footed steeds,
With manes of flowing gold, to draw his car,
And put on golden mail, and took his scourge,
Wrought of fine gold, and climbed the chariot-seat,
And rode upon the waves. The whales came forth
From their deep haunts, and frolicked round his way:
They knew their king. The waves rejoicing smoothed
A path, and rapidly the coursers flew;
Nor was the brazen axle wet below.
And thus they brought him to the Grecian fleet.

Deep in the sea there is a spacious cave,

Between the rugged Imbrus and the isle
Of Tenedos. There Neptune, he who shakes
The shores, held back his steeds, took off their yoke,
Gave them ambrosial food, and, binding next
Their feet with golden fetters which no power
Might break or loosen, so that they might wait
Their lord's return, he sought the Grecian host.
  Still did the Trojans, rushing on in crowds,
Like flames or like a tempest, follow close
Hector, the son of Priam; still their rage
Abated not; with stormy cries they came;
They hoped to seize the fleet and slay the Greeks
Beside it. But the power who swathes the earth
And shakes it, Neptune, coming from the deep,
Revived the valor of the Greeks. He took
The shape of Calchas and his powerful voice,
And thus to either Ajax, who yet stemmed
The battle with a resolute heart, he spake:—
  "O chieftains! yours it is to save the host,
Recalling your old valor, with no thought
Of fatal flight. Elsewhere I feel no dread
Of what the daring sons of Troy may do
Who climb the wall in throngs; the well-greaved Greeks
Will meet them bravely. But where Hector leads,

Fierce as a flame, his squadrons, he who boasts
To be a son of sovereign Jove, I fear
Lest we should sorely suffer. May the gods
Strengthen your hearts to stand against the foe,
And flinch not, and exhort the rest to stand,
And drive him back, audacious as he is,
From the swift ships, though Jove should urge him on."
  Thus earth-surrounding Neptune said, and touched
Each hero with his sceptre, filled their hearts
With valor, gave new lightness to their limbs
And feet and hands, and then, as when a hawk
Shoots swiftly from some lofty precipice
And chases o'er the plain another bird,
So swiftly Neptune, shaker of the shores,
Darted from them away. Oïleus' son
Perceived the immortal presence first, and thus
At once to Telamonian Ajax spake:—
  "Some god, O Ajax, from the Olympian hill,
Wearing the augur's form, hath bid us fight
Beside the ships; nor can it be the seer
Calchas, for well I marked his feet and legs
As he departed; easily by these
The gods are known. I feel a spirit roused
In my own bosom eager to engage

In the fierce strife; my very feet below,
And hands above, take part in the desire."
  And thus the son of Telamon replied:—
"So also these strong hands that grasp the spear
Burn eagerly to wield it, and my heart
Is full of courage. I am hurried on
By both my feet, and vehemently long
To try alone the combat with this chief
Of boundless valor, Hector, Priam's son."
  Thus they conferred, rejoicing as they felt
That ardor for the battle which the god
Had breathed into their hearts. Meantime he roused
The Achaians at the rear, who in their ships
Sought respite, and whose limbs were faint with toil,
And their hearts sad to see the Trojan host
With tumult pouring o'er the lofty wall.
As they beheld, the tears came gushing forth
From underneath their lids; they little hoped
For rescue from destruction; but when came
The power that shakes the shores, he woke anew
The spirit of their valiant phalanxes.
Teucer he first addressed, and Leïtus,
The hero Peneleus and Thoas next,
Deipyrus, Meriones expert

In battle, and Antilochus his peer,
And thus exhorted them with wingèd words:—
"Shame on you, Argive youths! I put my trust
In your tried valor to defend our fleet;
But if ye fear to face the perilous fight,
The day has risen which shall behold us fall
Vanquished before the Trojans. O ye gods!
These eyes have seen a marvel, a strange sight
And terrible, which I had never thought
Could be,—the Trojans close upon our ships,
They who, erewhile, were like the timid deer
That wander in the wood an easy prey
To jackals, pards, and wolves,—weak things, unapt
For combat, fleeing, but without an aim.
Such were the Trojans, who till now ne'er dared
Withstand the might and prowess of the Greeks
Even for an hour. But now, afar from Troy
They give us battle at the hollow ships,
All through our general's fault, and through the sloth
Of the Greek warriors, who, displeased with him,
Fight not for their swift galleys, but are slain
Beside them. Yet although our sovereign chief,
Atrides Agamemnon, may have done
Foul wrong, dishonoring the swift-footed son

Of Peleus, still ye cannot without blame
Decline the combat. Let us then repair
The mischief done; the hearts of valiant men
Are soon appeased. And not without the loss
Of honor can your fiery courage sleep,
Since ye are known the bravest of the host.
I would not chide the weak, unwarlike man
For shrinking from the combat; but for you,—
I look on you with anger in my heart.
Weaklings! ye soon will bring upon yourselves
Some sorer evil if ye loiter thus.
Let each of you bethink him of the shame
And infamy impending. Terrible
The struggle is before us. Hector storms
The ships, loud-shouting Hector; he has burst
The gate and broken the protecting bar."

So Neptune spake, encouraging the Greeks.
While firmly stood the serried phalanxes
Round either Ajax, nor could Mars himself,
Nor Pallas, musterer of armèd hosts,
Reprove their order. There the flower of Greece
Waited the Trojans and their noble chief,
Spear beside spear, and shield by shield, so close
That buckler pressed on buckler, helm on helm,

And man on man. The plumes of horse-hair touched
Each other as they nodded on the crests
Of the bright helms, so close the warriors stood,
The lances quivered in the fearless hands
Of warriors eager to advance and strike
The enemy. But the men of Troy began
The assault; the fiery Hector was the first
To rush against the Greeks. As when a stone
Rolls from a cliff before a wintry flood
That sweeps it down the steep, when mighty rains
Have worn away the props that held it fast;
It rolls and bounds on high; the woods around
Crash, as it tears its unresisted way
Along the slope until it reach the plain,
And there, however urged, moves on no more;—
So Hector, menacing to cut his way
Through tents and galleys to the very sea,
Slaying as he went forward, when he now
Met the firm phalanxes and pressed them close,
Stopped suddenly; the sons of Greece withstood
His onset and repulsed it, striking him
With swords and two-edged spears, and made the chief
Give way before the shock. He lifted up
His voice and shouted to the Trojans thus:—

"Trojans and Lycians and Dardanians skilled
In fighting hand to hand, stand firm. Not long
Will the Greeks bide my onset, though drawn up
Square as a tower in close array. My spear,
I trust, will scatter them, if true it be
That Juno's husband, Sovereign of the gods,
And Lord of thunders, prompts my arm to-day."
He spake, and kindled in the breasts of all
Fresh courage. In the band Deiphobus
Marched proudly, Priam's son, with his round shield
Before him, walking with a quick, light step
Behind its shelter. Then Meriones
Aimed at the chief his glittering spear; the point
Missed not; it struck the orb of bullock's hide,
Yet did not pierce it, for the weapon broke
Just at the neck. Deiphobus held forth
His shield far from him, dreading to receive
A spear-thrust from the brave Meriones.
Vexed thus to lose the victory, and the spear
Snapped by the blow, Meriones fell back
Into the column of his friends, and passed
Hastily toward the camp and ships, to bring
A powerful spear that stood within his tent,
While others fought, and fearful was the din.

Then Teucer first, the son of Telamon,
Smote gallant Imbrius, son of Mentor, lord
Of many steeds. He, ere the Greeks had come
To Troy, dwelt at Pedæum and espoused
Medesicasta, Priam's spurious child.
But when the well-oared galleys of the Greeks
Mustered at Troy, he also came, and there
Was eminent among her chiefs, and dwelt
With Priam, and was honored as his son.
The son of Telamon beneath the ear
Pierced him with his long javelin, and drew forth
The weapon. Headlong to the earth he fell.
As on a mountain height, descried from far,
Hewn by a brazen axe, an ash is felled
And lays its tender sprays upon the ground,
Thus Imbrius fell, and round him in his fall
Clashed his bright armor. Teucer sprang in haste
To spoil the dead, but Hector hurled at him
His shining spear; the wary Teucer stepped
Aside, and just escaped the brazen blade.
It struck Amphimachus, Cteatus' son,
And Actor's grandson; as he came to join
The battle, he was smitten in the breast,
And fell, his armor clashing round his limbs.

Then Hector flew in haste to tear away
From the large-souled Amphimachus the helm
That cased his temples. Ajax saw, and hurled
His glittering spear at Hector as he came:
It made no wound; for Hector stood equipped
All o'er in formidable brass. The spear
Struck on the bossy shield with such a shock
As forced him to recoil, and leave unspoiled
The bodies, which the Achaians dragged away.
For Stichius and Menestheus, chief among
The Athenians, bore the dead Amphimachus
To the Greek camp, while the two men of might,
The chieftains Ajax, lifted Imbrius up;
And as two lions, bearing off among
The close-grown shrubs a goat, which they have snatched
From sharp-toothed dogs, uplift it in their jaws
Above the ground, so the two warriors raised
The corpse of Imbrius, and stripped off the mail,
While, angered that Amphilochus was slain,
Oïleus' son struck from the tender neck
The head, and sent it far among the crowd,
Whirled like a ball, to fall at Hector's feet.
Meantime was Neptune moved with grief to see
His grandson perish in that desperate fray,

And passed among the Achaian tents and ships
Encouraging the men, and planning woes
For Ilium. There he met Idomeneus,
Expert to wield the spear, as he returned
From caring for a comrade who had left
The battle, wounded in the knee, and whom
His friends had carried in. Idomeneus
Had called the surgeons to his aid, and now
Was hastening to the field, intent to bear
His part in battle. Him the monarch god
Of ocean thus addressed, but first he took
The voice of Thoas, King Andræmon's son,
Whose father ruled the Ætolians through the bounds
Of Pleuron, and in lofty Calydon,
And like a god was honored in the land.
"O counsellor of Crete, Idomeneus!
Where are the threats which late the sons of Greece
Uttered against the Trojans?" Promptly came
The Cretan leader's answer: "No man here,
O Thoas, seems blameworthy, for we all
Are skilled in war, nor does unmanly fear
Hold any back; nor from the difficult strife
Does sloth detain one warrior. So it is
Doubtless that it seems good to Saturn's son,

The All-disposer, that the Greeks, afar
From Argos, should ingloriously fall
And perish. Thoas, thou wert ever brave,
And didst exhort the laggards. Cease not now
To combat, cease not to exhort the rest."

And Neptune, he who shakes the earth, rejoined:—
"Idomeneus, whoever keeps aloof
From battle, willingly, to-day, may he
Never return from Troy, but be the prey
Of dogs. Take thou thy arms and come with me,
For we must quit ourselves like men, and strive
To aid our cause, although we be but two.
Great is the strength of feeble arms combined,
And we can combat even with the brave."

So speaking, Neptune turned to share the toils
Of war. Idomeneus, who now had reached
His princely tent, put on his glorious mail,
And seized two spears, and flew upon his way,
Like lightning grasped by Saturn's son and flung
Quivering above Olympus' gleaming peak,
A sign to mortals, dazzled by the blaze,
So glittered, as he ran, his brazen mail.
His fellow-warrior, good Meriones,
Met him beside the tent, for he had come

To fetch a brazen javelin thence, and thus
The stout Idomeneus addressed his friend:—
"O son of Molus, swift Meriones,
Dearest of all my comrades! Why hast thou
Thus left the battle-field? Hast thou a wound,—
A weapon's point that galls thee? Dost thou bring
A message to me? Think not that I sit
Within my tent an idler; I must fight."
Discreetly did Meriones reply:—
"Idomeneus, whose sovereign counsels rule
The well-armed Cretans, I am come to seek
A spear if one be left within thy tents.
I broke the one I bore, in hurling it
Against the shield of fierce Deiphobus."
The Cretan chief, Idomeneus, rejoined:—
"If spears thou seek, there stand within my tent
Twenty and one against the shining walls.
I took them from slain Trojans. 'T is my wont
Never to fight at distance from the foe,
And therefore have I spears, and bossy shields,
And helms, and body-mail of polished brass."
Then spake in turn discreet Meriones:—
"Within my tent are also many spoils
Won from the Trojans, and in my black ship;

But they are far away. I do not think
That I forget what valor is. I fight
Among the foremost in the glorious strife
Where'er the battle calls me. Other men
Among the well-armed Greeks may not have seen
What I perform, but thou must know me well."
  Idomeneus, the Cretan leader, spake:—
"I know thy courage well. What need hast thou
To speak as thou hast done? If all of us,
The bravest of the Greeks, were set apart
To form an ambush;—for an ambush tries
And shows men's valor; there the craven, there
The brave, is known; the coward's color comes
And goes; his spirit is not calm within
His bosom, so that he can rest awhile
And tremble not; he shifts his place; he sits
On both his feet; his heart beats audibly
Within his breast; his teeth at thought of death
Chatter; the brave man's color changes not,
Nor when with other warriors he sits down
In ambush is he troubled, but he longs
To rise and mingle in the desperate fray;—
For thee, in such an ambush, none could blame
Thy courage or thy skill. If there the foe

Should wound thee from afar, or smite thee near,
The weapon would not strike thy neck behind,
Or pierce thy back, but enter at thy breast
Or stomach, as thou wert advancing fast
Among the foremost. But enough of this.
Come! stand we here no longer, idiot-like,
Lest some one chide us sharply. Hasten thou,
And bring a sturdy javelin from the tent."
He spake. Meriones, like Mars in port
And swiftness, hastened to the tent and brought
A brazen spear, and joined Idomeneus,
Eager for battle. As the god of war,
The man-destroyer, comes into the field,
With Terror, his strong-limbed and dauntless son,
Following and striking fear into the heart
Of the most resolute warrior, when from Thrace
They issue armed against the Ephyri,
Or else against the Phlegyans large of soul,
And hearken not to both the hosts, but give
To one the victory; so Meriones
Advanced to battle with Idomeneus,
Leaders of heroes both, and both equipped
In glittering helms. And first Meriones
Spake and addressed his fellow-warrior thus:—

"Son of Deucalion, at which point wilt thou
Enter the throng? Upon the army's right,
Its centre, or its left? The long-haired Greeks
Seem most to need our aid upon the left."
Then spoke Idomeneus, in turn, the prince
Of Cretans: "At the centre of the fleet
Are others who will guard it. Posted there
Are either Ajax and the most expert
Of Grecian archers, Teucer, not less skilled
In standing fight, and amply will they task
The arm of Hector, Priam's son, though bent
On desperate conflict, and though passing fierce.
With all his fierceness, he will find it hard
To quell their prowess, never yet o'ercome,
And fire the ships, unless Saturnian Jove
Himself should cast on them the flaming torch.
Nor yet will Telamonian Ajax yield
To any man of mortal birth, or reared
Upon the grains of Ceres, or whom brass
Or ponderous stones can wound. He would not own
The warlike son of Peleus mightier
Than he in standing fight, although in speed
He vies not with him. Lead us then to join
The army's left, that we may learn at once

Whether our fate in battle shall confer
Glory on other men, or theirs on us."
  So spake the chief. Meriones, the peer
Of Mars in swiftness, hastened till he joined
The army where his comrade bade. The foe
Beheld Idomeneus, who like a flame
Swept on with his companion all in arms
Gloriously wrought; they raised from rank to rank
The battle-cry, and met him as he came,
And hand to hand, before the galleys' sterns
Was waged the combat. As when storms arise,
Blown up by piping winds, when dust lies loose
Along the roads, a spreading cloud of dust
Fills the wide air, so came the battle on
Between the bands that struggled eagerly
To slay each other. All along the line
The murderous conflict bristled with long spears
That tore the flesh; the brazen splendor, shot
From gleaming helmets and from burnished mail
And shining bucklers, all in narrow space,
Dazzled the eyes. Brave-hearted would he be,
The man who, gazing on it, could have seen
The furious strife rejoicing or unmoved.
  Meantime the potent sons of Saturn each

Favored a different side, and planned new toils
For all the warriors. Jupiter had willed
That Hector and the Trojans should prevail,
Yet had he not decreed the Achaian host
To perish before Troy; he only sought
To honor Thetis and her large-souled son.
But Neptune, mingling with the Greeks, aroused
Their martial spirit. From the hoary deep
He came unmarked, for deeply was he grieved
To see the Greeks give way before the host
Of Troy, and he was wroth with Jupiter.
Both gods were of one race, and owed their birth
To the same parents; but the elder-born
Was Jupiter, and wiser. For that cause
Not openly did Neptune aid the Greeks,
But, as by stealth, disguised in human form,
Moved through their army and encouraged them
To combat. Thus it was the potent twain
Each drew, with equal hand, the net of strife
And fearful havoc, which no power could break
Or loosen, stretched o'er both the warring hosts,
And laying many a warrior low in death.
And now, although his brows were strewn with gray,
Idomeneus, encouraging the Greeks,

Rushed on the Trojans, and revived the fight.
He slew Orthryoneus, who just before,
Drawn by the rumor of the war, had left
Cabesus, and now made a lover's suit
For Priam's fairest daughter. Without dower
He sought to wed Cassandra, promising
A vast exploit,—to drive the Greeks from Troy,
In spite of all their valor. The old king
Consented that the maiden should be his;
And now he fought, and trusted to fulfil
His promise. But Idomeneus took aim,
And cast his glittering javelin at the youth.
It struck him marching proudly on, nor stopped
The weapon at the brazen mail, but pierced
The stomach. With a clash the warrior fell,
And thus the victor boasted over him:—
"Orthryoneus, I deem thee worthy of praise
Beyond all other men, if thou perform
What thou hast undertaken,—to defend
Dardanian Priam, who has promised thee
His daughter. We would make a compact too,
And will perform it,—to bestow on thee
A spouse, the fairest daughter of the house
Of Atreus' son, and we will send for her

To Argos, if thou join us, and lay waste
The well-built Ilium. Now, then, follow me,
And at the ships which brought us we will treat
Of marriage, and will make no niggard terms."
So spake Idomeneus, and dragged the slain
Through the sharp conflict by the foot. He met
Asius, who walked before his car, and came
To avenge his friend. The attending charioteer
Behind him reined the steeds, that they should breathe
Over the shoulders of their lord, who sought
To smite Idomeneus. The Greek was first
To strike; he plunged the spear into his throat
Below the chin, and drave the weapon through.
The Trojan fell to earth as falls an oak,
Poplar, or stately pine, which woodmen fell
With their sharp axes on the mountain-side,
To form a galley's beam. So there he lay
Stretched out before his coursers and his car,
And gnashed his teeth, and clenched the bloody dust.
The charioteer, amazed, and losing power
Of action, dared not turn the horses back
To bear him from the foe. Antilochus
The warlike cast his spear, and in the midst
Transfixed him. Little did the brazen mail

Avail to stay the blade, which cleft its way
Into the stomach. With a sudden gasp
He toppled from the sumptuous chariot-seat,
And large-souled Nestor's son, Antilochus,
Drave with the chariot to the well-armed Greeks.
Deiphobus, who sorrowed for the fate
Of Asius, drawing near Idomeneus,
Hurled at him his bright spear. The Greek beheld,
As face to face they stood, and scaped the stroke,
Covered by his round shield, two-handled, strong
With bullocks' hides and glittering brass. With this
He hid himself, close couched within, and turned
The brazen point aside. The buckler rang
Shrilly; the weapon glanced away, yet flew
Not vainly from the Trojan's powerful hand:
It struck Hypsenor, son of Hippasus,
The shepherd of the people, on the side
Where lies the liver, just below the breast.
His knees gave way; he fell; Deiphobus
Thus shouted o'er the dead his empty boast:—
"Not unavenged lies Asius, and no doubt,
In journeying to the massy gates and wall
Of Hades, will rejoice that I have sent
A soul to be companion of his way."

He spake; and at his boast the Greeks were moved
With anger,—most of all Antilochus
The warlike; yet he left not to the foe
His slain companion, but made haste to hold
His shield above him. His beloved friends,
Mecisteus, son of Echius, and the prince
Alastor, lifted up, with many a groan,
The corpse, and bore it to the roomy ships.
Meantime the valor of Idomeneus
Remitted not; he vehemently longed
To cover many a Trojan with the night
Of death, or fall himself with clashing arms,
In warring to defend the ships of Greece.
The brave Alcathoüs, the beloved son
Of Æsyetus, whom Anchises made
His son-in-law,—for he had given to him
Hippodameia, eldest-born of all
His daughters, whom her parents, while she dwelt
With them, loved dearly, fair and wise beyond
All other maidens of her age, and skilled
In household arts; so that the noblest prince
Of the broad Trojan kingdom made her his;—
Him, by the weapon of Idomeneus,
Did Neptune bring to death. The sparkling eyes

Grew dim, and stiffened were the shapely limbs,
For neither could he flee nor turn aside;
But as he stood before him, column-like,
Or like a towering tree, Idomeneus
Transfixed him in the bosom with his spear.
The brazen coat of mail gave way, which oft
Had saved him, breaking with a sharp, shrill sound
Before the severing blade. He fell to earth
With noise; the spear stood planted in his heart,
And as he panted quivered through its length,
Yet soon its murderous force was spent and still.
And then the victor boasted thus aloud:—
 "Deiphobus, does this appear to thee
A fair return, when three are slain for one,
Or hast thou boasted idly? Yet do thou,
Vain as thou art, stand forth and face me here,
And I will teach thee of what race I am,—
An offshoot of the stock of Jove, whose son
Was Minos, guardian of our Crete, and he
Was father of the good Deucalion.
Deucalion's son am I, and I am king
O'er many men in the broad isle of Crete.
My galleys brought me thence to be the dread
Of thee, thy father, and the men of Troy."

He spake. Deiphobus, irresolute,
Stood doubting whether to retreat and bring
Some other of the heroic sons of Troy
To aid him, or to try the fight alone.
As thus he mused, it seemed most wise to seek
Æneas. Him he found withdrawn among
The rear of the army, for he was displeased
With noble Priam, who had paid his worth
With light esteem. Deiphobus approached,
And thus with wingèd words accosted him:—
"Æneas, counsellor of Troy, if thou
Hadst ever a regard to him who was
Thy sister's husband, it becomes thee now
To avenge him. Follow me, and help avenge
Alcathoüs, guardian of thy tender years,
Slain by the spear of famed Idomeneus."
He spake; and at his words Æneas felt
His courage rise. Impatient for the fight,
He went to meet Idomeneus; yet fear
Fell not upon the Greek as if he were
A puny boy: he stood and kept his ground.
As, when a mountain boar, unterrified,
Waits in the wilderness the hunter-crew,
That come with mighty din, his bristly back

Rises, his eyes shoot fire, he whets his tusks,
And fiercely keeps both dogs and men at bay,—
So did Idomeneus, expert to wield
The spear, await Æneas hastening on
With fury. Not a backward step he made,
But called upon his warrior-friends aloud,
Looking at Aphareus, Ascalaphus,
Deïpyrus, Meriones, and last
Antilochus, all skilled in arts of war,
And thus exhorted them with wingèd words:—
"Haste hither, O my friends, and bring me aid.
I stand alone, in dread of the approach
Of swift Æneas, who comes fiercely on,
Powerful to slay, and in his prime of youth,
The highest vigor of the human frame.
Yet, were our years the same, that chief or I
Would quickly triumph at the other's cost."
He spake, and all with one accord drew near
And stood by him, with shields obliquely held
Upon their shoulders. On the other side
Æneas cheered his comrades on. He fixed
His look on Paris, and Deiphobus,
And nobly-born Agenor, who, like him,
Were leaders of the Trojans. After these

The soldiers followed, as the thronging flock
Follow the ram that leads them to the fount
From pasture, and the shepherd's heart is pleased.
So was Æneas glad at heart to see
The multitude of warriors following him.
Then mingled they in battle hand to hand
Around Alcathoüs, with their ponderous spears,
And fearfully upon their bosoms rang
The brass, as through the struggling crowd they aimed
Their weapons at each other. Two brave men,
Æneas and Idomeneus, the peers
Of Mars, conspicuous o'er their fellows, strove
With cruel brass to rend each other's limbs.
And first Æneas cast his spear to smite
Idomeneus, who saw it as it came,
And shunned it. Plunging in the earth beyond,
It stood and quivered; it had left in vain
The Trojan's powerful hand. Idomeneus
Next smote Œnomaüs: the spear brake through
His hollow corslet at the waist; it pierced
And drank the entrails: down amid the dust
He fell, and grasped the earth with dying hand.
Idomeneus plucked forth the massy spear,
But, pressed by hostile weapons, ventured not

To strip the sumptuous armor from the dead;
Since now no more the sinews of his feet
Were firm to bear him rushing to retake
His spear, or start aside from hostile spears.
Wherefore in standing fight he warded off
The evil hour, nor trusted to his feet
To bear him fleetly from the field. He moved
Slowly away, and now Deiphobus,
Who long had hated him and bitterly,
Aimed at him his bright spear; it missed its mark,
And struck Ascalaphus, the son of Mars.
The weapon cleft the shoulder of the Greek,
Who fell amid the dust, and clenched the earth.
  Not yet the clamorous Mars, of passionate mood,
Had heard that in the fray his son was slain;
But on the summit of the Olympian mount
He sat, o'ercanopied by golden clouds,
Restrained from combat by the will of Jove,
With other gods, forbidden, like himself,
To aid the combatants. Meantime around
Ascalaphus the combat hand to hand
Still raged. Deiphobus had torn away
The slain man's shining helm, when suddenly
Meriones sprang forward, spear in hand,

And smote him on the arm; the wounded limb
Let fall the helm, resounding as it fell,
And with a vulture's leap Meriones
Rushed toward him, plucking out from the torn flesh
The spear, and falling back among the crowd.
Polites, brother of the wounded, threw
Both arms around his waist, and bore him off
From the loud din of conflict, till he reached
His swift-paced steeds, that waited in the rear
Of battle, with their chariot nobly wrought
And charioteer. These took him back to Troy,
Heavily groaning and in pain, the blood
Yet gushing from the newly wounded limb.
  Still fought the other warriors, and the noise
Of a perpetual tumult filled the air.
Æneas, rushing upon Aphareus,
Caletor's son, who turned to face him, thrust
A sharp spear through his throat. With drooping head,
And carrying shield and helmet to the ground,
He fell, and rendered up his soul in death.
Antilochus, as Thoön turned away,
Attacked and smote him, cutting off the vein
That passes through the body to the neck.
This he divided sheer; the warrior fell

Backward, and lay in dust, with hands outstretched
To his beloved friends. Antilochus
Flew to the slain, and from his shoulders stripped
The armor, casting cautious glances round;
While toward him pressed the Trojans on all sides,
Striking the fair broad buckler with their darts,
Yet could not even score with pointed brass
The tender skin of Nestor's son; for still
Neptune, the shaker of the sea-coast, kept
Watch o'er him while the weapons round him showered.
Yet he withdrew not from his foes, but moved
Among the crowd, nor idle was his spear,
But wielded right and left, and still he watched
With resolute mind the time to strike the foe
At distance, or assault him near at hand.

The son of Asius, Adamas, beheld
The hero meditating thus, and struck,
In close attack, the middle of his shield
With a sharp brazen spear. The dark-haired god
Who rules the deep denied to Adamas
The life he sought, and weakened the hard stroke.
Part of the Trojan's weapon, like a stake
Hardened by fire, stood fixed within the shield,
Part lay on earth, and he who cast it slunk

Among his comrades to avoid his fate.
Meriones, pursuing with his spear,
Smote him between the navel and the groin,
Where deadliest are the wounds in battle given
To man's unhappy race. He planted there
The cruel blade, and Adamas, who fell,
Writhed panting round it, as a bullock bound
By cowherds on the mountain with strong cords
Pants as they lead him off against his will.
So wounded, Adamas drew heavy breath,
And yet not long. The brave Meriones,
Approaching, plucked the weapon forth, and night
Came o'er the eyes of Adamas. At hand
Stood Helenus, and struck Deipyrus
Upon the temple with his ponderous sword,
Of Thracian make, and cut the three-coned helm
Away, and dashed it to the ground; it rolled
Between a Grecian warrior's feet, who stooped
And took it up, while o'er its owner's eyes
The darkness gathered. Grieved at this, the son
Of Atreus, Menelaus great in war,
Rushed forward, threatening royal Helenus.
He brandished his sharp spear; the Trojan drew
His bow; advancing, one to hurl a lance,

And one to send an arrow. Priam's son
Let fly a shaft at Menelaus' breast.
The bitter missile from the hollow mail
Glanced off. As when from the broad winnowing-fan
On some wide threshing-floor the swarthy beans,
Or vetches, bound before the whistling wind
And winnower's force, so, bounding from the mail
Of gallant Menelaus, flew afar
The bitter shaft. Then Menelaus, great
In battle, smote the hand of Helenus
That held the polished bow; the brazen spear
Passed through the hand, and reached the bow, and there
Stood fixed, while Helenus, avoiding death,
Drew back among his comrades, with his hand
Held low, and trailing still the ashen stem.
Magnanimous Agenor from the wound
Drew forth the blade, and wrapped the hand in wool,
Carefully twisted, taken from a sling
Carried by an attendant of the chief.

To meet the glorious Menelaus sprang
Pisander, led by his unhappy fate
To perish, Menelaus! by thy hand
In that fierce conflict. When the two were near,
Advancing toward each other, Atreus' son

Took aim amiss; his spear flew far aside.
Pisander smote the buckler on the arm
Of mighty Menelaus, yet drave not
The weapon through. The broad shield stopped its force,
And broke it at the neck; yet hoped he still
For victory, and exulted. Then the son
Of Atreus drew his silver-studded sword
And sprang upon his foe, who from beneath
His buckler took a brazen battle-axe,
With a long stem of polished olive-wood.
Both struck at once. Pisander hewed away,
Below the crest, the plumèd helmet-cone
Of Atreus' son, who smote, above the nose,
Pisander's forehead, crashing through the bones.
Both bleeding eyes dropped to the ground amid
The dust; he fell; he writhed; the conqueror,
Advancing, set his heel upon his breast,
And stripped the armor off, and, boasting, said:—
"Thus shall ye leave unharmed the fleet that brought
The knights of Greece, ye treaty-breaking sons
Of Ilium, never satisfied with war!
Yet lack ye not still other guilt and shame,—
Wrong done to me, ye dogs! Ye have not feared
The wrath of Hospitable Jove, who flings

The thunder, and will yet destroy your town,
With all its towers,—ye who, without a cause,
Bore off my youthful bride, and heaps of wealth,
When she had given you welcome as our guests.
And now ye seek to burn with fire the fleet
With which we cross the ocean, and to slay
The Grecian heroes. Ye shall yet be forced,
Eager for battle as ye are, to pause.
O Father Jupiter, who hast the praise
Of highest wisdom among gods and men!
All this is of thy ordering. How hast thou
Favored this arrogant crew of Troy, in love
With violence, who never have enough
Of war and all its many miseries!
All other things soon satisfy desire,—
Sleep, love, and song, and graceful dance, which most
Delight in more than warlike toils,—yet they
Of Troy are never satisfied with war."

So spake the illustrious man, and, having stripped
The bloody armor from the dead, he gave
The spoil to his companions, and rejoined
The warriors in the van. Harpalion then,
A son of King Pylæmenes, with whom
He left his home to join the war at Troy,
Assaulted him. He never saw again

His native land. Close to Atrides' shield,
He struck it in the centre with his lance,
Yet could not drive the weapon through the brass,
And backward shrank, in fear of death, among
His comrades, looking round him lest some foe
Should wound him with the spear. Meriones
Let fly a brazen arrow after him,
Which, entering his right flank below the bone,
Passed through and cleft the bladder. Down he sank
Where the shaft struck him, breathing out his life
In the arms of his companions. Like a worm
He lay extended on the earth; his blood
Gushed forth, a purple stream, and steeped the soil.
The large-souled Paphlagonians came around,
And placed him in a chariot, sorrowing,
And bore him to the gates of sacred Troy.
The father followed weeping, but no hand
Was raised to avenge the slaughter of his son.
  Yet deeply moved was Paris at his death,
For he had been Harpalion's guest among
The Paphlagonians. Grieving for the slain,
He sent a brazen arrow from his bow.
Now there was one Euchenor, rich and brave,
The son of Polyïdus, hoary seer;

His dwelling was in Corinth, and he came,
Forewarned and conscious of his fate, to Troy;
For often Polyïdus, good old man,
Warned him that he within his palace halls
Should perish by a grievous malady,
Or else be slain by Trojan hands beside
The Grecian fleet. So, to escape at once
The censure of the Achaians and disease,
He came, lest he in after times might rue
His choice. And now between the jaw and ear
Did Paris smite him; from the warrior's limbs
Life fled, and darkness gathered o'er his eyes.
  And then they fought; like a devouring fire
That battle was; but Hector, dear to Jove,
Had not yet learned that on the left the Greeks
Made havoc of his men; for in that hour
The Greeks had almost made the victory theirs,
So greatly had the god who shakes the shores
Kindled their courage, and with his own arm
Brought timely aid. Still Hector, pressing on
Where first he leaped within the gates and wall,
Broke the close phalanxes of shielded Greeks.
There, ranged beside the hoary deep, the ships
Of Ajax and Protesilaus lay.

The wall that guarded them was low, and there
Warriors and steeds in fiercest conflict met;
There the Bœotians, there in their long robes
The Iäonians, there the Locrians, there
The men of Phthia, and the Epeians famed
For valor, held back Hector, struggling on
To reach the ships, yet found they had no power
To drive the noble warrior from the ground,
For he was like a flame. The chosen men
Of Athens formed the van. Menestheus, son
Of Peteus, was their leader, after whom
Phidas and Stichius followed, and with them
The gallant Bias. Meges, Phyleus' son,
With Dracius and Amphion, marshalled there
The Epeians; while the Phthian band were led
By Medon and Podarces, warlike chief.
And Medon was the great Oïleus' son,
And brother of the lesser Ajax, born
Without the tie of wedlock, and he dwelt
Far from his native land, in Phylacè;
For by his violent hand the brother died
Of Eryopis, whom Oïleus made
His lawful spouse. Podarces was the son
Of Iphiclus, and dwelt in Phylacè.

These, at the head of Phthia's valiant youth,
And cased in massive armor, fought beside
Bœotia's warriors for the Grecian fleet.
  But Ajax swift of foot, Oïleus' son,
From him of Telamon departed not
Even for an instant. As when two black steers
Of equal vigor o'er a fallow draw
The strongly jointed plough, till near their horns
Streams the warm sweat; the polished yoke alone
Holds them asunder, as they move along
The furrow, and the share divides the soil
That lies between them;—so the heroic twain
Kept near each other. Many men and brave
Followed to Troy the son of Telamon
As his companions, and, when weariness
Came o'er his sweaty limbs, relieved their chief
Of his broad buckler. But the Locrian host
Attended not Oïleus' great-souled son,
Nor could they ever venture to engage
In combat hand to hand. No brazen helms
Were theirs, with horse-hair plumes, no orbèd shields,
Nor ashen spears. They came with him to Troy,
Trusting in their good bows, and in their slings
Of twisted wool, from which they showered afar

Stones that dispersed the phalanxes of Troy.
The chieftains Ajax, warring in the van,
Clad in their shining armor, fought to check
The Trojans and their leader, brazen-mailed,
While in the rear the Locrians lurked unseen,
And sent their shafts, so that the men of Troy,
All order lost, were fain to cease from fight.
  Then had the Trojans from the ships and tents
Turned back, and fled, with fearful loss of life,
To lofty Ilium, if Polydamas
Had not accosted valiant Hector thus:—
  "Hector, thou hearkenest not to warning words.
Deem'st thou, because a god has given thee strength
Beyond all other men for feats of war,
That therefore thou art wiser than they all
In council? Think not for thyself to claim
All gifts at once. On one the god bestows
Prowess in war, upon another grace
In dance, upon another skill to touch
The harp and sing. In yet another, Jove
The Thunderer, implants the prudent mind,
By which the many profit, and by which
Communities are saved; and well doth he
Who hath it know its worth. Now let me speak

What seems to me the wisest. Round thee flames
The encircling war; the valiant sons of Troy,
Since they have crossed the ramparts, stand aloof,
Armed as they are, or fight against large odds
Scattered among the galleys. Yield thou now
The ground, and, summoning the chiefs, decide
What plan to follow,—whether we shall storm
The well-oared galleys, should the God vouchsafe
The victory to us,—or else depart
In safety from the fleet. I greatly fear
The Achaians may repay to us the debt
Of yesterday. There yet is at the fleet
One who, I think, no longer will refrain
Wholly from battle." Thus Polydamas
Spake, and the sage advice pleased Hector well,
Who, leaping from his chariot to the ground,
With all his weapons, said these wingèd words:—
"Remain with all the bravest warriors here,
Polydamas, while I depart to give
The due commands, and instantly return."
He spake, and with a shout he rushed away,
Seen from afar, like a snow-mountain's peak,
And flew among the Trojans and allies,
Who crowded round the brave Polydamas,

The son of Panthöus, at Hector's call.
Among the foremost combatants he sought
Deiphobus, and mighty Helenus,
The king; he looked for Adamas, the son
Of Asius, and for Asius of the house
Of Hyrtacus. Some not unharmed he found,
Yet not o'ercome; while others lay in death
Beneath the galley-sterns, where Grecian hands
Had slain them; others on the wall, struck down
By missiles, or in combat hand to hand.
There on the left of that disastrous fray
He met the noble Alexander, spouse
Of fair-haired Helen, as he cheered his men,
And rallied them to battle. Hector thus
Addressed his brother with reproachful words:—
"Accursed Paris! noble but in form,
Effeminate seducer! where are now
Deiphobus, and mighty Helenus?
And Adamas, the son of Asius, where?
And Asius, son of Hyrtacus? and where
Orthryoneus? Now towering Ilium sinks
From her high summit, and thy fate is sure."
And then the godlike Paris answered thus:—
"Since it hath pleased thee, Hector, thus to cast

Reproach on me, though innocent, I may
Another day neglect the toils of war,
Although in truth my mother brought me forth
Not quite unapt for combat. Since the hour
When thou didst lead the battle to the ships
With thy companions, we have held our ground,
Here on this spot, contending with the Greeks.
Three chiefs for whom thou askest have been slain.
Deiphobus and mighty Helenus,
Both wounded in the hand by massive spears,
Have left the field; the son of Saturn saved
Their lives. Now lead us wheresoe'er thou wilt,
And we will follow thee with resolute hearts,
Nor deem that thou wilt find in us a lack
Of valor while our strength of arm remains.
The boldest cannot fight beyond his strength."
  With such persuasive words the warrior calmed
His brother's anger, and they went where raged
The hottest conflict round Cebriones,
Phalces, Orthæus, and the excellent
Polydamas, with Palmys at his side,
And Polyphœtes, godlike in his form,
And where Ascanius and Morys fought,
Sons of Hippotion. They the day before

Came marching from Ascania's fertile fields,
Moved by the will of Jove to share the war.
All these swept on, as when a hurricane,
A thunder-gust, from Father Jupiter
Buffets the plain, and mingles with the deep,
In mighty uproar, and the billows rise
All over the resounding brine, and swell,
Whitening with foam, and chase each other on.
So moved the Trojans on, man after man,
In close array, all armed in glittering brass,
Following their generals. Hector, Priam's son,
And peer of Mars in battle, led the van,
His round shield held before him, tough with hides
And overlaid with brass. Upon his brow
The gleaming helmet nodded as he moved.
On every side he tried the phalanxes,
If haply they might yield to his assault,
Made from beneath that buckler; but the Greeks
In spirit or in order wavered not.
And Ajax, striding forth, defied him thus:—
"Draw nearer, friend! Think'st thou to frighten thus
The Greeks? We are not quite so inexpert
In war, although so cruelly chastised
By Jupiter. Thou thinkest in thy heart

That thou shalt make our ships thy spoil; but we
Have also our strong arms to drive thee back,
And far more soon the populous town of Troy,
Captured and sacked, shall fall by Grecian hands.
And now I warn thee that the hour is near
When, fleeing, thou shalt pray to Father Jove
And all the immortals, that thy long-maned steeds,
Bearing thee townward 'mid a cloud of dust
Along the plain, may be more swift than hawks."
  As thus he spake, an eagle, to the right,
High in the middle heaven, flew over him,
And, gladdened by the omen, all the Greeks
Shouted; but then illustrious Hector spake:—
  "Babbler and boaster, what wild words are these?
O Ajax! would that I were but as sure
To be the child of ægis-bearing Jove,
Brought forth by Juno the august, and held
In honor everywhere like that which crowns
Apollo and Minerva, as I know
That to the Greeks this very day will bring
Destruction, and that thou shalt also lie
Slain with the others, if thou dare abide
The stroke of my long spear, which yet shall tear
Thy dainty flesh, and thou, with thy full limbs,

Shalt be the feast of Trojan dogs and birds,
Unburied by the galleys of the Greeks."
  So Hector spake, and led his warriors on.
They followed with a mighty shout; the rear
Sent up as loud a cry. On the other side
Shouted the Greeks, nor intermitted now
Their wonted valor, but stood firm to breast
The onset of the chosen men of Troy.
The mingled clamor of both hosts went up
To heaven, and to the shining seat of Jove.

## *BOOK XIV.*

THE mighty uproar was not unperceived
By Nestor's ear, who, sitting at the wine,
Addressed the son of Æsculapius thus:—
"Noble Machaon, what will happen now?
Bethink thee: for the clamor grows more loud
From our young warriors at the ships. Stay here
And drink the purple wine, while for thy limbs
The fair-haired Hecamede warms the bath
And washes the dark blood away, and I
Will climb the watch-tower, and will know the worst."
He spake, and took a buckler, fairly wrought,
Glittering with brass, and left within the tent
By Thrasymedes, his own knightly son,
Who to the war had borne his father's shield;
He grasped a ponderous spear, with brazen blade,
And stood without the tent, and saw a sight
Of shame,—the routed Greeks, and close behind
The haughty Trojans putting them to flight,

And the Greek wall o'erthrown. As when the face
Of the great deep grows dark with weltering waves,
That silently forebode the swift descent
Of the shrill blast, the yet uncertain seas
Roll not to either side, till from the seat
Of Jupiter comes down the violent wind,—
So paused the aged chief, uncertain yet
Of purpose,—whether he should join the throng
Of Greeks, with their swift coursers, or repair
To sovereign Agamemnon, Atreus' son.
This to his thought seemed wiser, and he went
To seek Atrides. Meantime both the hosts
Urged on the work of slaughter; still they fought,
And still the solid brass upon their limbs
Rang, smitten with the swords and two-edged spears.
  Then, coming from the fleet, the wounded kings,
Nurslings of Jove, met Nestor; toward him came
Tydides, and Ulysses, and the son
Of Atreus, Agamemnon. On the beach
Of the gray deep their ships were ranged afar
From that fierce conflict. There the Greeks had drawn,
To the plain's edge, the first that touched the land,
And built a rampart at their sterns. Though long
The shore-line, it sufficed not to contain

The galleys, and the host had scanty room;
Wherefore they drew the galleys up in rows,
Row behind row, and filled the shore's wide mouth
Between the promontories. There the kings
Walked, leaning on their lances, to behold
The tumult and the fight, and inly grieved.
The sight of aged Nestor startled them,
And thus the royal Agamemnon spake:—
"Neleian Nestor, glory of the Greeks,
Why hast thou left the murderous fray, and why
Come hither? Much I fear the fiery chief,
Hector, will make the menace good which once
He uttered, speaking to the men of Troy,—
Not to return to Ilium from the fleet
Till he had burned our ships with fire, and slain
Us also; thus he spake, and now fulfils
His menace. O ye gods! the other Greeks,
And not Achilles only, cherish hate
Against me in their hearts, and now refuse
To combat even where our galleys lie."
And Nestor, the Gerenian knight, replied:—
"Thus is the threat accomplished, nor can Jove
The Thunderer reverse the event. The wall
In which we trusted as impregnable,

Our fleet's defence and ours, is overthrown;
But obstinately still the Greeks maintain
The combat at the ships, nor couldst thou now
Distinguish with thy sharpest sight where most
The ranks are routed, so confusèdly
They fall, and the wild uproar reaches heaven.
Meantime consult we what may yet be done,
If counsel aught avail; yet can I not
Advise to mingle in the strife again.
It is not meet that wounded men should fight."
  And then the royal Agamemnon said:—
"Since at our ships, beneath their very sterns,
The combat rages; since the wall we built
Avails not, nor the trench, at which the Greeks
Labored and suffered, hoping it might be
A sure defence for us and for our fleet,
Certain it is that to Almighty Jove
It hath seemed good that here the Greeks, afar
From Argos, should be shamefully cut off;
For well was I aware when he designed
To aid the Greeks, and well can I perceive
That he is honoring now the men of Troy
Like to the blessed gods, and fettering
Our valor and our hands. Hear my advice,

And follow it. Let us draw down the ships
Nearest the sea, and launch them on the deep,
And moor them, anchored, till the lonely night
Shall come, when, if the Trojans pause from war,
Haply we may draw down the other barks;
For he who flees from danger, even by night,
Deserves no blame; and better is his fate
Who flees from harm than his whom harm o'ertakes."
Then wise Ulysses, with stern look, replied:—
"What words, Atrides, have escaped thy lips?
Unhappy man, thou shouldst have held command
O'er some effeminate army, and not ours,—
Ours to whom Jupiter, from youth to age,
Hath granted to accomplish difficult wars,
Until we pass away. And wouldst thou then
Depart from Troy, the city of broad streets,
For which we have endured so much and long?
Nay, be thou silent, lest the other Greeks
Hear words that never should be said by one
Who knows to speak with wisdom, and who bears
The sceptre, and who rules so many Greeks
As thou dost. I contemn with my whole soul
The counsel thou hast given, commanding us,
While yet the battle rages, to draw down

Our good ships to the sea, that so the foe
May see his wish more easily fulfilled,
Even in the hour of triumph, and our fate
Be certain ruin; for the Greeks no more
Will combat when they draw their galleys down,
But, looking backward to the shore, will leave
The battle there; and thus, O king of men!
Will mischief flow from what thou counsellest."
  And Agamemnon, king of men, rejoined:—
"Thou touchest me, Ulysses, to the heart
With thy harsh censure; yet I did not give
Command to drag our good ships to the sea,
Against the will of the Greeks. And would there were
Some other, young or old, to counsel them
More prudently, for that would please me well."
  Then spake the great in battle, Diomed:—
"The man is here, nor have ye far to look
If ye will be persuaded, and refrain
To blame me angrily, because my years
Are fewest 'midst you all. I too can boast
Of noble birth; my father, Tydeus, lies
Buried beneath a mound of earth at Thebes.
To Portheus three illustrious sons were born,
Who dwelt in Pleuron, and in Calydon

The lofty,—Agrius, Melas, and the knight,
My father's father, Œneus, eminent
Among the rest for valor; he remained
At home, but, wandering thence, my father went
To Argos, for the will of Jove was such,—
Jove and the other gods. He wedded there
A daughter of Adrastus, and he dwelt
Within a mansion filled with wealth; broad fields
Fertile in corn were his, and many rows
Of trees and vines around him; large his flocks,
And great his fame as one expert to wield,
Beyond all other Greeks, the spear in war.
This should ye know, for this is true; nor yet
Contemn my counsel given with careful thought
And for your good, nor deem it comes from one
Unwarlike and low-born. Now let us join
The battle, wounded as we are, for much
It needs our presence, keeping carefully
Beyond the reach of weapons, to avoid
Wound upon wound, and, cheering on the rest,
Send back into the combat those who stand
Apart, indulgent to their weariness."

He spake: they hearkened, and with hasty steps
Went on, King Agamemnon at their head.

Nor was the glorious power that shakes the earth
Unmindful of his charge. He went among
The warriors in the semblance of a man
Stricken in years, and, seizing the right hand
Of Agamemnon, spake these wingèd words:—
"O son of Atreus, the revengeful heart
Of Peleus' son must leap within his breast
For joy, to see the slaughter and the rout
Of the Achaians, since with him there dwells
No touch of pity. May he perish too,
Like us, and may some god o'erwhelm his name
With infamy. With thee the blessed gods
Are not so far incensed, and thou shalt see
The Trojan chiefs and princes of their host
Raising the dust-clouds on the spacious plain
In fleeing from our ships and tents to Troy."
He spake, and, shouting, strode across the field.
As loud a cry as from nine thousand men,
Or from ten thousand hurrying to engage
In battle, such the cry that ocean's king
Uttered from his deep lungs. It woke anew
Invincible resolve in every heart
Among the Greeks to combat to the end.
Now, Juno of the golden throne beheld

As, standing on the Olympian height, she cast
Downward her eyes to where her brother moved,
Bearing his part with glory in the fray;
And inly she rejoiced. She also saw
Jove on the peak of Ida, down whose side
Glide many brooks, and greatly was displeased.
Then the majestic goddess with large eyes
Mused how to occupy the mind of him
Who bears the ægis. This at length seemed best:
To deck herself in fair array, and haste
To Ida, that the God might haply yield
To amorous desire, and in that hour
Her hand might pour into his lids, and o'er
His watchful mind, a soft and pleasant sleep.
She went to her own chamber, which her son
Vulcan had framed, with massive portals made
Fast to the lintels by a secret bolt,
Which none but she could draw. She entered in
And closed the shining doors; and first she took
Ambrosial water, washing every stain
From her fair limbs, and smoothed them with rich oil,
Ambrosial, soft, and fragrant, which, when touched
Within Jove's brazen halls, perfumed the air
Of earth and heaven. When thus her shapely form

Had been anointed, and her hands had combed
Her tresses, she arranged the lustrous curls,
Ambrosial, beautiful, that clustering hung
Round her immortal brow. And next she threw
Around her an ambrosial robe, the work
Of Pallas, all its web embroidered o'er
With forms of rare device. She fastened it
Over the breast with clasps of gold, and then
She passed about her waist a zone which bore
Fringes an hundred-fold, and in her ears
She hung her three-gemmed ear-rings, from whose gleam
She won an added grace. Around her head
The glorious goddess drew a flowing veil,
Just from the loom, and shining like the sun;
And, last, beneath her bright white feet she bound
The shapely sandals. Gloriously arrayed
In all her ornaments, she left her bower,
And calling Venus to herself, apart
From all the other gods, addressed her thus:—
"Wilt thou, dear child, comply with what I ask?
Or, angered that I aid the Greeks, while thou
Dost favor Troy, wilt thou deny my suit?"
And thus Jove's daughter, Venus, made reply:—
"O Juno, whom I reverence, speak thy thought,

Daughter of mighty Saturn! for my heart
Commands me to obey thy wish in all
That I can do, and all that can be done."
  And thus imperial Juno, planning guile,
Rejoined: "Give me the charm and the desire
With which thou overcomest gods and men.
I go to the far end of this green earth,
To visit Ocean, father of the gods,
And Mother Tethys, who, receiving me
From Rhea, cherished me, and brought me up
In their abodes, when Jove the Thunderer
Cast Saturn down to lie beneath the earth
And barren sea. I go to visit them,
And end their hateful quarrel. For too long
Have they been strangers to the marriage-bed.
But if my words persuade them, and bring back
Their hearts to their old love, my name will be
Honored by them, and dear throughout all time."
  And laughter-loving Venus answered thus:—
"What thou desirest should not be denied,
And shall not, for thou sleepest in the arms
Of Jupiter, the mightiest of the gods."
  She spake, and from her bosom drew the zone,
Embroidered, many colored, and instinct

With every winning charm — with love, desire,
Dalliance, and gentle speech — that stealthily
O'ercomes the purpose of the wisest mind,
And, placing it in Juno's hands, she said: —
"This many-colored zone, and all that dwells
Within it, take, and in thy bosom hide,
And thou, I deem, wilt not return and leave
Thy purpose unfulfilled." As thus she spake,
The large-eyed stately Juno smiled and took,
And, smiling, in her bosom placed the zone,
While Venus, daughter of the Thunderer,
Went to the palace. Juno took her way
From high Olympus o'er Pieria's realm
And rich Emathia, o'er equestrian Thrace,
With snowy peaks exceeding high; her feet
Touched not the ground. From Athos suddenly
She stooped upon the tossing deep, and came
To Lemnos, seat of Thoas the divine,
And there she met Death's brother, Sleep, and took
His hand in hers, and thus accosted him: —
"O Sleep, whose sway is over all the gods
And all mankind, if ever thou didst heed
My supplication, hearken to me now,
And I shall be forever grateful. Close

The glorious eyes of Jove beneath his lids
Midst our embracings, and for thy reward
Thou shalt possess a sumptuous throne of gold
Imperishable. Vulcan, my lame son,
Shall forge it for thee, and adorn its sides,
And place below a footstool, upon which
Thy shining feet shall rest in banqueting."
  Then gentle Sleep made answer, speaking thus:—
"Great Saturn's daughter, Juno the august,
On any other of the deathless gods
Could I bring slumber,—even on the tides
Of the swift Ocean, parent of them all;
Yet may I not approach Saturnian Jove
If he command me not. Already once
He made me quail with fright before his threats,
When his magnanimous son, Alcides, sailed
From Troy, which he had ravaged. Then I lulled
The senses of the Ægis-bearer, Jove,
Wrapping myself around him, while thy mind
Was planning mischiefs for his son, and thou
Didst wake the blasts of all the bitter winds
To sweep the ocean, and to bear away
The hero on its billows from his friends
To populous Cos. When Jupiter awoke

His anger rose; he seized and flung the gods
Hither and thither; me he chiefly sought,
And would have cast me to destruction, down
From the great heavens into the deep, if Night,
Whose power o'ercomes the might of gods and men,
Had not preserved me, fleeing to her shade.
So Jove refrained, indignant as he was,
For much he feared to offend the swift-paced Night.
And now thou bid'st me tempt my fate again."
Imperial, large-eyed Juno thus rejoined: —
"Why rise such thoughts, O Sleep, within thy heart?
Deem'st thou that Jove the Thunderer favors Troy
As much as he was angered for the sake
Of Hercules, his son? Do what I ask,
And thou shalt have from me a wedded spouse.
One of the younger Graces shall be thine, —
Pasithea, whom thou hast desired so long."
She spake, and Sleep, delighted, answered thus: —
"Swear now to me, O goddess, by the Styx,
The inviolable river. Lay one hand
Upon the food-producing earth, and place
The other on the glimmering sea, that all
The gods below, round Saturn, may attest
Thy promise, — that thou wilt bestow on me

One of the younger Graces for my bride,—
Pasithea, whom I have desired so long."
  He spake, and white-armed Juno willingly
Complied; she took the oath, and called on all
The gods who dwell in Tartarus below,
And bear the name of Titans. When the oath
Was taken, and the accustomed rites performed,
From Lemnos and from Imbrus forth they went,
Shrouded in mist; and swiftly moving on
Toward Ida, seamed with rivulets and nurse
Of savage beasts, they came to Lectos first,
And there they left the sea. Their way was now
Over the land, and underneath their feet
The forest summits shook. Sleep halted there
Ere yet the eye of Jupiter descried
His coming, and upon a lofty fir,
The tallest growing on the Idæan mount,
High in the air among the clouds of heaven,
Springing from earth, he took his perch within
The screen of branches, like the shrill-voiced bird,
Called Chalcis by the immortals, and by men
Cymindis, haunting the high mountain-side.
  And Juno hastened on to Gargarus,
The peak of lofty Ida. Jupiter

The Cloud-compeller, saw her, and at once
Love took possession of his mighty heart,
As when they first were wedded, and withdrew
From their dear parents' sight. The God drew near
And stood before her, and addressed her thus:—
"Why art thou hastening from Olympus thus,
And whither; yet without thy steeds and car?"
And Juno answered with dissembled guile:—
"To the far ends of the green earth I go,
To visit Ocean, father of the gods,
And Mother Tethys, in whose palace halls
They nourished me, and brought me up. I go
To end their hateful quarrels, for too long
Have they been strangers to the marriage-bed,
Incensed against each other. Now my steeds,
Waiting to bear me over land and sea,
Stand at the foot of Ida seamed with rills,
And now I come to thee, lest thou perchance
Be wroth if I unknown to thee repair
To where old Ocean dwells amid his deeps."
The Cloud-compeller, Jupiter, rejoined:—
"Hereafter, Juno, there will be a time
For such a journey; meantime let us give
This hour to rest and dalliance. Never yet

Did love of goddess or of mortal maid
Possess and overcome my heart as now;
Not even when I loved Ixion's dame,
Who bore Pirithoüs, prudent as a god
Among the counsellors; nor when I loved
Acrisius' daughter with the dainty feet,
Danaë, who brought forth Perseus, eminent
Above the other warrior-chiefs; nor when
I carried off from Phœnix the renowned
His daughter, who bore Minos afterward,
And Rhadamanthus. Never so I loved
Semele, nor Alcmena who in Thebes
Brought forth to me the great-souled Hercules,
My valiant son, while Bacchus, the delight
Of men, was born of Semele; nor yet
So loved I Ceres, fair-haired queen, nor yet
Latona, gloriously beautiful,
Nor even thee, as now I love, and yield
My spirit to the sweetness of desire."
   Imperial Juno artfully replied:—
"Importunate Saturnius, what is this
That thou hast said? If on this summit height
Of Ida we recline, where all around
Is open to the sight, how will it be

Should any of the ever-living gods
Behold us sleeping, and to all the rest
Declare it? I could never, rising thence,
Enter again thy palace, save with shame.
Yet if thou truly speakest thy desire,
Thou hast a marriage-chamber of thine own,
Which Vulcan, thy beloved son, for thee
Framed, fitting to its posts the solid doors;
And thither let us go to take our rest
Within it, since thou hast declared thy will."

Then spake again the Cloud-compeller Jove:—
"O Juno! fear thou not that any god
Or man will look upon us. I shall throw
A golden cloud around us, which the Sun
Himself cannot look through, although his eye
Is piercing, far beyond all other eyes."

The son of Saturn spake, and took his wife
Into his arms, while underneath the pair
The sacred Earth threw up her freshest herbs,—
The dewy lotus, and the crocus-flower,
And thick and soft the hyacinth. All these
Upbore them from the ground. Upon this couch
They lay, while o'er them a bright golden cloud
Gathered, and shed its drops of glistening dew.

So slumbered on the heights of Gargarus
The All-Father, overcome by sleep and love,
And held his consort in his arms. Meanwhile
The gentle Sleep made haste to seek the fleet
Of Greece. He bore a message to the god
Neptune, who shakes the shores, and, drawing near,
He thus accosted him with wingèd words:—
"Now, Neptune, give the Greeks thy earnest aid,
And though it be but for a little space,
While Jupiter yet slumbers, let them win
The glory of the day; for I have wrapt
His senses in a gentle lethargy,
To which he is betrayed by Juno's wiles."
He spake, and took his way, departing thence
Among the tribes of men. These words inflamed
The god's desire to aid the Greeks; he sprang
Far on among the foremost, and exclaimed:—
"O Greeks! do ye again submit to yield
The victory to Hector, Priam's son,
That he may seize our fleet and bear away
The glory of the day? This is his hope,
And this his boast, since now Achilles lies
Inactive at his ships, in sullen wrath.
Yet little should we need him, if the rest

Stood bravely by each other. Hear me now,
And do what I advise. Let all of us,
The best and bravest, bearing shields, and capped
With glittering helms, and wielding in our hands
The longest spears, advance, and I will lead
The charge; nor do I think that Hector, son
Of Priam, daring as he seems, will yet
Abide our onset. Whoso has the heart
To make a stand with me, and yet who bears
A narrow shield, let it be given to one
Less warlike, and a broader shield be found."

He spake; they hearkened and obeyed. The kings
Tydides, and Ulysses, and the son
Of Atreus, Agamemnon, though their wounds
Still galled them, marshalled and reviewed the ranks,
And changed their arms; they made the braver wear
The better armor, and the worse they gave
To the less warlike. Now, when o'er their breasts
The burnished mail was girded, they began
Their march; the great earth-shaker, Neptune, led
The onset, grasping in his sinewy hand
A sword of fearful length and flashing blade,
Like lightning. No man dared encounter it
In combat; every arm was stayed by fear.

Right opposite, illustrious Hector ranged
His Trojans. Dark-haired Neptune and the son
Of Priam now engaged in desperate strife,
One on the side of Troy, and one for Greece.
The sea swelled upward toward the Grecian tents
And fleet, while both the armies flung themselves
Against each other with a loud uproar.
Not with such noise the ocean-billows lash
The mainland, when the violent north wind
Tumbles them shoreward; not with such a noise
Roar the fierce flames within the mountain glen,
When leaping upward to consume the trees;
And not so loudly howls the hurricane
Among the lofty branches of the oaks
When in its greatest fury, as now rose
The din of battle from the hosts that rushed
Against each other with terrific cries.
At Ajax glorious Hector cast his spear,
As face to face they stood. It missed him not,
But struck him where two belts upon his breast
O'erlapped each other,—that which held the shield
And that which bore the silver-studded sword.
These saved the tender muscles. Hector, vexed
That thus his weapon should have flown in vain,

Retreated toward his comrades, shunning death.
As he drew back, the Telamonian hurled
A stone,—for stones in multitude, that propped
The galleys, lay around, and rolled among
The feet of those who struggled. One of these
He lifted, smiting Hector on the breast,
Above the buckler's orb and near the neck.
He sent it spinning like a top; it fell
And whirled along the ground. As when beneath
The stroke of Father Jupiter an oak
Falls broken at the root, and from it fumes
A stifling smell of sulphur, and the heart
Of him who stands and sees it sinks with dread,—
For fearful is the bolt of mighty Jove,—
So dropped the valiant Hector to the earth
Amid the dust; his hand let fall the spear;
His shield and helm fell with him, and his mail
Of shining brass clashed round him. Then the Greeks
Rushed toward him, yelling fiercely, for they hoped
To drag him thence; and many a lance they cast;
But none by javelin or by thrust could wound
The shepherd of the people, for there came
Around him all the bravest of his host,—
Polydamas, Æneas, and the great

Agenor, and Sarpedon, he who led
The Lycian bands, and Glaucus the renowned;
These flung themselves into the strife, while none
Of all the rest refrained, but firmly held
Their broad round shields before him. Then his friends
Lifted him in their arms, and bore him off,
Out of the conflict, to his fiery steeds
That waited for him in the battle's rear,
With charioteer and sumptuous car; and these
Bore him to Ilium, sorely suffering.
  But when they now had reached the crossing-place
Of Xanthus, full of eddies, pleasant stream,
The progeny of ever-living Jove,
They lifted out the hero from the car,
And laid him on the ground, and on him poured
Water, at which his breath and sight returned.
He sat upon his knees, and from his throat
Gave forth the purple blood, and then he fell
Back to the ground, and darkness veiled his eyes,
For still his senses felt the stunning blow.
  The Greeks saw Hector leave the field, and pressed
The foe more hotly, and bethought themselves
Of their old valor. Then the swift of foot,
Oïlean Ajax, darted to the van,

And with his fir-tree spear smote Satnius, son
Of Enops, whom a Naiad eminent
For beauty among all the nymphs brought forth
To Enops, when on Satnio's banks he kept
His flocks. Oïleus' son, expert to wield
The spear, drew near, and pierced him in the flank.
Prostrate he fell, and suddenly the Greeks
And Trojans gathered round in desperate fray.
Polydamas, the mighty spearman, son
Of Panthoüs, coming to avenge him, smote
On the right shoulder Prothoënor, son
Of Areïlochus. The pitiless spear
Passed through, and falling in the dust he grasped
The earth with dying hands. Polydamas
Shouted aloud, exulting over him:—
"Not vainly, as I think, hath flown the spear
From the strong hand of the magnanimous son
Of Panthoüs. Some Achaian hath received
The weapon in his side, to lean upon
In going down to Pluto's dim abode."
He spake; the Achaians chafed to hear his boast,
And most the warlike son of Telamon;
For the slain Greek fell near him. Instantly,
Just as the Trojan moved away, he hurled
His shining lance. Polydamas, to escape

The death-stroke, sprang aside. Archilochus,
Antenor's son, received the blow: the gods
Had doomed him to be slain. It pierced the spine
Where the head joins the neck, and severed there
The tendons on each side. His head and mouth
And nostrils struck the ground before his knees.
  And thus to excellent Polydamas
Did Ajax shout in turn: "Bethink thee now,
And tell me truly, was not this a man
Worthy to die for Prothoënor's sake?
No man of mean repute or meanly born
He seems, but either brother to the knight
Antenor, or his son; for certainly
His looks declare him of Antenor's race."
  He spake; but well he knew the slain. Meanwhile
The Trojans heard and grieved. Then Acamas,
Stalking around his fallen brother, slew
Promachus, the Bœotian, with his spear,
While dragging off the dead man by the feet.
  Then o'er the fallen warrior, Acamas
Boasted aloud: "O measureless in threats!
Bowmen of Argos! not to us alone
Shall woe and mourning come; ye also yet
Will perish. See your Promachus o'erthrown,
And by my spear, that so my brother's death

May not be unrequited. Every man
Should wish a brother left to avenge his fall."
He ended, and the Greeks were vexed to hear
His boast; the brave Peneleus most of all
Was angered, and he rushed on Acamas,
Who waited not the onset of the king,
And in his stead was Ilioneus slain,
The son of Phorbas, who was rich in flocks,
Whom Mercury, of all the sons of Troy,
Loved most, and gave him ample wealth; his wife
Brought Ilioneus forth, and only him;
And him Peneleus smote beneath the brow,
In the eye's socket, forcing out the ball;
The spear passed through, and reappeared behind.
Down sat the wounded man with arms outstretched,
While, drawing his sharp sword, Peneleus smote
The middle of his neck, and lopped away
The helmèd head, which fell upon the ground,
The spear still in the eye. He lifted it
As one would lift a poppy up, and thus
He shouted, boasting, to the Trojan host:—
"Go now, ye Trojans, and inform from me
The father and the mother of the slain
That they may mourn within their palace walls
Illustrious Ilioneus. After this

Shall the sad wife of Promachus, the son
Of Alegenor, never hasten forth
To meet her husband with glad looks, when we
The Greeks return from Ilium with our fleet."
He spake; the Trojans all grew pale with fear,
And gazed around for an escape from death.
Say, Muses, ye who on the Olympian height
Inhabit, who was first among the Greeks
To gather bloody spoil, when now the power
That shakes the shores had turned the tide of war.
First, Ajax, son of Telamon, struck down
Hyrtius, the leader of the Mysian band,
And son of Gyrtias, while Antilochus
Spoiled Mermerus and Phalces. Morys next,
Slain by the weapon of Meriones,
Fell with Hippotion. Teucer overthrew
Prothoüs and Periphœtes. Atreus' son
Smote Hyperenor, prince among his tribe,
Upon the flank; the trenchant weapon drank
The entrails, and the soul, driven forth, escaped
Through the deep wound, and darkness veiled his eyes.
But Ajax swift of foot, Oïleus' son,
O'erthrew the most, for none could equal him
In swift pursuit when Jove ordained a flight.

## *BOOK XV.*

NOW when the Trojans in their flight had crossed
Rampart and trench, and many had been slain
By the pursuing Greeks, they made a halt
Beside their chariots, in despair and pale
With terror. Meanwhile Jupiter awoke,
On Ida's height, from slumber by the side
Of Juno, goddess of the golden throne.
At once he rose and saw the Trojan host
Routed, and, following close upon their flight,
The Argive warriors putting them to rout,
Aided by Neptune, sovereign of the sea,
And Hector lying on the field among
His fellow-warriors, breathing painfully,
Vomiting blood, and senseless, for the arm
That smote was not the feeblest of the Greeks.
The Father of immortals and of men
Beheld and pitied him, and terribly
Frowned upon Juno, and bespake her thus:—

"O evil-minded Juno, full of guile!
Thy arts have made the noble Hector leave
The combat, and have forced his troops to flee.
I know not whether 'twere not well that thou
Shouldst taste the fruit of thy pernicious wiles,
Chastised by me with stripes. Dost thou forget
When thou didst swing suspended, and I tied
Two anvils to thy feet, and bound a chain
Of gold that none could break around thy wrists?
Then didst thou hang in air amid the clouds,
And all the gods of high Olympus saw
With pity. They stood near, but none of them
Were able to release thee. Whoso came
Within my reach I seized, and hurled him o'er
Heaven's threshold, and he fell upon the earth
Scarce breathing. Yet the passion of my wrath,
Caused by the wrongs of godlike Hercules,
Was not to be so calmed; for craftily
Hadst thou called up the violent northern blast,
To chase him far across the barren deep,
And drive him from his course to populous Cos.
I rescued him at length, and brought him back
To Argos famed for steeds, though after long
And many hardships. I remind thee now
Of this, that thou mayst see of what avail

Hereafter thy dissembled love and all
Thy cunning strategies will be to thee."
He spake, and Juno, large-eyed and august,
Shuddered, and answered Jove with wingèd words:—
"Be witness, Earth, and the great Heavens above,
And waters of the Styx that glide beneath,—
That dreadful oath which most the blessed gods
Revere,—be witness, too, that sacred head
Of thine, and our own nuptial couch, by which
I would not rashly swear at any time,
That not by my persuasion Neptune went—
The shaker of the shores—to harass Troy
And Hector, and to aid the cause of Greece.
He went self-counselled; he had seen the Greeks
Pressed grievously beside their fleet, and took
Compassion on them. Yet would I advise
That he obey thy word, and take his place
Where thou, the Cloud-compeller, bid'st him go."
She ended, and the Father of the gods
And mortals smiled, and said, in wingèd words:—
"Large-eyed, imperial Juno, wouldst thou sit
In council with the immortals, and assist
My purposes, then Neptune, though at heart
He were averse, would yet conform his will

To mine and thine. If thou dost truly speak,
And from thy heart, go now to where the gods
Assemble, summon Iris, and with her
The archer-god Apollo. Give in charge
To Iris that she hasten to the host
Of the mailed Greeks, and bid king Neptune leave
The battle for his palace. Let the god
Phœbus, preparing Hector for the fight,
Breathe strength into his frame, that so he lose
The sense of pain which bows his spirit now,
And he shall force the Greeks again to flee
In craven fear. Then shall their flying host
Fall back upon the galleys of the son
Of Peleus, who shall send into the fight
His friend Patroclus. Him the mighty spear
Of Hector shall o'erthrow before the walls
Of Ilium, after many a Trojan youth
Shall by his hand have fallen, and with them
My noble son, Sarpedon. Roused to rage,
Then shall the great Achilles take the life
Of Hector. Be it from this time my care
That all the assaults of Trojans in the fleet
Be beaten back, till by Minerva's aid
The Greeks possess the lofty town of Troy.

Still am I angry, nor will I allow
One of the ever-living gods to aid
The Greeks, until the prayer of Peleus' son
Shall fully be accomplished, as my word
And nod were given, when Thetis clasped my knees,
Entreating me to honor, signally,
Her son, Achilles, spoiler of walled towns."
He spake; the white-armed goddess willingly
Obeyed him, and from Ida's summit flew
To high Olympus. As the thought of man
Flies rapidly, when, having travelled far,
He thinks, "Here would I be, I would be there,"
And flits from place to place, so swiftly flew
Imperial Juno to the Olympian mount,
And there she found the ever-living gods
Assembled in the halls of Jupiter.
These, as they saw her, starting from their seats,
Reached forth their cups to greet her. All the rest
She overlooked, and took the beaker held
By blooming Themis, who in haste had run
To meet her, and in wingèd accents said: —
"Why comest thou, O Juno! with the look
Of one o'ercome with fear. Hath Saturn's son,
Thy lord, disquieted thy soul with threats?"

The white-armed goddess Juno answered her:—
"Ask me not, heavenly Themis,—thou dost know
The cruel, arrogant temper that is his,—
But sit presiding at the common feast,
In this fair palace of the gods, and thou
And all in heaven shall hear what evils Jove
Has threatened. All, I think, will not rejoice
To hear the tidings, be they gods or men,
Though some contentedly are feasting now."
Thus having said, imperial Juno took
Her place, and all the gods within the halls
Of Jupiter were grieved. The goddess smiled,
But only with the lips; her forehead wore
Above the jetty brows no sign of joy,
While thus she spake in anger to the rest:—
"Vainly, and in our madness, do we strive
With Father Jove. We come and seek by craft
Or force to move his stubborn will; he sits
Apart, unyielding, unregarding, proud
Of the vast strength and power in which he stands
Above all other of the deathless gods.
Bear therefore patiently whatever ill
He sends to each. Already, as I learn,
Hath Mars his share of sorrow. In the war

Ascalaphus hath perished, whom he loved
Dearly, beyond all other men, and whom
The fiery god acknowledged as his son."
  As thus she spake, Mars smote his sinewy thighs
With his dropped hands, and sorrowfully said: —
  "Be not offended with me, ye who make
Your dwelling on Olympus, if I go
Down to the Achaian fleet, and there avenge
The slaughter of my son, though I be doomed
To fall before the thunderbolt of Jove,
And lie in blood and dust among the dead."
  He spake, and summoned Fear and Flight to yoke
His steeds, and put his glorious armor on.
Then greater and more terrible had been
The avenging wrath of Jupiter inflamed
Against the gods, if Pallas in her fear
For all the heavenly dwellers had not left
Her throne, and, rushing through the portals, snatched
The helmet from his head, and from his arm
The shield, and from his brawny hand the spear,
And laid the brazen weapon by, and thus
Rebuked the fiery temper of the god: —
  "Thou madman, thou art frantic, thou art lost!
Hast thou not ears to hear, nor any shame

Nor reason left? Hast thou not heard the words
Of white-armed Juno, who so lately left
Olympian Jupiter? Wouldst thou return
In pain and sorrow to the Olympian heights,
Driven back ingloriously, and made the cause
Of many miseries to all the gods?—
For Jove would leave the Trojans and their foes,
The gallant Greeks, and turn on us, and bring
Ruin upon Olympus. He would seize
Guilty and guiltless in his rage alike.
Wherefore I counsel thee to lay aside
Resentment for the slaughter of thy son,
Since braver men and stronger have been slain,
And will be slain hereafter. Vain it were
To seek from death to save the race of man."

She said, and, leading back the fiery Mars,
Seated him on his throne, while Juno called
Apollo forth, with Iris, messenger
Of heaven, and thus in wingèd accents spake:—

"Jove calls you both to Ida. When ye reach
Its heights, and look upon his countenance,
Receive his sovereign mandate and obey."

So spake imperial Juno, and withdrew
And took her seat again, while they in haste

Flew toward the mount of Ida, seamed with rills
And nurse of savage beasts. Upon the top
Of Gargarus they found the Thunderer,
The son of Saturn, sitting. In a cloud
Of fragrant haze he sat concealed; the twain
Entered and stood before the God of Storms,
Who saw them not displeased, so speedily
Had they obeyed his consort. First he turned
To Iris, and in wingèd accents said:—

"Haste thee, swift Iris, and report my words
To royal Neptune, and report them right.
Bid him, withdrawing from the battle-field,
Repair to the assembly of the gods,
Or the great ocean. If he disobey,
Contemning my command, then bid him think
Maturely, whether, mighty though he be,
He can withstand when I put forth my power
Against him. Greater is my strength than his,
And elder-born am I. Yet in his pride
Of heart he dares to call himself my peer,
Though all the others look on me with awe."

Thus spake the god, and Iris, whose swift feet
Are like the wind, obeyed, and downward plunged
From Ida's height to sacred Troy. As when

Snow-flakes or icy hail are dropped to earth
From clouds before the north wind when it sweeps
The sky, so darted Iris to the ground,
And stood by mighty Neptune's side, and said:—
"O dark-haired shaker of the shores, I bring
A message from the Ægis-bearer, Jove,
That thou, withdrawing from the battle-field,
Repair to the assembly of the gods,
Or the great ocean. If thou disobey,
Contemning his command, then hear his threat:
He will come hither and put forth his power
Against thee, and he warns thee not to tempt
The strife; for greater is his power than thine,
And he is elder-born, though in thy pride
Of heart thou dost declare thyself the peer
Of him whom all the rest regard with awe."
Illustrious Neptune answered with disdain:—
"In truth an arrogant speech; he seeks by force
To bar me from my purpose, who can claim
Rights equal to his own, though great his power.
We are three brothers,—Rhea brought us forth,—
The sons of Saturn,—Jupiter, and I,
And Pluto, regent of the realm below.
Three parts were made of all existing things,

And each of us received his heritage.
The lots were shaken; and to me it fell
To dwell forever in the hoary deep,
And Pluto took the gloomy realm of night,
And, lastly, Jupiter the ample heaven
And air and clouds. Yet doth the earth remain,
With high Olympus, common to us all.
Therefore I yield me not to do his will,
Great as he is; and let him be content
With his third part. He cannot frighten me
With gestures of his arm. Let him insult
With menaces the daughters and the sons
Of his own loves, and give them law, since they
Perforce must hear, and patiently submit."
Then the fleet-footed Iris spake again:—
"O dark-haired Neptune, shall I bear from thee
This harsh, defiant answer back to Jove,
Or shall it yet be changed? The prudent mind
Yields to the occasion, and thou knowest well
The Furies wait upon the elder-born."
Then spake in turn the god who shakes the shores:—
"O goddess Iris, thou hast wisely said.
An excellent thing it is when messengers
Know how to counsel well. But in my heart
And soul a wrathful sense of injury

Arises when he chides with insolent words
Me, who was equal with him in my lot,
And born to equal destinies. Yet now,
Although offended, I give way; but this
I tell thee, and 't is from my heart,—if he,
In spite of me and Pallas, spoiler-queen,
And Juno, Mercury, and Vulcan, spare
The towers of Troy,—if he refuse to bring
Ruin on her, and glory on the Greeks,
Then let him know that hatred without end
Or intermission is between us two."

As thus he spake, the shaker of the shores
Quitted the Grecian army, took his way
Seaward, and plunged into the deep. The host
Perceived their loss. Then Cloud-compelling Jove
Turned to Apollo and addressed him thus:—

"Now go at once to Hector, mailed in brass,
Belovèd Phœbus, for the god who shakes
The earth, departing to the ocean-deeps,
Avoids our wrath; else had the other gods,
Even they who far beneath the earth surround
Old Saturn, heard our quarrel. Well it is
For both of us that he, although enraged,
Braved not my arm, for otherwise the strife

Had not been ended without sweat. Now take
The fringèd ægis in thy hands, and shake
Its orb before the warrior Greeks, to fill
Their hearts with fear. I give, O archer-god,
Illustrious Hector to thy charge. Revive
The might that dwelt within him, till the Greeks
Reach, in their flight, the fleet and Hellespont;
Then shall it be my care, by word and deed,
To give them rest and respite from their toils."
He spake: Apollo hearkened and obeyed
His father, darting down from Ida's height
Like the fleet falcon, chaser of the dove,
And swiftest of the race of birds. He found
Hector, the warlike Priam's noble son,
No longer on his bed. He sat upright;
The life was coming back; he knew again
His friends; the heavy breathing ceased; the sweat
Was stanched; the will of ægis-bearing Jove
Revived the warrior's strength. The archer-god,.
Phœbus, approached, and, standing by him, said:—
"Why, Hector, son of Priam, dost thou sit
Languishing thus, apart from all the host?
Has aught of evil overtaken thee?"
And then the crested Hector feebly said:—

"Who may'st thou be, O kindest of the gods,
That thus dost question me? Hast thou not heard
That the great warrior Ajax, with a stone,
Smote me upon the breast, and made me leave
The battle-field, where I o'ertook and slew
His comrades by the galleys of the Greeks?
I thought to be this day among the dead
In Pluto's mansion; even now it seemed
That I was breathing my dear life away."
Then spake again Apollo, archer-god:—
"Take courage, for the son of Saturn sends
From Ida's summit one who will attend
And aid thee,—Phœbus of the golden sword,
Long practised to defend thy Troy and thee.
Rise now, encouraging thy numerous host
Of charioteers to press with their swift steeds
Straight toward the roomy galleys of the Greeks.
I go before to smooth for them the way,
And turn the Achaian bands, and make them flee."
He spake, and into the great ruler's breast
Breathed strength and courage. As a stabled horse,
Fed at his crib with barley, breaks the thong
That fastened him, and, issuing, scours the plain
Where he was wont in some smooth-flowing stream

To bathe his sides,—he holds his head aloft
Proudly, and o'er his shoulders streams the mane,—
Consciously beautiful, he darts away
On nimble knees, that bear him to the fields
He knows so well, and pastures of the mares;—
So after he had hearkened to the god
Moved the swift feet of Hector, and he flew
To cheer his horsemen on. As peasant men
Rush with their dogs in chase of hornèd stag
Or mountain goat, whose refuge is among
Thickets and lofty rocks, nor can they take
Their prey, for at their clamor there appears
A manèd lion in the way, and turns
The chasers back, although in hot pursuit,—
Thus did the Greeks embattled close pursue
The men of Ilium, striking with their swords
And two-edged spears; but when at length they saw
Hector among the ranks of armèd men,
Their hearts were troubled, and their courage sank.
  Thoas, Andræmon's son, the bravest far
Among the Ætolians, skilled to cast the spear
And combat hand to hand, addressed the Greeks.
In council few excelled him, when the youths
Assembled for debate. With prudent speech

Thoas bespake his fellow-warriors thus:—
"Gods! what a marvel do mine eyes behold;
Hector has risen from death! We fully thought,
Each one of us, that, smitten by the hand
Of Telamonian Ajax, he had died.
Some god hath rescued and restored to strength
This Hector who hath slain, and yet will slay,
I fear, so many Greeks. He comes not thus
Leading the charge without the aid of Jove,
The God of Thunders. Now let all of us
Follow this counsel: bid the multitude
Retreat upon the ships, and let the rest,
Who boast ourselves the bravest of the host,
Stand firm and breast his onset, and so break
Its fury with our lifted spears. I think,
With all his rage, he will be slow to fling
Himself into a band of armèd Greeks."
  He spake; they hearkened and at once complied;
The Ajaxes, the Prince Idomeneus,
Teucer, Meriones, and Meges, peer
Of Mars, assembled all the chiefs, and ranked
Their files to encounter Hector and his band
Of Trojans, while the multitude fell back
To the Greek galleys. Then, in close array,

The Trojan host moved forward. Hector led
The van in rapid march. Before him walked
Phœbus, the terrible ægis in his hands
Dazzlingly bright within its shaggy fringe,
By Vulcan forged, the great artificer,
And given to Jupiter, with which to rout
Armies of men. With this in hand he led
The assailants on. The Achaians kept their ground
In serried ranks, and a sharp yell arose
From Greeks and Trojans. Arrows from the string
Flew through the air, and spears from valiant hands.
Some pierced the breasts of warrior-youths, but more
Fell half-way ere they reached their aim, and plunged
Into the ground, still hungering for their prey.
As long as Phœbus held the ægis still,
The weapons reached and wounded equally
Both armies, and in both the people fell;
But ever when the god looked face to face
On the Greek knights, and shook the orb, and gave
A mighty shout, he made their hearts to sink
Within their bosoms, and their courage fled.
As when two beasts of prey at dead of night
Suddenly, while their keeper is away,
Scatter a herd of beeves or flock of sheep,

So the disheartened Greeks were put to rout,
For Phœbus sent among them fear, and gave
Victory to Hector and the men of Troy.
Then, as the lines were broken, man slew man.
First Stichius fell by Hector's hand, and next
Arcesilaus; one was chief among
The mailed Bœotians, one the trusty friend
Of brave Menestheus. Medon fell before
Æneas, and with him Iasus died.
Medon was great Oïleus' base-born son,
And Ajax was his brother, and he dwelt
In Phylacè, an exile, for his hand
Had slain the brother of his father's wife,
The step-dame Eriopis, late espoused.
Iasus was appointed to command
The warriors sent from Athens, and he claimed
His birth from Sphelus, son of Bucolus.
Mecistes fell before Polydamas.
Polites struck down Echius in the van,
And Clonius died by great Agenor's hand;
And Paris, when Deïochus had turned
To flee, among the foremost combatants,
Smote him upon the shoulder from behind,
And drave the brazen weapon through his heart.

Then, while the Trojans stripped the dead, the Greeks
Fled every way, and, falling as they ran
Into the trench and on the stakes, were driven,
Back o'er the rampart. Hector lifted up
His mighty voice, and bade the Trojans leave
The bloody spoil and hasten to the ships.
"And whomsoever I shall find apart
In any place, at distance from the ships,
There will I slay him. None of all his kin,
Women or men, shall build his funeral pile,
But dogs shall tear his limbs in sight of Troy."
He spake; and on the shoulders of his steeds
He laid the lash, and urged them toward the foe,
And cheered the Trojans on. They joined their shouts
To his, and charged with all their steeds and cars;
And fearful was the din. Apollo marched
Before them, treading down with mighty feet
The banks of the deep ditch, and casting them
Back to the middle, till a causey rose,
Broad, and of length like that to which a spear
Reaches when thrown by one who tries his strength.
O'er this the Trojans poured into the camp
By squadrons, with Apollo still in front,
Holding the marvellous ægis. He with ease

O'erthrew the rampart. As a boy at play
Among the sea-shore sands in childish sport
Scatters with feet and hands the little mounds
He reared, thus didst thou cause the mighty work,
O archer Phœbus, which the Greeks had reared
With so much toil, to crumble. Thou didst fill
Their hearts with eager thoughts of flight, till, hemmed
Between the assailants and their ships, they stopped
And bade each other stand, and raised their hands
To all the gods, and offered vows aloud.
Gerenian Nestor, guardian of the Greeks,
With arms extended toward the starry skies,
Prayed earnestly: "O Father Jove, if e'er
In fruitful Argos there were burned to thee
The thighs of fattened oxen or of sheep,
By one who asked a safe return to Greece,
And thou didst promise it, remember him,
God of Olympus, and avert from us
The day of evil. Suffer not the Greeks
To perish, slaughtered by the sons of Troy."
So spake he supplicating. Jupiter
The All-disposer thundered as he heard
The old man's prayer. The Trojans by that voice
Of ægis-bearing Jove were moved to press

The Greeks more resolutely, and were filled
With fiercer valor. As a mighty wave
On the great ocean, driven before a gale
Such as rolls up the hugest billow, sweeps
O'er the ship's side, so swept the Trojan host
With dreadful tumult o'er the wall. They drave
Their steeds into the camp, and there they fought
Beside the galley-sterns, and hand to hand,
With two-edged spears,—they from their cars, the Greeks
From their black ships on high with long-stemmed poles
Which lay upon the decks, prepared for fight
At sea, and strongly joined to blades of brass.
 Patroclus, while the Greeks and Trojans fought
Around the wall, at distance from the fleet
Sat with the brave Eurypylus in his tent,
Amusing him with pleasant talk, and dressed
His wound with balms that calmed the bitter pain.
But when he saw the Trojans bursting in
Over the wall, and heard the din, and saw
The Achaians put to rout, he gave a cry
Of sudden grief, and with his open hands
Smote both his thighs, and sorrowfully said:—
 "Eurypylus, I cannot stay with thee,
Much as thou needest me, for desperate grows

The struggle. Now let thine attendant take
The charge of thee. I hasten to persuade
Achilles to the field. Who knows but I,
With Jove's good help, may change his purpose yet?
For potent are the counsels of a friend."
The hero spake, and instantly his feet
Bore him away. Meanwhile the Achaian host
Firmly withstood the onset of their foes.
And yet, though greater was their multitude,
They could not drive the Trojans from the fleet,
Nor could the Trojans break, with all their power,
The serried lines, and reach the tents and ships.
As when a plumb-line, in the skilful hands
Of shipwright well instructed in his art
By Pallas, squares the beam that builds a bark,
So even was the fortune of the fray.
While some beside one galley waged the war,
And others round another, Hector came
To encounter Ajax the renowned, and both
Fought for one ship. The Trojan could not drive
The Greek away, and burn his ship with fire,
Nor the Greek drive the Trojan, for a god
Had brought him thither. Then did Ajax smite
Caletor, son of Clytius, with his spear

Upon the breast, as he was bringing fire
To burn the ship; he dropped the torch, and fell,
With clashing armor. Hector, as he saw
His kinsman lying slain amid the dust
By the black galley, raised his voice, and thus
Called to the Lycians and the men of Troy: —
"Hear, men of Troy and Lycia, and ye sons
Of Dardanus, who combat hand to hand,
Stand firm, and never yield this narrow ground.
Rescue the son of Clytius, who has fallen
Before the ships, nor let the Achaians make
His arms their spoil." The hero spake, and aimed
His shining spear at Ajax, whom it missed,
But smote Lycophron, Mastor's son, who served
Ajax, and dwelt with him, for he had left
His native land, Cythera, having slain
One of the gallant Cytherean race.
Him Hector smote upon the head beneath
The ear with his keen weapon, as he stood
Near Ajax; from the galley's stern he fell
Headlong upon the ground, with lifeless limbs.
Then to his brother Teucer Ajax spake: —
"Dear Teucer, see, our faithful friend is gone,
The son of Mastor, from Cythera's isle,

Whom we had learned to honor equally
With our own parents in our palaces.
He falls before the great-souled Hector's hand.
Where, then, are now thy shafts that carry death,
And where the bow that Phœbus gave to thee?"
  He spake, and Teucer, hearkening, came in haste,
With his bent bow, and quiver full of shafts,
And, standing near him, sent his arrows forth
Among the Trojan warriors. There he smote
Clitus, Pisenor's eminent son, the friend
Of the renowned Polydamas, who claimed
His birth from Panthoüs. Clitus held the reins,
Guiding the coursers of Polydamas
Where most the crowded Grecian phalanxes
Wavered and broke, that so he might support
Hector and his companions. Soon he met,
Brave as he was, disaster which no hand
Had power to avert: the bitter arrow struck
His neck behind, and from the chariot-seat
He fell to earth; the startled steeds sprang back;
The empty chariot rattled. This the king
Polydamas perceived, and came to meet
His steeds, and gave them to Astinoüs,
The son of Protiäon, charging him

To keep them ever near, and in his sight,
While he, returning, mingled with the throng
That struggled in the van. Then Teucer aimed
Another shaft at Hector mailed in brass,
Which, had it reached him fighting gallantly,
Had made him leave the battle, for his life
Had ended there. The act was not unseen
By All-disposing Jupiter, whose power
Protected Hector, and denied the Greek
The glory hoped for; for he snapped in twain
The firmly twisted cord as Teucer drew
That perfect bow; the brazen arrow flew
Aside; the warrior's hands let fall the bow,
And, shuddering, he bespake his brother thus:—
"Now woe is me! some deity, no doubt,
Brings all our plans to nought. 'T is he whose touch
Strikes from my hand the bow, and snaps in twain
The cord just twisted, which I bound myself
This morning to the bow, that it might bear
The frequent arrow bounding toward the foe."
He spake, and thus replied the man of might,
The Telamonian Ajax: "Lay aside
Thy bow, my brother, and thy store of shafts,
Since, in displeasure with the Greeks, a god

Has made them useless. Haste to arm thy hand
With a long spear, and on thy shoulders lay
A buckler, and with these attack the foe,
And bid thy fellows stand. Let Trojans see
That, even though the day thus far be theirs,
They cannot lay their hands on our good ships
Without a mighty struggle. Let us all
Be mindful of our fame for gallant deeds."

He spake, and Teucer went to place the bow
Within the tents, and on his shoulders hung
A fourfold shield, and placed on his grand brows
A stately helmet with a horse-hair crest
That nodded fearfully. He took in hand
A ponderous spear with brazen blade, and sprang
Forward with hasty steps, and stood beside
His brother Ajax. Hector, when he saw
That Teucer's shafts had failed him, called aloud
Upon the men of Lycia and of Troy: —

"Ye men of Troy and Lycia, and ye sons
Of Dardanus who combat hand to hand,
Acquit yourselves like men, my friends, and prove
Your fiery valor by these roomy ships;
For I have seen with mine own eyes the shafts
Of their chief warrior rendered impotent

By Jupiter. His hand is plainly seen
Among the sons of men; to some he gives
Glory above the rest; from some he takes
The glory, and withdraws from their defence.
He withers now the courage of the Greeks,
And succors us. Press closely round the fleet,
And combat. Whosoe'er among you all,
Wounded or beaten down, shall meet his death,
So let him die; 't is no inglorious fate
To perish fighting in his country's cause;
And he shall leave his wife and children safe,
His home and household store inviolate,
If now the Greeks depart to their own land."
  With words like these he filled their hearts anew
With strength and courage. On the other side
Ajax exhorted thus his warrior friends:—
  "Shame on you, Greeks! We perish here, unless
We rescue with strong arms our host and fleet.
Think ye that, should the crested Hector seize
Our galleys, ye may reach your homes on foot?
Hear ye not Hector's voice, who, fiercely bent
To burn our ships with fire, is cheering on
His warriors? To no dance he summons them,
But to the battle. Nought is left for us,

And other counsel there is none, save this:
Close with the foe; let every hand put forth
Its strength; far better 't were to die at once,
Or make at once our safety sure, than thus
To waste away, in lingering fight, beside
Our ships, destroyed by weaker arms than ours."
 So spake the chief, and all who heard received
Courage and strength. Then Hector put to death
Schedius, the son of Perimedes, prince
Of the Phocæans. Ajax also slew
Laodamas, Antenor's honored son,
A chief of infantry. Polydamas
Struck down Cyllenian Otus, who had come,
The comrade of Phylides, at the head
Of the high-souled Epeians. Meges saw,
And rushed upon Polydamas, who sprang
Aside unharmed, for Phœbus suffered not
The son of Panthoüs thus to be o'erthrown,
Fighting among the foremost. But the spear
Of Meges wounded Crœsmus in the breast;
He fell with clanging arms. The slayer stripped
The corpse; but Dolops, son of Lampus, skilled
To wield the spear, leaped on him in the act.
Lampus, the father, best of men, was son

Of king Laomedon, and eminent
For warlike prowess. Dolops struck the shield
Of Meges in the midst; the corselet stayed
The blade with its close-jointed plates, and saved
The warrior's life. That corselet Phyleus brought
From Ephyre, beside the Selleïs,
Given by his host, Euphetes, king of men,
For his defence in battle, and it now
Preserved his son from death. Then Meges smote
With his sharp spear the helm that Dolops wore,
And from its summit struck the horse-hair crest,
New-tinged with purple, and the cone entire
Fell midst the dust. While Meges, standing firm,
Fought thus, and hoped the victory, to his aid
Came warlike Menelaus, unobserved,
And, standing near, smote Dolops from behind,
Beneath the shoulder, and drave through the spear
Till it appeared beyond. The Trojan fell
Upon his face, and both the Greeks rushed on
To wrench the brazen armor from his limbs,
When Hector saw his fall and called aloud
Upon the kindred of the slain. He first
Rebuked the valiant Melanippus, son
Of Hicetaon, who but lately fed

His slow-paced beeves at Percotè, while yet
The enemy was far from Troy; but when
The Achaians landed from their well-oared barks,
He came to Troy, and took an eminent place
Among the Trojans. Near to Priam's halls
He had his dwelling, honored equally
With Priam's sons. Him Hector thus rebuked:—
"Why, Melanippus, are we loitering thus?
Grievest thou not to see thy kinsman slain?
And see'st thou not how eagerly the Greeks
Are spoiling Dolops of his arms? Come on
With me. No time is this for distant fight,
But either we must rout the Greeks, or they
Will level to the ground the lofty towers
Of Ilium, and will slay its citizens."
He spake, and led the way; his godlike friend
Followed him, while the son of Telamon,
Ajax, exhorted thus the sons of Greece:—
"Be men, my friends, and let a noble dread
Of shame possess your hearts, and jealously
Look to each other's honor in the heat
Of battle; for to men who flee there comes
No glory, and that way no safety lies."
He spake, and all were eager to drive back

The assaulting foe; they heeded well his words,
And drew around their barks a fence of mail,
While Jove urged on the Trojans. Then it was
That Menelaus, brave in battle, spake
To rouse the courage of Antilochus:—
"Antilochus, there is no other Greek
Younger than thou, or fleeter; none so strong
For combat. Would that, springing on the foe,
Thou mightest strike some Trojan warrior down."
So speaking, he drew back; but he had roused
The courage of his friend, who, springing forth
From midst the foremost combatants, took aim,
First looking keenly round, with his bright spear,
From which the Trojans shrank as they beheld
The hero cast it. Not in vain he threw
The weapon, for it struck upon the breast
Brave Melanippus, Hicetaon's son;
Beneath the pap it smote him as he came.
He fell with ringing arms; Antilochus
Sprang toward him like a hound that springs to seize
A wounded fawn, which, leaping from its lair,
Is stretched disabled by the hunter's dart.
So sprang the stout Antilochus on thee,
O Melanippus!—sprang to spoil thy limbs

Of armor; but the noble Hector saw,
And, hastening through the thick of battle, came
Against him. Mighty as he was in war,
Yet ventured not Antilochus to wait
His coming; but as flees a savage beast,
Conscious of guilty deed, when, having slain
Herdsman or hound, that kept the pastured kine,
He steals away before a crowd of men,
So fled the son of Nestor. On his rear
The Trojans under Hector poured a storm
Of weapons, and the din was terrible.
Yet when he reached the serried ranks of Greece
He turned and stood. Meanwhile the Trojan host,
Like ravening lions, fiercely rushed against
The galleys, that the will of Jupiter
Might be fulfilled; for now he nerved their limbs
With vigor ever new, while he denied
Stout hearts and victory to the Greeks, and cheered
Their foes with hope. His purpose was to give
The victory to Hector, Priam's son,
Till he should cast upon the beakèd ships
The fierce, devouring fire, and bring to pass
The end for which the cruel Thetis prayed.

Therefore did Jove the All-disposer wait

Till from a burning galley he should see
The flames arise. Then must the Trojan host,—
Such was his will,—retreating from the fleet,
Yield to the Greeks the glory of the day.
For this he moved the already eager heart
Of Hector, son of Priam, to attack
The roomy ships. The hero was aroused
To fury fierce as Mars when brandishing
His spear, or as a desolating flame
That rages on a mountain-side among
The thickets of a close-grown wood. His lips
Were white with foam; his eyes from underneath
His frowning brows streamed fire; and as he fought,
Upon the hero's temples fearfully
The helmet nodded. Jupiter himself
Sent aid from his high seat, and heaped on him
Honor and fame beyond the other chiefs,—
And they were many,—for his term of life
Was to be short. Minerva even now
Was planning to bring on its closing day,
Made fatal by the might of Peleus' son.
And now he strove to break the Grecian ranks,
Assaulting where he saw the thickest crowd
And the best weapons; yet in vain he strove

With all his valor. Through the serried lines
He could not break; the Greeks in solid squares
Resisted, like a rock that huge and high
By the gray deep abides the buffetings
Of the shrill winds and swollen waves that beat
Against it. Firmly thus the Greeks withstood
The Trojan host, and fled not. In a blaze
Of armor, Hector, rushing toward their ranks,
Fell on them like a mighty billow raised
By the strong cloud-born winds, that flings itself
On a swift ship, and whelms it in its spray,
While fearfully among the cordage howls
The blast; the sailors tremble and are faint
With fear, as men who deem their death-hour nigh.
So the Greek warriors were dismayed at heart.

As when a hungry lion suddenly
Springs on a herd of kine that crop the grass
By hundreds in the broad moist meadow-grounds,
Beneath the eye of one who never learned
To guard his hornèd charge from beasts of prey,
But ever walks before them or behind,
While the grim spoiler bounds into the midst
And makes a prey of one, and all the rest
Are scattered in affright, so all the Greeks

Were scattered by the will of heaven before
Hector and Father Jove. Yet only one,
Young Periphœtes of Mycenæ, fell,
The son of Copreus. Once his father went
An envoy from Eurystheus to the court
Of mighty Hercules. The son excelled
The father in all gifts of form and mind,
In speed, in war, in council eminent
Among the noblest of his land. His death
Brought Hector new renown; for as he turned,
Stepping by chance upon his buckler's rim,
That reached the ground, — the buckler which had been
His fence against the enemy's darts, — he fell
Backward, his helmet clashing fearfully
Around his temples. Hector saw, and came
In haste, and pierced his bosom with his spear,
Among his fellow-warriors, who with grief
Beheld, yet dared not aid him, such their awe
Of noble Hector. Now the Greeks retired
Among that row of galleys which were first
Drawn up the beach; the foe poured after them,
In hot pursuit; again the Greeks fell back,
Constrained, and left that foremost row behind,
And stood beside their tents in close array,

And not dispersed throughout the camp, for shame
And fear restrained them, and unceasingly
With shouts they bade each other bravely stand.
Chiefly Gerenian Nestor, wise to guide
The counsels of the Greeks, adjured them all,
And in their parents' name, to keep their ground.
"O friends, be men; so act that none may feel
Ashamed to meet the eyes of other men.
Think each one of his children and his wife,
His home, his parents, living yet or dead.
For them, the absent ones, I supplicate,
And bid you rally here, and scorn to fly."
He spake, and his brave words to every heart
Carried new strength and courage. Pallas then
Lifted the heaven-sent cloud that veiled the fight,
And all things in the clear full light were seen
On either side, both where the galleys lay
And where the warriors struggled. They beheld
Hector the great in war, and all his host,
Both those who formed the rear and wielded not
Their arms, and those who combated in front
Beside the ships. And now it pleased no more
The soul of valiant Ajax to remain
In the thick squadrons with the other Greeks,

But, striding on the galley-decks, he bore
A sea-pike two and twenty cubits long,
Huge, and beset with iron nails. As when
One who is skilled to vault on running steeds
Chooses four horses from a numerous herd,
And on the highway to a populous town
Drives them, while men and women in a crowd
Behold his feats with wonder, as he leaps
Boldly, without a fall, from steed to steed,
And back again, and all the while they run,
So on the lofty decks of those good ships
From ship to ship flew Ajax, lifting up
His mighty voice, — a shout that reached to heaven, —
And bade the Greeks defend their fleet and tents
Nor loitered Hector in those armèd throngs
Of Troy, but as a tawny eagle swoops
Upon a flock of birds that seek their food
Along a river's border, — geese or cranes,
Or long-necked swans, — so Hector in hot haste
Sprang toward a galley with an azure prow,
While mightily the power of Jove impelled
The hero onward, and inflamed his train
With courage. Fiercely then around the ships
The struggle was renewed. Thou wouldst have said

No toils of war could tire those resolute arms,
So stubbornly they fought. In every mind
The thought was this: the Greeks were in despair
Of rescue, and believed their hour had come
To perish; every Trojan hoped to give
The fleet to flames, and slay the sons of Greece.
With thoughts like these the hostile warriors closed.
  Then Hector laid his hand upon the stern
Of a stanch galley, beautiful and swift,
In which Protesilaüs came to Troy,—
It never bore him back. Around its keel
The Trojans and the Greeks fought hand to hand,
And slew each other. For no more they sent
The arrow or the javelin from afar,
Waiting to see the wound it gave, but each
With equal fury pressed upon his foe
With halberd and with trenchant battle-axe,
Huge sword and two-edged spear. Upon the ground
Had fallen many a fair black-hilted sword
With solid handles, some from slain men's hands,
Some from lopped arms of warriors; the dark earth
Ran red with blood. But Hector, having laid
His hand upon the galley's stern, held fast
To the carved point, and called upon his men:—

"Bring fire, and press in throngs upon the foe;
For now doth Jove vouchsafe to us a day
Worth all the past,—a day on which we make
The ships our prey. Against the will of Heaven
They landed on our coast, and brought on us
Disasters many, through the coward fears
Of our own elders, who denied my wish
To combat at the galleys, and held back
The people. But if then the Thunderer
Darkened our minds, his spirit moves us now
In what we do, and we obey his will."
He spake; and they with fiercer valor fell
Upon the Greeks. Even Ajax could no more
Withstand the charge, but, fearing to be slain,
Amid a storm of darts withdrew a space,
To where the seven-foot bench of rowers lay,
And left the galley's stern. There, as he stood,
He watched the assailants keenly, and beat back
With thrusts of his long spear whoever brought
The firebrand. With terrific shouts he called
Upon the Greeks to combat manfully:—
"O friends, Achaian heroes, ministers
Of Mars, be men, be mindful of your fame
For valor. Do ye dream that in your rear

Are succors waiting us, or firmer walls
That may protect us yet? Nay, no fenced town
Have we for refuge, flanked with towers from which
Fresh troops may take our place. Between the sea
And country of the well-armed Trojans lie
Our tents; our native land is far away;
And now our only hope of safety left
Is in our weapons: there is no retreat."

He spake, and mightily with his sharp spear
Thrust at whoever of the men of Troy
At Hector's bidding came with fire to burn
The galleys. On the blade of that long spear
The hero took them as they came, and slew
In close encounter twelve before the fleet.

## *BOOK XVI.*

SUCH was the struggle for that gallant bark.
Meanwhile Patroclus stood beside his friend,
The shepherd of the people, Peleus' son,
And shed hot tears, as when a fountain sheds
Dark waters streaming down a precipice.
The great Achilles, swift of foot, beheld
And pitied him, and spake these wingèd words: —
"Why weepest thou, Patroclus, like a girl, —
A little girl that by her mother's side
Runs, importuning to be taken up,
And plucks her by the robe, and stops her way,
And looks at her, and cries, until at last
She rests within her arms? Thou art like her,
Patroclus, with thy tears. Dost thou then bring
Sad tidings to the Myrmidons or me?
Or hast thou news from Phthia? It is said
That still Menœtius, son of Actor, lives,
And Peleus also, son of Æacus,

Among the Myrmidons. Full bitterly
Should we lament to hear that either died.
Or mournest thou because the Achaians fall
Through their own folly by the roomy ships?
Speak, and hide nothing, for I too would know."
 And thou, O knight Patroclus, with a sigh
Deep-drawn, didst answer thus: "Be not displeased,
Achilles, son of Peleus, bravest far
Of all the Achaian army! for the Greeks
Endure a bitter lot. The chiefs who late
Were deemed their mightiest are within the ships,
Wounded or stricken down. There Diomed,
The gallant son of Tydeus, lies, and there
Ulysses, the great spearman, wounded both;
And Agamemnon; and Eurypylus,
Driven from the field, an arrow in his thigh.
Round them the healers, skilled in remedies,
Attend and dress their painful wounds, while thou,
Achilles, sittest here implacable.
O, never be such fierce resentments mine
As thou dost cherish, who art only brave
For mischief! Whom wilt thou hereafter aid,
If now thou rescue not the perishing Greeks?
O merciless! it cannot surely be

That Peleus was thy father, or the queen
Thetis thy mother; the green sea instead
And rugged precipices brought thee forth,
For savage is thy heart. But if thou heed
The warning of some god, if thou hast heard
Aught which thy goddess-mother has received
From Jove, send me at least into the war,
And let me lead thy Myrmidons, that thus
The Greeks may have some gleam of hope. And give
The armor from thy shoulders. I will wear
Thy mail, and then the Trojans, at the sight,
May think I am Achilles, and may pause
From fighting, and the warlike sons of Greece,
Tired as they are, may breathe once more, and gain
A respite from the conflict. Our fresh troops
May easily drive back upon their town
The weary Trojans from our tents and fleet."

So spake he, sighing; rash and blind, he asked
Death for himself and evil destiny.
Achilles the swift-footed also drew
A heavy sigh, and thus in turn he spake:—

"What, O divine Patroclus, hast thou said?
I fear no omen yet revealed to me;
Nor has my goddess-mother told me aught

From Jove; but ever in my heart and soul
Rankles the painful sense of injury done
By one who, having greater power, deprives
An equal of his right, and takes away
The prize he won. This is my wrong, and this
The cause of all my bitterness of heart.
Her whom the sons of Greece bestowed on me
As my reward, a trophy of my spear,
After the sack of a fenced city,—her
Did Agamemnon, son of Atreus, take
Out of my hands, as if I were a wretch,
A worthless outcast. But let that affront
Be with the things that were. It is not well
To bear a grudge forever. I have said
My anger should not cease to burn until
The clamor of the battle and the assault
Should reach the fleet. But go thou and put on
My well-known armor; lead into the field
My Myrmidons, men that rejoice in war,
Since like a lowering cloud the men of Troy
Surround the fleet, and the Achaians stand
In narrow space close pressed beside the sea,
And all the city of Ilium flings itself
Against them, confident of victory,

Now that the glitter of my helm no more
Flashes upon their eyes. Yet very soon
Their flying host would fill the trenches here
With corpses, had but Agamemnon dealt
Gently with me; and now their squadrons close
Around our army. Now no more the spear
Is wielded by Tydides Diomed
In rescue of the Greeks; no more the shout
Of Agamemnon's hated throat is heard;
But the man-queller Hector, lifting up
His voice, exhorts the Trojans, who, in throngs,
Raising the war-cry, fill the plain, and drive
The Greeks before them. Gallantly lead on
The charge, Patroclus; rescue our good ships;
Let not the enemy give them to the flames,
And cut us off from our desired return.
Follow my counsel; bear my words in mind;
So shalt thou win for me among the Greeks
Great honor and renown, and they shall bring
The beautiful maiden back with princely gifts.
When thou hast driven the assailants from the fleet,
Return thou hither. If the Thunderer,
Husband of Juno, suffer thee to gain
That victory, seek no further to prolong

The combat with the warlike sons of Troy,
Apart from me, lest I be brought to shame,
Nor, glorying in the battle and pursuit,
Slaying the Trojans as thou goest, lead
Thy men to Troy, lest from the Olympian mount
One of the ever-living gods descend
Against thee: Phœbus loves the Trojans well.
But come as soon as thou shalt see the ships
In safety; leave the foes upon the plain
Contending with each other. Would to Jove
The All-Father, and to Pallas, and the god
Who bears the bow, Apollo, that of all
The Trojans, many as they are, and all
The Greeks, not one might be reprieved from death,
While thou and I alone were left alive
To overthrow the sacred walls of Troy."

So talked they with each other. Ajax, whelmed
Beneath a storm of darts, meantime but ill
Endured the struggle, for the will of Jove
And the fierce foe prevailed. His shining helm
Rang fearfully, as on his temples fell,
Stroke following after stroke, the weapons hurled
Against its polished studs. The buckler borne
Firmly on his left arm, and shifted oft

From side to side, had wearied it, and yet
The Trojans, pressing round him, could not drive,
With all their darts, the hero from his place.
Heavily heaved his panting chest; his limbs
Streamed with warm sweat; there was no breathing-time;
On danger danger followed, toil on toil.
  Now, Muses, dwellers of Olympus, tell
How first the galleys of the Greeks were fired.
  Hector drew near, and smote with his huge sword
The ashen spear of Ajax just below
The socket of the blade, and cut the stem
In two. The son of Telamon in vain
Brandished the severed weapon, while afar
The brazen blade flew off, and ringing fell
To earth. Then Ajax in his mighty mind
Acknowledged that the gods were in the war,
And shuddered, knowing that the Thunderer
Was thwarting all his warlike purposes,
And willed the victory to Troy. The chief
Withdrew beyond the reach of spears, while fast
The eager enemy hurled the blazing brands
At the swift ship, and wrapped the stern in flames
Unquenchable. Achilles saw, and smote
His thigh, and spake: "Patroclus, noble friend

And knight, make haste: already I behold
The flames that rage with fury at the fleet.
Now, lest the enemy seize our ships and we
Be barred of our return, put quickly on
Thy armor; be my task to call the troops."
He spake: Patroclus then in glittering brass
Arrayed himself; and first around his thighs
He put the beautiful greaves, and fastened them
With silver clasps; around his chest he bound
The breastplate of the swift Æacides,
With star-like points, and richly chased; he hung
The sword with silver studs and blade of brass
Upon his shoulders, and with it the shield
Solid and vast; upon his gallant head
He placed the glorious helm with horsehair plume,
That grandly waved on high. Two massive spears
He took, that fitted well his grasp, but left
The spear which great Achilles only bore,
Heavy and huge and strong, and which no arm
Among the Greeks save his could poise; his strength
Alone sufficed to wield it. 'Twas an ash
Which Chiron felled in Pelion's top, and gave
To Peleus, that it yet might be the death
Of heroes. Then he called, to yoke with speed

The steeds, Automedon, whom he esteemed
Next to Achilles, that great scatterer
Of armies; for he found him ever firm
In battle, breasting faithfully its shock.
Automedon led forth to take the yoke
Xanthus and Balius, coursers that in speed
Were like the wind. Podargè brought them forth
To Zephyrus, while she, the Harpy, grazed
By ocean's streams. Upon the outer side
He joined to them the noble Pedasus,
Brought by Achilles from the captured town
Where ruled Eëtion. Though of mortal stock,
Well might he match with those immortal steeds.
  Meanwhile Achilles armed the Myrmidons,
Passing from tent to tent. Like ravening wolves,
Terribly strong, that, having slain among
The hills an antlered stag of mighty size,
Tear and devour it, while their jaws are stained
With its red blood, then gather in a herd
About some darkly flowing stream, and lap
The sullen water with their slender tongues,
And drop the clots of blood from their grim mouths,
And, although gorged, are fierce and fearless still, —
So came the leaders of the Myrmidons,

In rushing crowds, about the valiant friend
Of swift Æacides. Among them stood
Achilles, great in war, encouraging
The charioteers and warriors armed with shields.
Achilles, dear to Jupiter, had led
Fifty swift barks to Ilium, and in each
Were fifty men, companions at the oar.
O'er these he gave command to five; himself,
Supreme in power, was ruler over all.
One band, the nobly armed Menestheus led,
Son of Spercheius. To that river-god,
Beautiful Polydora brought him forth,
Daughter of Peleus; she, a mortal maid,
Met an immortal's love. Yet Borus, son
Of Periëres, owned the boy and took
The mother for his bride, with princely dower.
Eudorus led the second band, a youth
Of warlike mould, whom Polymela bore,
Daughter of Phylas, graceful in the dance.
In secrecy she brought him forth, for once
The mighty Argus-queller saw the maid
Among the choir of those who danced and sang
At Dian's festival, the huntress-queen,
Who bears the golden shafts; he saw and loved

And, climbing to her chamber, met by stealth
The damsel, and she bore a gallant son,
Eudorus, swift of foot and brave in war.
When Ilithyia, midwife goddess, gave
The boy to see the pleasant light of day,
The stout Echecleus, son of Actor, brought
The mother to his house, with liberal dower.
The aged Phylas reared the child she left
Tenderly as a son, and loved him well.
Pisander, warlike son of Mæmalus,
Commanded the third squadron; none like him
Among the Myrmidons could wield the spear
Except Pelides. Phœnix, aged knight,
Led the fourth squadron. With the fifth and last
There came Alcimedon, Laerceus' son,
As leader. When their ranks were duly formed,
Achilles spake to them in earnest words:—
"Now, Myrmidons, forget no single word
Of all the threats ye uttered against Troy
Since first my wrath began. Ye blame me much,
And say: 'Hard-hearted son of Peleus, sure
Thy mother must have suckled thee on gall;
For sternly thou dost keep us in the ships,
Unwilling as we are. We might, at least,

Crossing the sea, return in our good ships,
If thus thine anger is to last.' These words
Ye utter oft when our assemblies meet,
And now the great occasion is at hand
Which ye have longed for; now let him whose heart
Is fearless meet the Trojans valiantly."
He spake, and roused their courage and their might;
And as they heard their king they brought their ranks
To closer order. As an architect
Builds up, with closely fitting stones, the wall
Of some tall mansion, proof against the blast,
So close were now the helms and bossy shields.
Shield leaned on shield, and helm on helm, and man
On man, and on the glittering helmet-cones
The horse-hair plumes with every motion touched
Each other, so compact the squadrons stood.
Two heroes, nobly armed, were at their head,
Patroclus and Automedon, and both
Had but one thought, — to combat in the van.
Entering his tent, Achilles raised the lid
Of a fair coffer, beautifully wrought,
Which silver-footed Thetis placed on board
His bark, and filled with tunics, cloaks well lined,
And fleecy carpets. There he also kept

A goblet richly chased, from which no lip
Of man, save his, might drink the dark red wine,
Nor wine be poured to any god save Jove,
The mighty Father. This he took in hand
And purified with sulphur first, and then
Rinsed with clear water. Next, with washen hands,
He drew the dark red wine, and stood without,
In the open space, and, pouring out the wine,
Prayed with his eyes turned heavenward, not unheard
By Jupiter, who wields the thunderbolt.
"Dodonian Jove, Pelasgian, sovereign King,
Whose dwelling is afar, and who dost rule
Dodona winter-bound, where dwell thy priests,
The Selli, with unwashen feet, who sleep
Upon the ground! Thou once hast heard my prayer,
And thou hast honored me, and terribly
Avenged me on the Greeks. Accomplish yet
This one request of mine. I shall remain
Among the rows of ships, but in my stead
I send my comrade, who will lead to war
My vast array of Myrmidons. With him,
O God of Thunders, send the victory.
Make his heart bold; let even Hector learn
Whether my follower, though alone, can wage

Successful war, or conquer only then
When I go forth with him into the field
Of slaughter. When he shall have beaten back
The assailants from the fleet, let him return
Unharmed to my good galleys and to me,
With all his arms and all his valiant men."

So spake he, offering prayer, and Jupiter,
The Great Disposer, hearkened. Half the prayer
The All-Father granted him, and half denied:
To drive the storm of battle from the fleet
He granted, but denied his friend's return
In safety. When the warrior thus had prayed,
And poured the wine to Father Jove, he went
Into his tent again, and there replaced
The goblet in the coffer. Coming forth,
He stood before the entrance to behold
The terrible encounter of the hosts.

The newly armed, led by their gallant chief,
Patroclus, marched in warlike order forth,
And in high hope, to fall upon the foe.
As wasps, that by the wayside build their cells,
Angered from time to time by thoughtless boys,—
Whence mischief comes to many,—if by chance
Some passing traveller should unwittingly

Disturb them, all at once are on the wing,
And all attack him, to defend their young;
So fearless and so fierce the Myrmidons
Poured from their fleet, and mighty was the din.
Patroclus with loud voice exhorted them:—
"O Myrmidons, companions of the son
Of Peleus, bear in mind, my friends, your fame
For valor, and be men, that we who serve
Achilles, we who combat hand to hand,
May honor him by our exploits, and teach
Wide-ruling Agamemnon how he erred
Slighting the bravest warrior of the Greeks."
These words awoke the courage and the might
Of all who heard them, and in close array
They fell upon the Trojans. Fearfully
The fleet around them echoed to the sound
Of Argives shouting. When the Trojans saw,
In glittering arms, Menœtius' gallant son
And his attendant, every heart grew faint
With fear; the close ranks wavered; for they thought
That the swift son of Peleus at the fleet
Had laid aside his wrath, and was again
The friend of Agamemnon. Eagerly
They looked around for an escape from death.

Then first Patroclus cast his shining spear
Into the crowd before him, where they fought
Most fiercely round the stern of the good ship
Of brave Protesilaus. There it smote
Pyræchmes, who had led from Amydon,
On the broad Axius, his Pæonian knights.
Through his right shoulder went the blade; he fell,
Heavily groaning, to the earth. His band
Of warriors from Pæonia, panic-struck,
Fled from Patroclus as they saw their chief
Cut off, their bravest in the battle-field.
So from the ship he drave the foe, and quenched
The blazing fire. There lay the half-burnt bark,
While with a mighty uproar fled the host
Of Troy, and from between the beakèd ships
Poured after them with tumult infinite
The Greeks. As when from some high mountain-top
The God of Lightnings, Jupiter, sweeps off
The overshadowing cloud, at once appear
The watch-towers and the headland heights and lawns
All in full light, and all the unmeasured depth
Of ether opens, so the Greeks, when thus
Their fleet was rescued from the hostile flame,
Breathed for a space; and yet they might not cease

From battle, for not everywhere alike
Were chased the Trojans from the dark-hulled ships
Before the Greeks, but struggled still to keep
The mastery, and yielded but to force.
  Then in that scattered conflict of the chiefs
Each Argive slew a warrior. With his spear
The brave son of Menœtius made a thrust
At Areïlochus, and pierced his thigh,
Just as he turned away, and through the part
Forced the keen weapon, splintering as it went
The bone, and brought the Trojan to the ground;
And warlike Menelaus pierced the breast
Of Thoas where the buckler left it bare,
And took his life. The son of Phyleus saw
Amphiclus rushing on, and with his spear
Met him and pierced his leg below the knee,
Where brawniest is the limb. The blade cut through
The sinews, and his eyes were closed in night.
There fought the sons of Nestor. One of these,
Antilochus, transfixed with his good spear
Atymnius through the flank, and brought him down
At his own feet. With sorrow Maris saw
His brother fall, and toward Antilochus
Flew to defend the corpse; but ere he strook,

The godlike Thrasymedes, with a blow
That missed not, smote his shoulder, tearing off
With the spear's blade upon the upper arm
The muscles from the bone. With ringing arms
He fell, and darkness gathered o'er his eyes.
Thus were two brothers by two brothers slain,
And sent to Erebus; two valiant friends
Were they of King Sarpedon, and the sons
Of Amisodarus, who reared and fed
Chimera, the destroyer of mankind.

Oïlean Ajax, springing forward, seized
On Cleobulus, for the struggling crowd
Hindered his flight. He took the Trojan's life,
Smiting the neck with his huge-handled sword;
The blade grew warm with blood, and cruel fate
Brought darkness o'er the dying warrior's eyes.
Peneleus fought with Lycon; each had cast
His spear and missed his aim, and now with swords
The twain encountered. Lycon dealt a stroke
Upon the crested helmet of his foe,
And the blade failed him, breaking at the hilt.
Meantime Peneleus smote beneath the ear
The neck of Lycon: deep the weapon went;
The severed head, held only by the skin,
Dropped to one side, and life forsook the limbs.

Meriones, o'ertaking Acamas,
In rapid flight, discharged a mighty blow
On his left shoulder as he climbed his car;
He fell, and darkness gathered o'er his eyes.
Then plunged Idomeneus the cruel spear
Into the mouth of Erymas. The blade
Passed on beneath the brain, and pierced the neck,
And there divided the white bones. It dashed
The teeth out; both the eyes were filled with blood,
Which gushed from mouth and nostrils as he breathed;
And the black cloud of death came over him.
Thus every Grecian leader slew his man.
As ravening wolves that spring on lambs and kids,
And seize them, wandering wide among the hills
Beyond the keeper's care, and bear them off,
And rend with cruel fangs their helpless prey,
So fiercely did the Achaians fling themselves
Upon the men of Troy, who only thought
Of flight from that tumultuous strife, and quite
Forgot their wonted valor. All the while
The greater Ajax sought to hurl his spear
At Hector, clad in brazen mail, who yet,
Expert in battle, kept his ample chest
Hid by his bull's-hide shield, and, though he heard

The hiss of darts and clash of spears, and saw
The fortune of the field deserting him,
Lingered to rescue his beloved friends.
   As from the summit of Olympus spreads
A cloud into the sky that late was clear,
When Jove brings on the tempest, with such speed
In clamorous flight the Trojans left the fleet,
Yet passed they not the trench in seemly plight.
The rapid steeds of Hector bore him safe
Across with all his arms, while, left between
The high banks of the trench, the Trojan host
Struggled despairingly. The fiery steeds,
Harnessed to many a chariot, left it there
With broken pole. Patroclus followed close,
With mighty voice encouraging the Greeks,
And meditating vengeance on the foe,
That noisily ran on, and right and left
Were scattered, filling all the ways. The dust
Rose thick and high, and spread, and reached the clouds,
As with swift feet the Trojan coursers held
Their way to Ilium from the tents and ships.
Patroclus where he saw the wildest rout
Drave thither, shouting threats. Full many a chief
Fell under his own axle from his car,

And chariots with a crash were overthrown.
The swift, immortal horses which the gods
Bestowed on Peleus leaped the trench at once,
Eager to reach the plain. As eagerly
Patroclus longed to overtake and smite
Hector, whose steeds were hurrying him away.
As when, in autumn time, the dark-brown earth
Is whelmed with water from the stormy clouds,
When Jupiter pours down his heaviest rains,
Offended at men's crimes who override
The laws by violence, and drive justice forth
From the tribunals, heedless of the gods
And their displeasure, — all the running streams
Are swelled to floods, — the furious torrents tear
The mountain slopes, and, plunging from the heights
With mighty roar, lay waste the works of men,
And fling themselves into the dark-blue sea, —
Thus with loud tumult fled the Trojan horse.
Patroclus, having cut the nearest bands
Of Troy in pieces, made his warriors turn
Back to the fleet, and, eager as they were,
Stopped the pursuit that led them toward the town.
Then, in the area bounded by the sea,
River, and lofty wall, he chased and smote

And took full vengeance. With his glittering spear
He wounded Pronoüs where the buckler left
The breast exposed; the Trojan with a clash
Fell to the earth, and life forsook his limbs.
Advancing in his might, Patroclus smote
Thestor, the son of Enops, as he sat
Cowering upon his sumptuous seat, o'ercome
With fear, and dropped the reins. Through his right cheek
Among the teeth Patroclus thrust his spear,
And o'er the chariot's border drew him forth
With the spear's stem. As when an angler sits
Upon a jutting rock, and from the sea
Draws a huge fish with line and gleaming hook,
So did Patroclus, with his shining spear,
Draw forth the panting Trojan from his car,
And shook him clear: he fell to earth and died.
 As Eryalus then came swiftly on,
Patroclus flung a stone, and on the brow
Smote him; the Trojan's head, beneath the blow,
Parted in two within the helm; he fell
Headlong to earth, a prey to ghastly death.
Then slew he Erymas, Amphoterus,
Epaltes, Pyris, Ipheus, Echius,
Tlepolemus, Damastor's son, and next

Euippus; nor was Polymelus spared,
The son of Argias,—smitten all, and thrown,
Slain upon slain, along their mother earth.
  And now Sarpedon, as he saw his friends,
The unbelted Lycians, falling by the hand
Of Menœtiades, exhorted thus
The gallant Lycians: "Shame upon you all,
My Lycians! whither do you flee? Be bold!
For I myself will meet this man, and learn
Who walks the field in triumph thus, and makes
Such havoc in our squadrons; for his hand
Has laid full many a gallant warrior low."
  He spake, and from his car with all his arms
Sprang to the ground, while on the other side
Patroclus, as he saw him come, leaped down
And left his chariot. As on some tall rock
Two vultures, with curved talons and hooked beaks,
Fight screaming, so these two with furious cries
Advanced against each other. When the son
Of crafty Saturn saw them meet, his heart
Was touched with pity, and he thus bespake
His spouse and sister Juno: "Woe is me!
Sarpedon, most beloved of men, is doomed
To die, o'ercome by Menœtiades.

And now I halt between two purposes,—
Whether to bear him from this fatal fight,
Alive and safe, to Lycia's fertile fields,
Or let him perish by his enemy's hand."
  Imperial, large-eyed Juno answered thus:—
"What words, dread son of Saturn, hast thou said!
Wouldst thou deliver from the common lot
Of death a mortal doomed long since by fate?
Do as thou wilt, but be thou sure of this,—
The other gods will not approve. And bear
In mind these words of mine. If thou shouldst send
Sarpedon home to Lycia safe, reflect
Some other god may claim the right, like thee,
To rescue his beloved son from death
In battle; for we know that in the war
Round Priam's noble city are many sons
Of gods, who will with vehement anger see
Thy interposing hand. Yet if he be
So dear to thee, and thou dost pity him,
Let him in mortal combat be o'ercome
By Menœtiades, and when the breath
Of life has left his frame, give thou command
To Death and gentle Sleep to bear him hence
To the broad realm of Lycia. There his friends

And brethren shall perform the funeral rites;
There shall they build him up a tomb, and rear
A column,—honors that become the dead."

He ceased, nor did the All-Father disregard
Her words. He caused a bloody dew to fall
Upon the earth in sorrow for the son
Whom well he loved, and whom Patroclus soon
Should slay upon the fertile plain of Troy,
Far from the pleasant land that saw his birth.

The warriors now drew near. Patroclus slew
The noble Thrasymelus, who had been
Sarpedon's valiant comrade in the war.
Below the belt he smote him, and he fell
Lifeless. Sarpedon threw his shining lance;
It missed, but struck the courser Pedasus
In the right shoulder. With a groan he fell
In dust, and, moaning, breathed his life away.
Then the two living horses sprang apart,
And the yoke creaked, and the entangled reins
Were useless, fastened to the fallen horse.
Automedon, the mighty spearman, saw
The remedy, and from his brawny thigh
He drew his sword, and cut the outside horse
Loose from his fellows. They again were brought

Together, and obeyed the reins once more;
And the two chiefs renewed the mortal fight.
  And now, again, Sarpedon's shining spear
Was vainly flung; the point, in passing o'er
Patroclus's left shoulder, gave no wound.
In turn, Patroclus, hurling not in vain
His weapon, smote him where the midriff's web
Holds the tough heart. He fell as falls an oak
Or poplar or tall pine, which workmen hew
Among the mountains with their sharpened steel
To frame a ship. So he before his steeds
And chariot fell upon the bloody dust,
And grasped it with his hands, and gnashed his teeth.
As when a lion coming on a herd
Seizes, amid the crowd of stamping beeves,
A tawny and high-mettled bull, that dies
Bellowing in fury in the lion's jaws,—
Like him, indignant to be overcome,
The leader of the bucklered Lycian host,
Laid prostrate by Patroclus, called by name
His dear companion, and addressed him thus:—
  "Beloved Glaucus, mighty among men!
Now prove thyself a hero, now be bold.
Now, if thou have a warrior's spirit, think

Of naught but battle. Go from rank to rank,
Exhorting all the Lycian chiefs to fight
Around Sarpedon. Combat thou for me
With thy good spear, for I shall be to thee
A shame and a reproach through all thy days,
If here the Greeks, beside whose ships I fall,
Bear off my armor. Stand thou firm, and stir
Thy people up to combat valiantly."
  While he was speaking, death crept o'er his sight
And stopped his breath. Patroclus set his heel
Against his bosom, and plucked out the spear;
The midriff followed it, and thus he drew
The life and weapon forth at once. Meantime
The Myrmidons held fast the snorting steeds,
That, loosened from the Lycian's car, were bent
On flight. The grief of Glaucus as he heard
His comrade's voice was bitter, and his heart
Ached at the thought that he could bring no aid.
He seized his arm and pressed it in his grasp,
For there the wound which Teucer's arrow left,
When Glaucus stormed the wall and Teucer's shafts
Defended it, still pained him grievously,
And thus he prayed to Phœbus, archer-god:—
  "Give ear, O king! wherever thou abide

In the opulent realm of Lycia, or in Troy;
For everywhere thou hearest those who cry
To thee in sorrow, and great sorrow now
Is on me. Grievous is the wound I bear;
Sharp are the pains that pierce my hand; the blood
Cannot be stanched; my very arm becomes
A burden; I can wield the spear no more
With a firm grasp, nor combat with the foe.
A mighty chief—Sarpedon, son of Jove—
Has perished, and the father came not nigh
To aid his son. Yet come thou to my aid,
O monarch-god! and heal this painful wound,
And give me strength to rally to the fight
The Lycian warriors, and myself contend
Valiantly for the rescue of the dead."
  So prayed he: Phœbus hearkened, and at once
Assuaged the pain, and stanched the purple blood
In the deep wound, and filled his frame with strength.
The warrior felt the change, rejoiced to know
That with such friendly speed the mighty god
Granted his prayer. And first he went among
The Lycian chiefs, exhorting them to wage
Fierce battle for Sarpedon. Then he sought,
Walking with rapid strides, the Trojan chiefs,

Agenor, nobly born, Polydamas,
The son of Panthoüs, Æneas next,
And Hector mailed in brass. By him he stood,
And thus accosted him with wingèd words:—
"O Hector, thou art careless of the fate
Of thine allies, who for thy sake, afar
From those they love, and from their native land,
Pour out their lives; thou bringest them no aid.
Sarpedon lies in death, the chief who led
The bucklered Lycians, who with justice swayed
The realm of Lycia, and defended it
With valor. Him hath brazen Mars beneath
The weapon of Patroclus smitten down.
Come then, my friends, repulse we gallantly
These Myrmidons; else will they bear away
His armor and insult his corpse, to avenge
The havoc we have made among the Greeks
Who perished by our weapons at the fleet."
He spake, and grief immitigable seized
The Trojans; for the slain, though stranger-born,
Had been a pillar of the realm of Troy,
And many were the troops that followed him,
And he was bravest of them all in war.
Then rushed the Trojans fiercely on the Greeks,

With Hector, sorrowing for Sarpedon's fall,
Leading them on, while the bold-hearted chief
Patroclus Menœtiades, aroused
The courage of the Greeks. He thus addressed
The warriors Ajax, eager like himself
For combat: "Be it now your welcome task,
O warriors Ajax, to drive back the foe;
He who first sprang across the Grecian wall,
Sarpedon, lies a corpse, and we must now
Dishonor the dead chief, and strip from him
His armor, and strike down with our good spears
Whoever of his comrades shall resist."
He spake, and all were resolute to beat
The enemy back; and when, on either side,
Trojans and Lycians, Myrmidons and Greeks,
Had put their phalanxes in firm array,
They closed, with dreadful shouts and horrid clash
Of arms, in fight around the dead, while Jove
Drew o'er that deadly fray an awful veil
Of darkness, that the struggle for the corpse
Of his dear son might rage more furiously.
The Trojans first drave back the dark-eyed Greeks,
For one was in the onset smitten down,
Not the least valiant of the Myrmidons,—

The son of brave Agacles, nobly born
Epeigeus, who aforetime, when he ruled
The populous Budeium, having slain
A noble kinsman, fled a suppliant
To Peleus and the silver-footed queen,
Thetis, his consort, and by them was sent,
With terrible Achilles, to the coast
Of courser-breeding Ilium and the siege
Of Troy. As now he stooped to seize the dead,
Illustrious Hector smote him with a stone
Upon the forehead, cleaving it in two
In the strong helmet; headlong on the corse
He fell, and cruel death crept over him.
With grief Patroclus saw his comrade slain,
And broke his way among the foremost ranks.
As a swift hawk that chases through the air
Starlings and daws, so didst thou dart among
Trojans and Lycians, for thy wrath was roused,
O knight Patroclus! by thy comrade's death.
And now his hand struck Sthenelaüs down,
The dear son of Ithæmenes; he flung
A stone that crushed the sinews of the neck.
Back drew illustrious Hector, and with him
The warriors who were fighting in the van.

As far as one can send a javelin,
When men contend in martial games, or meet
Their deadly enemies in war, so far
Withdrew the Trojans, and the Greeks pursued.
The leader of the bucklered Lycian host,
Glaucus, was first to turn against his foes.
He slew the brave Bathycles, the dear son
Of Chalcon, who in Hellas had his home,
And was the richest of the Myrmidons.
The Lycian, turning on him suddenly
As he drew near pursuing, sent his spear
Right through his breast, and with a clash he fell.
Great was the sorrow of the Greeks to see
That valiant warrior fall; the men of Troy
Exulted, and pressed round him in a crowd.
Nor lacking was the valor of the Greeks,
Who met them manfully. Meriones
Struck down a Trojan chief, Laogonus,
Onetor's valiant son. His father stood
Priest at the altar of Idæan Jove,
And like a god was honored by the realm.
Below the jaw and ear Meriones
Smote him, and instantly the life forsook
His limbs, and fearful darkness shrouded him.

Straight at Meriones Æneas aimed
His brazen spear to smite him, as he came,
Beneath his buckler; but the Greek beheld
The weapon in the air, and, stooping low,
Escaped it; over him it passed, and stood
Fixed in the earth behind him, where its stem
Trembled, for now the rapid steel had spent
Its force. As thus it quivered in the ground,
Æneas, who perceived that it had left
His powerful hand in vain, was vexed, and said:
"Had I but struck thee, dancer as thou art,
Meriones, my spear had suddenly
Ended thy dancing." Then Meriones,
The skilful spearman, answered: "Thou art brave,
But thou wilt find it hard to overcome
The might of all who gather to repulse
Thy onset. Thou art mortal, and if I,
Aiming at thee with my good spear, should pierce
Thy bosom, valiant as thou art and proud
Of thy strong arm, thy death would bring me praise,
And send thy soul where gloomy Pluto dwells."

He spake; the brave Patroclus heard, and thus
Rebuked him: "Why wilt thou, Meriones,
With all thy valor, stand to make a speech.

The foe, my friend, will not be forced to leave
The corpse by insults; some of them must die.
In deeds the issue of a battle lies;
Words are for counsel. Now is not the time
To utter swelling phrases, but to fight."
He ended, and went on; the godlike man
Followed his steps. As when from mountain dells
Rises, and far is heard, a crashing sound
Where woodmen fell the trees, such was the noise
From those who fought on that wide plain,—the din
Of brass, of leather, and of tough bull's-hide
Smitten with swords and two-edged spears. No eye,
Although of keenest sight, would then have known
Noble Sarpedon, covered as he lay,
From head to foot, with weapons, blood, and dust;
And still the warriors thronged around the dead.
As when in spring-time at the cattle-stalls
Flies gather, humming, when the milk is drawn,
Round the full pails, so swarmed around the corpse
The combatants; nor once did Jove withdraw
His bright eyes from the stubborn fray, but still
Gazed, planning how Patroclus should be slain.
Uncertain whether, in the desperate strife
Over the great Sarpedon, to permit

Illustrious Hector with his spear to lay
The hero dead, and make his arms a spoil,
Or spare him yet a while, to make the war
More bloody. As he pondered, this seemed best:
That the brave comrade of Achilles first
Should put to flight the Trojans and their chief,
Hector the brazen-mailed, pursuing them
Toward Troy with slaughter. To this end he sent
Into the heart of Hector panic fear,
Who climbed his car and fled, and bade the rest
Flee also, for he saw how Jove had weighed
The fortunes of the day. Now none remained,
Not even the gallant Lycians, when they saw
Their monarch lying wounded to the heart
Among a heap of slain; for Saturn's son
In that day's strife had caused a multitude
To fall in death. Now when the Greeks had stripped
Sarpedon of the glittering brazen mail,
The brave son of Menœtius bade his friends
Convey it to the hollow ships. Meanwhile
The Cloud-compeller spake to Phœbus thus:—
"Go now, beloved Phœbus, and withdraw
Sarpedon from the weapons of the foe;
Cleanse him from the dark blood, and bear him thence,

And lave him in the river-stream, and shed
Ambrosia o'er him. Clothe him then in robes
Of heaven, consigning him to Sleep and Death,
Twin brothers, and swift bearers of the dead,
And they shall lay him down in Lycia's fields,
That broad and opulent realm. There shall his friends
And kinsmen give him burial, and shall rear
His tomb and column,—honors due the dead."
  He spake: Apollo instantly obeyed
His father, leaving Ida's mountain height,
And sought the field of battle, and bore off
Noble Sarpedon from the enemy's spears,
And laved him in the river-stream, and shed
Ambrosia o'er him. Then in robes of heaven
He clothed him, giving him to Sleep and Death,
Twin brothers and swift bearers of the dead,
And they, with speed conveying it, laid down
The corpse in Lycia's broad and opulent realm.
  Meantime Patroclus, urging on his steeds
And charioteer, pursued, to his own hurt,
Trojans and Lycians. Madman! had he then
Obeyed the counsel which Pelides gave,
The bitter doom of death had not been his.
But stronger than the purposes of men

Are those of Jove, who puts to flight the brave,
And takes from them the victory, though he
Impelled them to the battle; and he now
Urged on Patroclus to prolong the fight.
Who first, when thus the gods decreed thy death,
Fell by thy hand, Patroclus, and who last?
Adrastus first, Autonoüs next, and then
Echeclus; then died Perimus, the son
Of Meges; then with Melanippus fell
Epistor; next was Elasus o'ercome,
And Mulius, and Pylartes. These he slew,
While all the rest betook themselves to flight.
Then had the Greeks possessed themselves of Troy,
With all its lofty portals, by the hand
And valor of Patroclus, for his rage
Was terrible beyond the rage of all
Who bore the spear, had not Apollo stood
On a strong tower to menace him with ill,
And aid the Trojans. Thrice Patroclus climbed
A shoulder of the lofty wall, and thrice
Apollo, striking his immortal hands
Against the glittering buckler, thrust him down;
And when, for the fourth time, the godlike man
Essayed to mount the wall, the archer-god,

Phœbus, encountered him with fearful threats:
"Noble Patroclus, hold thy hand, nor deem
The city of the warlike Trojans doomed
To fall beneath thy spear, nor by the arm
Of Peleus' son, though mightier far than thou."
He spake; Patroclus, fearful of the wrath
Of the archer-god, withdrew, and stood afar,
While Hector, at the Scæan gates, restrained
His coursers, doubtful whether to renew
The fight by mingling with the crowd again,
Or gather all his host within the walls
By a loud summons. As he pondered thus,
Apollo stood beside him in the form
Of Asius, a young warrior and a brave,
Uncle of Hector, the great horse-tamer,
And brother of Queen Hecuba, and son
Of Dymas, who in Phrygia dwelt beside
The streams of the Sangarius. Putting on
His shape and aspect, thus Apollo said:—
"Why, Hector, dost thou pause from battle thus?
Nay, it becomes thee not. Were I in might
Greater than thou, as I am less, full soon
Wouldst thou repent this shrinking from the war.
Come boldly on, and urge thy firm-paced steeds

Against Patroclus; slay him on the field,
And Phœbus will requite thee with renown."
He spake, and mingled in the hard-fought fray,
While noble Hector bade his charioteer,
The brave Cebriones, ply well the lash,
And join the battle. Phœbus went before,
Entering the crowd, and spread dismay among
The Greeks, and gave the glory of the hour
To Hector and the Trojans. Little heed
Paid Hector to the rest, nor raised his arm
To slay them, but urged on his firm-paced steeds
To meet Patroclus, who, beholding him,
Leaped from his car. In his left hand he held
A spear, and with the other lifting up
A white, rough stone, the largest he could grasp,
Flung it with all its force. It flew not wide,
Nor flew in vain, but smote Cebriones,
The warlike chief who guided Hector's steeds,
A spurious son of Priam the renowned.
The sharp stone smote his forehead as he held
The reins, and crushed both eyebrows in; the bone
Resisted not the blow; the warrior's eyes
Fell in the dust before his very feet.
Down from the sumptuous seat he plunged, as dives

A swimmer, and the life forsook his limbs.
And this, Patroclus, was thy cruel jest:—
"Truly a nimble man is this who dives
With such expertness. Were this, now, the sea,
Where fish are bred, and he were searching it
For oysters, he might get an ample store
For many men, in leaping from a ship,
Though in a storm, so skilfully he dives
Even from the chariot to the plain. No doubt
There must be divers in the town of Troy."
He spake, and sprang upon Cebriones.
With all a lion's fury, which attacks
The stables and is wounded in the breast,
And perishes through his own daring; thus,
Patroclus, didst thou fall upon the slain,
While Hector, hastening also, left his steeds,
And both contended for Cebriones.
As lions for the carcass of a deer
Fight on a mountain summit, hungry both,
And both unyielding, thus two mighty men
Of war, Patroclus Menœtiades
And glorious Hector, eager each to smite
His adversary with the cruel spear,
Fought for Cebriones. The slain man's head

Was seized by Hector's powerful hand, whose grasp
Relaxed not, while Patroclus held the foot;
And, thronging to the spot, the other Greeks
And Trojans mingled in the desperate strife.
As when the east wind and the south contend
In the open mountain grounds, and furiously
Assail the deep old woods of beech and ash
And barky cornel, flinging their long boughs
Against each other with a mighty roar,
And crash of those that break, so did the Greeks
And Trojans meet with mutual blows, and slay
Each other; nor had either host a thought
Of shameful flight. Full many a trenchant spear
Went to its mark beside Cebriones,
And many a wingèd arrow that had left
The bowstring; many a massive stone was hurled
Against the ringing bucklers, as they fought
Around the dead, while he, the mighty, lay
Stretched on the ground amid the eddying dust,
Forgetful of his art of horsemanship.
While yet the sun was climbing to his place
In middle heaven, the men of either host
Were smitten by the weapons, and in both
The people fell; but when he stooped to the west

The Greeks prevailed, and from that storm of darts
And tumult of the Trojans they drew forth
Cebriones, and stripped him of his arms.
  Still rushed Patroclus onward, bent to wreak
His fury on the Trojans. Fierce as Mars,
He charged their squadrons thrice with fearful shouts,
And thrice he laid nine warriors in the dust.
But as with godlike energy he made
The fourth assault, then clearly was it seen,
Patroclus, that thy life was near its end,
For Phœbus terribly in that fierce strife
Encountered thee. Patroclus saw him not
Advancing in the tumult, for he moved
Unseen in darkness. Coming close behind,
He smote, with open palm, the hero's back
Between the ample shoulders, and his eyes
Reeled with the blow, while Phœbus from his head
Struck the tall helm, that, clanking, rolled away
Under the horses' feet; its crest was soiled
With blood and dust, though never till that hour
Had dust defiled its horse-hair plume; for once
That helmet guarded an illustrious head,
The glorious brows of Peleus' son, and now
Jove destined it for Hector, to be worn

In battle; and his death was also near.
The spear Patroclus wielded, edged with brass,
Long, tough, and huge, was broken in his hands;
And his broad buckler, dropping with its band,
Lay on the ground, while Phœbus, son of Jove,
Undid the fastenings of his mail. With mind
Bewildered, and with powerless limbs, he stood
As thunderstruck. Then a Dardanian named
Euphorbus, son of Panthoüs, who excelled
His comrades in the wielding of the spear,
The race, and horsemanship, approaching, smote
Patroclus in the back with his keen spear,
Between the shoulder-blades. Already he
Had dashed down twenty warriors from their cars,
Guiding his own, a learner in the art
Of war. The first was he who threw a lance
At thee, Patroclus, yet o'ercame thee not;
For, plucking from thy back its ashen stem,
He fled, and mingled with the crowd, nor dared
Await thy coming, though thou wert unarmed,
While, weakened by that wound and by the blow
Given by the god, Patroclus turned and sought
Shelter from danger in the Grecian ranks;
But Hector, when he saw the gallant Greek

Thus wounded and retreating, left his place
Among the squadrons, and, advancing, pierced
Patroclus with his spear, below the belt,
Driving the weapon deep. The hero fell
With clashing mail, and all the Greeks beheld
His fall with grief. As when a lion bears
A stubborn boar to earth, what time the twain
Fight on the mountains for a slender spring,
Both thirsty and both fierce, the lion's strength
Lays prone his panting foe, so Priam's son
Slew, fighting hand to hand, the valiant Greek,
Son of Menœtius, who himself had slain
So many. Hector gloried over him
With wingèd words: "Patroclus, thou didst think
To lay our city waste, and carry off
Our women captive in thy ships to Greece.
Madman! in their defence the fiery steeds
Of Hector sweep the battle-field, and I,
Mightiest of all the Trojans, with the spear
Will guard them from the doom of slavery.
Now vultures shall devour thee, wretched youth!
Achilles, mighty though he be, has brought
No help to thee, though doubtless when he sent
Thee forth to battle, and remained within,

He charged thee thus: 'Patroclus, flower of knights,
Return not to the fleet until thy hand
Hath torn the bloody armor from the corpse
Of the man-queller Hector.' So he spake,
And filled with idle hopes thy foolish heart."
  Then thou, Patroclus, with a faltering voice,
Didst answer thus: "Now, Hector, while thou mayst,
Utter thy boast in swelling words, since Jove
And Phœbus gave the victory to thee.
Easily have they vanquished me; 't was they
Who stripped the armor from my limbs, for else,
If twenty such as thou had met me, all
Had perished by my spear. A cruel fate
O'ertakes me, aided by Latona's son,
The god, and by Euphorbus among men.
Thou who shalt take my spoil art but the third;
Yet hear my words, and keep them in thy thought.
Not long shalt thou remain alive; thy death
By violence is at hand, and thou must fall,
Slain by the hand of great Æacides."
  While he was speaking, death stole over him
And veiled his senses, while the soul forsook
His limbs and flew to Hades, sorrowing
For its sad lot, to part from life in youth

And prime of strength. Illustrious Hector thus
Answered the dying man: "Why threaten me,
Patroclus, with an early death? Who knows
That he, thy friend, whom fair-haired Thetis bore
Achilles, may not sooner lose his life,
Slain by my spear?" He spake, and set his heel
Upon the slain, and from the wound drew forth
His brazen spear and pushed the corpse aside,
And with the weapon hurried on to smite
Godlike Automedon, the charioteer
Of swift Æacides; but him the steeds
Fleet-footed and immortal, which the gods
Bestowed on Peleus, swiftly bore away.

## *BOOK XVII.*

THE warlike Menelaus, Atreus' son,
Beheld Patroclus fall by Trojan hands,
And came in glittering armor to the van
To guard the body of the slain. As walks
A heifer moaning round her new-born young,
So fair-haired Menelaus stalked around
The body of Patroclus, holding forth
His spear and great round shield, intent to slay
Whoever came against him. But the son
Of Panthoüs, mighty spearman, not the less
Intent to spoil the illustrious dead, drew near,
And spake to warlike Menelaus thus:—
"Atrides Menelaus, reared by Jove,
And leader of thy host, give way and leave
The dead, and quit to me his bloody spoil;
For none of our brave Trojans and allies
Smote him in deadly combat with the spear,
Before me. Leave me therefore to receive

The glory due me from the sons of Troy,
Else will I smite thee too, and thou wilt lose
Thy precious life!" Indignant at the word,
The fair-haired Menelaus answered him:—
"O Father Jove! unseemly boasts are these!
For not the panther's nor the lion's might,
Nor that of the fierce forest-boar whose rage
Is heightened into fury, is as great
As that which these distinguished spearmen, sons
Of Panthoüs, utter with their lips. And yet
The horseman Hyperenor did not long
Enjoy his youth when he with insolent words
Assailed me, and withstood me,—when he said
That I was the most craven wretch who bore
Arms in the Grecian host. He never turned,
I think, his footsteps homeward to delight
His reverend parents and beloved wife;
And I, like his, will take thy life, if thou
Oppose me. Heed my counsel, and withdraw
Among the crowd, and so avoid my stroke
Before thou come to harm. He is a fool
Who only sees the mischiefs that are past."
He said: Euphorbus, heeding not his words
Of warning, spake again: "Now is my time,

Jove-nurtured Menelaus, to avenge
My brother, slain by thee, and over whom
Thou utteredst such swelling words, whose wife
In her new bridal chamber thou hast made
A widow, and upon her parents brought
Mourning and endless sorrow. It may make
The sorrow less, should I into the hands
Of Panthoüs and the noble Phrontis give
Thy head and armor. Let us now delay
The strife no longer: it will show with whom
The valor dwells, and who is moved by fear."
  He spake, and smote his enemy's round shield,
But pierced it not; the stubborn metal turned
The weapon's point. Then Menelaus, son
Of Atreus, with a prayer to Jupiter,
Struck, as Euphorbus made a backward step,
His throat, and drave the weapon with strong hand
Through the soft neck. He fell with clashing arms.
His locks, which were like those the Graces wear,
And ringlets, bound with gold and silver bands,
Were drenched with blood. As when some husbandman
Rears in a lonely and well-watered spot
An olive-tree with widely spreading boughs,
Beautiful with fresh shoots, and putting forth

White blossoms, gently waved by every wind,
A sudden blast descends with mighty sweep
And tears it from its bed, and lays it prone
Upon the earth,—so lay Euphorbus, skilled
To wield the spear and son of Panthoüs, slain
And spoiled by Menelaus, Atreus' son.
As when a lion of the mountain wilds,
Fearless and strong, bears from the browsing herd
The fairest of the kine, and breaks her neck
With his strong teeth, and, tearing her, devours
The bloody entrails, while a clamorous throng
Of dogs and herdsmen, with incessant cries,
Gather around him, yet approach him not,
Withheld by fear, so of the warriors round
The gallant Menelaus none could find
The courage to encounter him; and then
Atrides easily had borne away
The sumptuous armor worn by Panthoüs' son,
If envious Apollo had not moved
Hector to meet him. Putting on the form
Of Mentes, chief of the Ciconian band,
He said to him aloud, with wingèd words:—
"Hector, thou art pursuing what thy feet
Will never overtake, the steeds which draw

The chariot of Achilles. Hard it were
For mortal man to tame them or to guide,
Save for Achilles, goddess-born. Meanwhile
Hath warlike Menelaus, Atreus' son,
Guarding the slain Patroclus, overthrown
Euphorbus, bravest of the Trojan host,
A son of Panthoüs; he will fight no more."

Thus spake the god, and disappeared among
The warring squadrons. Bitter was the grief
That seized the heart of Hector as he looked
Along the ranks and saw the Greek bear off
The sumptuous arms, and saw the Trojan lie
Weltering in blood. At once he made his way
To the front rank, all armed in glittering brass,
And with loud shouts. As terrible he came
As Vulcan's inextinguishable fires.
The son of Atreus heard that mighty shout,
And thus to his great soul lamenting said:—

"If I abandon these rich spoils and leave
Patroclus, who has perished in my cause,
I fear the Greeks will look upon the act
With indignation. If, through dread of shame,
I fight alone with Hector and his men,
I fear to be o'erwhelmed by multitudes,

For crested Hector leads the whole array
Of Trojans hither. Yet why question thus?
For when a warrior ventures to assault
One whom a god protects, a bitter doom
Is his. Then none of all the Greeks should blame
If I give way to Hector, whom a god
Hath sent against me. Yet could I but hear
The voice of mighty Ajax, we would both
Return, and even against a god renew
The combat, that we haply might restore
Patroclus to Achilles, Peleus' son.
Such in this choice of evils were the least."

As thus he mused, the men of Troy came on,
With Hector at their head. The Greek gave way
And left the slain. As when a lion, driven
With pikes and clamor from the herdsman's stalls
By men and dogs, unwillingly retreats,
His valiant heart still raging in his breast,
So did the fair-haired Menelaus leave
Patroclus. When he reached the Grecian ranks,
He turned and stood and looked about to find
The mighty Ajax, son of Telamon,
And him he soon beheld on the left edge
Of battle, rallying there and heartening

His men; for Phœbus from above had sent
A panic fear among them. To him then
The son of Atreus went in haste and said: —
"Ajax, my friend, come hither where we fight
Around Patroclus. Let us strive at least
To bring Achilles back the hero's corpse,
Though stripped; for crested Hector hath his arms."
He spake; the courage of the warlike son
Of Telamon was kindled by his words.
To the front rank he hastened, and with him
Went fair-haired Menelaus. Hector there
Had spoiled Patroclus of his glorious arms,
And now was dragging him apart to hew
The head away with his keen sword, and give
The body to the dogs of Troy. Just then
Came Ajax, bearing, like a tower, his shield,
And Hector mingled with the Trojan ranks,
And leaped into his car; but first he gave
His friends the glittering spoil to bear away
To Troy, — a glory to the conqueror;
While Ajax, over Menœtiades
Holding his ample shield, stood firm as stands
A lion o'er his whelps, when, as he comes
Leading them through the wood, the hunters rush

Upon him, and his look is terrible
As his knit eyebrows cover his fierce eyes.
So Ajax moved around the hero's corpse,
While warlike Menelaus by his side,
The son of Atreus, stood in bitter grief.
  Then, with a look of anger, Glaucus spake—
Son of Hippolochus, and chief among
The Lycians—thus to Hector: "Though thy form,
Hector, be noble, yet in prowess thou
Art wanting, and thy fame in feats of war
Is not deserved, since thou dost fly the foe.
Think whether thou alone, with others born
In Troy, canst save the city and the state.
For henceforth will no Lycian fight for Troy
Against the Greeks; this conflict without end
Has never earned them thanks. Inglorious chief!
How wilt thou be the shield of humbler men,
If thou canst leave Sarpedon, who has been
Thy comrade and thy guest, to be the prey
And spoil of the Greek warriors? While he lived,
Great was the aid he brought thy cause and thee,
And now thou dost not seek to drive away
The dogs from his neglected corpse. For this,
If any of the Lycians heed my words,

They will go home, and imminent will be
The ruin of thy city. If that firm
And resolute valor lived in Trojan hearts
Which they should cherish who in the defence
Of their own country bear the toils and face
The dangers of the field, we might this hour
Drag off the slain Patroclus into Troy.
And should we bear him from the thick of fight
To the great city of Priam, soon the Greeks
Would let us ransom the rich armor worn
By our Sarpedon, and bring back his corpse;
For he lies slain who was the bosom friend
Of the most valiant chieftain at the fleet
Of Greece, and leader of her bravest men.
But thou, when great-souled Ajax fixed his eye
Upon thee, didst not venture to remain
And fight with him; he is more brave than thou."

The crested Hector frowned and thus replied:—
"Why, Glaucus, should a warrior such as thou
Utter such violent words? My friend, I deemed
That thou wert wise above all other men
Of fertile Lycia, but I now must blame
Thy judgment when thou say'st I shrink to meet
The mighty Ajax. I do neither dread

The battle's fury nor the rush of steeds;
But all-prevailing are the purposes
Of ægis-bearing Jove, who makes the brave
To flee, and takes from him the victory,
And then again impels him to the fight.
Come then, my friend, stand by me; see if I
Skulk this time from the conflict, as thou say'st,
Or tame the courage of whatever Greek,
The bravest, who defends Patroclus slain."

He spake, and, shouting, cheered the Trojans on:
"Trojans and Lycians and Dardanians, trained
To combat hand to hand, let it be seen,
My friends, that ye are men, and still retain
Your ancient valor; while I buckle on
The glorious armor of the illustrious son
Of Peleus, taken from Patroclus slain."

So spake the crested Hector, and withdrew
From the fierce conflict, and with rapid steps
O'ertook his comrades as they bore away
Townward the glorious arms of Peleus' son.
There from that deadly strife apart he stood,
And changed his coat of mail. He gave his own
To his companions, to be carried thence
To sacred Ilium, and he buckled on

The immortal armor of Achilles, son
Of Peleus, which the gods of heaven bestowed
Upon his father, who in his old age
Consigned them to Achilles; but the son
Was never in that armor to grow old.
  And when the Cloud-compeller Jove beheld
Hector apart, accoutred in the arms
Of Peleus' godlike son, he shook his head,
And to himself he said: "Unhappy man!
Death even now is near to thee, and yet
Is not in all thy thoughts. Thou puttest on
The heavenly armor of the terrible chief,
Before whom others tremble; thou hast slain
His friend, the brave and gentle, and hast stripped,
To do him shame, the armor from his limbs.
Yet will I for the moment give to thee
Fresh triumphs, since Andromache shall ne'er
Receive, when thou returnest from the field,
The armor of Pelides from thy hands."
  The son of Saturn spake, and gave the nod
With his dark brows. Well did that coat of mail
Suit Hector's form. Meantime the god of war
In all his fierceness entered Hector's breast:
Fresh vigor filled and nerved his frame; he went

Along the ranks of his renowned allies
With shouts; that glittering armor made him seem
The large-souled son of Peleus. To them all
He spake in turn, encouraging their hearts,—
To Mesthles, Glaucus, and Thersilochus,
Medon, Deisenor, and Hippothoüs,
Asteropæus, Phorcys, Chromius,
And Ennomus the Augur; these the chief
Exhorted to the fight with wingèd words:—
"Hear me, ye mighty throng of our allies,
Dwellers of nations round us! Not to make
Our army vast in numbers did I send
To summon you, each from his native town,
But that your willing valor might defend
The wives and children of the sons of Troy
From the assailing Greeks. I therefore give
Most freely of our substance in large gifts
And banquets, that ye all may be content;
And now let some of you move boldly on
To do or die, which is the chance of war.
To him who from the field will drag and bring
The slain Patroclus to the Trojan knights,
Compelling Ajax to give way,—to him
I yield up half the spoil; the other half

I keep, and let his glory equal mine."
  He spake, and all that mighty multitude
With lifted lances threw themselves against
The Grecian ranks. They hoped to bear away
The dead from Ajax, son of Telamon.
Ah, idle hope! that hero o'er the dead
Took many a Trojan's life. Then Ajax thus
To Menelaus, great in battle, spake:—
  "O friend, O Menelaus, reared by Jove,
No longer now I hope our safe return
From battle. Not the greatest of my fears
Is for Patroclus, whom the dogs of Troy
And birds of prey full quickly will devour,
But for my life and thine. That cloud of war,
Hector, o'ershadows all, and over us
Impends the doom of death. Yet let us call
Our mighty men, if they perchance may hear."
  He spake, and Menelaus, great in war,
Obeyed his wish and shouted to the Greeks:—
  "O friends, the princes and the chiefs of Greece,
Who at the public feasts with Atreus' sons—
King Agamemnon and his brother chief—
Drink wine,—who each command a host, and hold
Your honors and your state from Jove,—my eyes

Cannot discern you in the thick of fight;
But some of you, who cannot bear to leave
Patroclus to the dogs of Troy, draw near!"
He spake; Oïlean Ajax, swift of foot,
Heard and came forward, hastening through the fight;
And after him Idomeneus, who brought
Meriones, his armor-bearer, fierce
As the man-slayer Mars. But who could tell
The names of all the other Greeks that sprang
To mingle in the strife? The Trojans made
The first assault, and Hector led them on.
As at the mouth of some great river, swoln
By rains from Jove, the mighty ocean-wave
Meets it with roaring, and the cliffs around
Rebellow, while the surges toss without,
With such a clamor came the Trojans on,
While round Patroclus closed, with one accord,
The Greeks, protected by their brazen shields,
And o'er their shining helmets Saturn's son
Poured darkness. For when Menœtiades
Yet lived, attendant upon Peleus' son,
Jove looked on him with no unkind regard,
And now he would not that his corse should feed
The enemy's dogs, and therefore moved his friends

To rescue him. At first the Trojans drave
The dark-eyed Greeks before them; back they fell
And left the dead; yet, fiercely as they came,
The Trojans slew no man, but dragged away
The dead. A moment, and no more, the Greeks
Fell back; for Ajax quickly rallied them,—
Ajax, who, next to Peleus' valiant son,
Excelled them all in form and feats of war;
He through the foremost warriors brake, as strong
As a wild boar that on the mountain's side
Breaks through the shrubs, and scatters with a bound
A band of youths and dogs. The illustrious son
Of honored Telamon thus put to rout
The Trojan phalanxes environing
Patroclus, in the hope to bear him thence
Townward with glory. There Hippothoüs, son
Of Lethus the Pelasgian, having bound
A thong about the sinewy ankle, toiled
To drag away the slain man by the foot
From that fierce strife,—a grateful spectacle
To Hector and the Trojans. Yet on him
A vengeance which no friendly arm could ward
Fell suddenly. The son of Telamon
Rushed through the crowd, and in close combat smote

His helmet's brazen cheek. That plumèd helm
Was cleft by the huge spear and vigorous hand,
And where the weapon struck Hippothoüs,
Mingled with blood the brain gushed forth; the life
Forsook his limbs; he dropped from nerveless hands
The foot of brave Patroclus, and beside
The corpse fell headlong,—far from the rich fields
Of his Larissa, never to repay
With gentle cares in their old age the love
Of his dear parents; for his life was short,
Slain by the spear of Ajax, large of soul.
 Then Hector aimed again his shining spear
At Ajax, who perceived it as it came,
And just avoided it. The weapon struck
Schedius, the valiant son of Iphitus,
And bravest of the Phocians, whose abode
Was Panopeus the famous, where he ruled
O'er many men. Beneath the collar-bone
It pierced him, and passed through; the brazen point
Came out upon the shoulder; to the ground
He fell, his armor clashing with his fall.
Then Ajax smote the valiant Phorcys, son
Of Phœnops, in the navel. Through the mail
The brazen weapon broke, and roughly tore

The entrails. In the dust he fell, and clenched
The earth with dying hands. The foremost ranks,
Led by illustrious Hector, at the sight
Yielded the ground; the Greeks with fearful shouts
Dragged off the bodies of Hippothoüs
And Phorcys, and despoiled them of their arms.
  Then would the Trojans have been put to flight
Before the warlike Greeks, and, craven-like,
Gone up to Troy, and great had been the fame
Gained by the might and courage of the Greeks,
Beyond what Jupiter designed to give,
Had not Apollo brought Æneas forth
By putting on the form of Periphas,
The herald and the son of Epytus,
Who in that office as a prudent friend
And counsellor had served, till he grew old,
The father of Æneas. In his shape
Thus spake Apollo, son of Jupiter:—
  "Æneas, ye might even hold the towers
Of lofty Ilium safe against a god,
Were ye to act as some whom I have seen,—
Valiant, and confident in their own might
And multitude of dauntless followers.
And now Jove favors us and offers us

The victory o'er the Greeks, and yet ye flee
In abject terror, and refuse to fight."
  He spake; Æneas, looking at him, knew
The archer-god, and with a mighty voice
Called out to Hector: "Hector! thou and all
Who lead the troops of Troy, and our allies,
Great shame it were if we were put to rout
Before the warlike Greeks, and beaten back
To Troy like cowards. Standing by my side,
One of the gods already hath declared
That Jupiter, All-wise, is our ally
In battle. Let us therefore boldly fall
Upon the Greeks, nor suffer them to bear
Patroclus unmolested to their fleet."
  He spake, and, springing to the foremost ranks,
Stood firm; the Trojans also turned and faced
The Achaians. Then Æneas with his spear
Struck down Leocritus, the gallant friend
Of Lycomedes and Arisbas' son.
The warlike Lycomedes saw his fall
With grief, and came and cast his shining spear
At Apisaon, son of Hippasus,
A shepherd of the people. Underneath
The midriff, through the liver went the spear,

And he fell lifeless. He had come to Troy
From rich Pæonia, and was great in war,
Next to Asteropæus. As he saw
His comrade fall, Asteropæus, moved
By grief, advanced to combat with the Greeks,
But could not; for the group that stood around
Patroclus showed a fence of shields, and held
Their spears before them. Ajax moved among
The warriors, charging them that none should leave
The corpse, and none should step beyond the rest
To strike the foe, but stay to guard the dead,
And combat hand to hand. Such was the charge
Of mighty Ajax. All the earth around
Was steeped with blood, and many a corpse was heaped
On corpse of Trojans and their brave allies,
And of the Greeks, for even on their side
The strife was not unbloody, though of Greeks
There perished fewer; each was on the watch
To ward the battle's dangers from the rest.
Then did they fight like fire. You could not say
The sun was safe, nor yet the moon, so thick
A darkness gathered over the brave men
Around the corpse of Menœtiades.
The other Trojans and the well-armed Greeks

Fought freely under the clear sky; the sun
Shed o'er them his full brightness; not a cloud
Shadowed the earth, or rested on the hills.
From time to time they paused, and warily
They shunned each other's cruel darts, and kept
Far from each other, while in the mid-war
Struggled the combatants in darkness, galled
By the remorseless weapons of their foes.
Yet Thrasymedes and Antilochus,
Two famous Grecian warriors, had not learned
That excellent Patroclus was no more,
But thought that, still alive, he led the war
Against the Trojans, fighting in the van.
They watched the flight and slaughter of the Greeks,
And fought apart, for Nestor so enjoined,
Who sent them to the battle from the fleet.

But they who held the middle space around
The friend of swift Æacides, maintained
A desperate strife all day; the knees, the thighs,
The feet, the hands, the eyes of those who fought
Were faint with weariness and foul with sweat.
As when an ample ox-hide, steeped in fat,
Is given to workmen to be stretched, they stand
Around it in a circle, pulling it,

Till forth the moisture issues, and the oil
Enters the skin, and by that constant strain
From many hands the hide is duly stretched,
So in small space the warriors drew the dead
Hither and thither; they of Ilium strove
To drag it to the city, they of Greece
To bear it to the fleet. The tumult then
Was terrible, and neither Mars himself,
The musterer of hosts, nor Pallas, roused
To her intensest wrath, had they been near
The struggle, would have seen it with disdain.
Such deadly strife of steeds and men was held
O'er slain Patroclus by the will of Jove.

The great Achilles knew not yet the fate
Of his Patroclus, for the warriors fought
Far from the fleet, beside the wall of Troy.
He never thought of him as one whose death
Was near, but trusted that, when once he reached
The Trojan wall, he would return alive;
Nor ever deemed he that without his aid,
Or even with it, would Patroclus sack
The city. This was what he oft had heard
From Thetis, who disclosed to him apart
The counsel of Almighty Jupiter.

Yet had his mother never once revealed
The present evil, — that the one whom most
He loved of all his friends should perish thus.
  Still round the dead they fought with their keen spears,
And slew each other. Then of the mailed Greeks
Some one would say: "O friends, it were disgrace
Should we fall back upon our roomy ships.
First let the dark earth swallow us; for this
Were better than to let the Trojan knights
Drag off the dead in triumph to their town."
  And some among the large-souled sons of Troy
Would say: "O friends, though all of us should fall
Beside this corpse, let no one turn and flee."
Thus they, encouraging each other, spake,
And thus the fight went on. The iron din
Rose through the waste air to the brazen heaven.
  Meantime aloof from battle stood the steeds
Of Peleus' son, and sorrowed when they knew
That he who guided them lay stretched in dust
By Hector's slaughtering hand. Automedon,
The brave son of Diores, often tried
The lash, and gentle words as oft, and oft
Shouted forth threats; yet neither would they move
Toward the broad Hellespont, where lay the fleet,

Nor toward the Greeks in combat, but remained
Motionless as a funeral column, reared
To mark a man's or woman's tomb. So stood
The coursers yoked to that magnificent car,
With drooping heads, and tears that from their lids
Flowed hot, for sorrow at the loss of him
Who was their charioteer, and their fair manes,
Sweeping the yoke below, were foul with dust.
The son of Saturn saw their grief, and shook
His head in pity, saying to himself: —
"Why did the gods bestow you, luckless pair,
On Peleus, — on a king of mortal birth, —
You who shall never feel old age or death?
Was it that ye might share with human-kind
Their sorrows? for the race of mortal men
Of all that breathe and move upon the earth
Is the most wretched. Yet of this be sure, —
That ye shall never in that sumptuous car
Bear Hector. Is it not enough that he
Should wear that armor, uttering idle boasts?
And now will I infuse into your limbs
Spirit and strength, that ye may safely bear
Automedon across the battle-field
To where the roomy galleys lie. I yet

Must give more glory to the men of Troy,
And they must slay until they come again
To the good ships of Greece,—until the sun
Goes down and sacred darkness covers all."

So spake the god, and breathed into the steeds
New life and vigor. From their manes they shook
The dust, and flew with that swift car among
The Greeks and Trojans. With the Trojan throng,
Automedon, though mourning his slain friend,
Maintained the fight; he rushed upon their ranks,
A vulture pouncing on a flock of geese.
Swiftly he passed from out the Trojan throng;
Swiftly again he charged their phalanxes
In fierce pursuit. Yet slew he none of those
Whom he pursued; he could not guide at once
The steeds and cast the spear, when seated thus
Alone within that sacred car. At last
A friend, the valorous Alcimedon,
Laërces' son, of Æmon's line, beheld
His plight, and, standing near his chariot, said:—

"What god, Automedon, hath prompted thee
To these mad acts, and stolen thy better sense,
Fighting alone among the foremost ranks
Of Trojan warriors, thy companion slain,

And Hector in the field, who boastfully
Stalks in the armor of Æacides?"
  And thus Automedon, Diores' son,
Made answer: "Who is there among the Greeks
Able like thee, Alcimedon, to rein
And curb the spirit of immortal steeds?
None were there save Patroclus while he lived,
Wise as a god in council. Death and fate
Now hold him. To thy hand I give the lash
And shining reins, while I descend and fight."
  He spake, and into his swift chariot sprang
Alcimedon, and took the lash and reins.
Automedon leaped down. As Hector saw,
He thus bespake Æneas at his side:—
  "Æneas, leader of the men of Troy,
Equipped in brazen armor, I have seen
Those coursers of the swift Æacides
Driven through the battle by unwarlike hands,
And 'tis my hope, if thou wilt give thine aid,
To seize them. They who guide them will not dare
To stand and face us when we make the charge."
  He spake; Anchises' valiant son complied,
And, sheltered by their shields of tough ox-hide,
Well dried and firm, and strong with plates of brass,

The twain went forward. With them at their side
Went Chromius and Aretus, nobly formed,
In hope to lead away the high-necked steeds,
Their guardians slain. Vain dreamers! they were doomed
Not without bloody penance to return
From that encounter with Automedon,
Who prayed to Father Jove, and whose faint heart
Was strengthened and made bold. And thus the chief
Said to his faithful friend Alcimedon:—

"Keep not the steeds thou guidest far from me,
Alcimedon, but let them ever breathe
Upon my shoulders. Hector, Priam's son,
I think, will not give over this assault
Before he either slays us, and ascends
The car to which these steeds with flowing manes
Are yoked, and puts to flight the phalanxes
Of Argive warriors, or himself is slain."

He spake, and called to both the Ajaxes
And Menelaus: "Ye who lead the Greeks,"
He said, and named the chieftains, "give in charge
The dead to your best warriors, to surround
And guard the corpse, and drive away the foe;
But hasten to avert the evil day
From us who are alive. For even now

Hector comes rushing through the deadly fight,
And brings Æneas; these are the most brave
Of all the Trojan army. On the knees
Of the great gods the issue rests. I too
Will cast the spear, and leave the rest to Jove."
He spake, and lifting his huge spear he smote
The round shield of Aretus. There the blade
Stopped not, but, entering, pierced him through the belt.
As, when a vigorous youth with a keen axe
Strikes a wild bull behind the horns, and there
Severs the sinews, forward leaps the beast
And falls, — Aretus, springing forward thus,
Fell headlong. In the Trojan's entrails still
Quivered the spear, and life forsook his limbs.
Then Hector aimed, to smite Automedon,
His shining spear. The Greek beheld and stooped,
And shunned the brazen weapon. Down it came,
And plunged into the earth, and stood, its stem
Still shaken with the blow, and spent its force.
Now would the twain have turned, and hand to hand
Fought with their swords, when suddenly came up
The warriors Ajax, hastening, at the call
Of their companion, through the crowd, and stayed
The combat. Hector and Æneas then,

And Chromius, of the godlike form, withdrew
Through caution, leaving on the battle-field
Aretus lying mangled. The fierce chief
Automedon despoiled the dead, and spake
Boastfully: "Somewhat lighter on my heart
Lies now my grief for Menœtiades,
Though I have slain a man of meaner note."
  As thus he spake, he threw the bloody spoils
Into his chariot, mounting to the seat,
His feet and hands all crimson with the blood,
As when a lion has devoured an ox.
Then round Patroclus raged the strife again,
Murderous and sad to see; for Pallas there
Inflamed the strife, sent down from heaven by Jove,
To rouse the courage of the Greeks, since such
Was now his will. As when the god displays
To men a purple rainbow in the skies,
A sign of war or of a bitter storm,
Which drives the laborer from his task, and makes
The cattle droop, so, in a purple cloud
Concealed, she went among the Greeks, and filled
Their hearts with valor. Taking first the form
Of Phœnix, and his clear, unwearied voice,
She spake in stirring words to Atreus' son,

The gallant Menelaus, standing near:
"Shame and dishonor will it be to thee,
O Menelaus, if, beneath the walls
Of Troy, the hungry dogs should tear the corpse
Of him who was in life the faithful friend
Of great Achilles. Fight thou therefore on
Bravely, and bid the other Greeks be brave."
And Menelaus, great in war, rejoined:
"O Phœnix, aged father, who wert born
In days long past, would but Minerva give
The needed strength, and ward from me the stroke
Of weapons, then would I stand by and guard
Patroclus, for his death hath filled my heart
With grief. But Hector's rage is like the rage
Of fire; he ceases not to slay; for Jove
Gives to his spear the glory of the day."
He spake, and well was blue-eyed Pallas pleased
That first to her of all the deities
He prayed; and therefore did she nerve his chest
And knees with strength, and put into his heart
The daring of the fly, that, often driven
From man, returns and bites, and finds how sweet
Is human blood. Such resolute zeal she woke
In his stern soul, as quickly he approached

Patroclus, and sent forth his shining spear.
Among the Trojans was Eëtion's son,
Podes, the rich and brave, whom Hector held
In highest honor, choosing him to be
Companion of his feasts. Him in the waist
The fair-haired Menelaus, as he fled,
Smote, driving home the weapon. With a clash
He fell to earth, and Menelaus drew
The slain away among the Grecian ranks.
Then came Apollo, putting on the form
Of Phænops, son of Asius, whose abode
Was in Abydos, and whom Hector most
Esteemed of all his guests. The archer-god
Drew near to Hector, and bespake him thus:—
"Hector, what other Greek will fear thee now,
Since thou dost shrink from Menelaus, deemed
Effeminate in war? Behold, he drags
Away a warrior from thy host; his hand
Hath slain thy faithful friend, Eëtion's son,
Brave Podes, fighting in the foremost ranks."
He spake: a cloud of sorrow overspread
The soul of Hector. Armed in glittering brass,
He went among the warriors in the van.
Then did the son of Saturn lift on high

His fringèd ægis, gleaming; with a cloud
He covered Ida, sent his lightnings down,
And thundered terribly, and made the mount
Shake to its base, and gave the victory
To Troy, and put to rout the Grecian host.
  Peneleus of Bœotia led the fight.
A spear that lighted on the shoulder-tip,
As he came forward, wounded him. The blade,
Hurled by Polydamas in close assault,
Entered and grazed the bone. Then Hector pierced
The wrist of Leïtus, Alectryon's son,
And made him leave the combat. As he fled
He looked around in fear, nor hoped again
To wield the spear against the men of Troy.
As Hector followed Leïtus, he met
The long spear of Idomeneus, which struck
His corselet near the pap; the weapon broke
Sheer at the socket, and the Trojans raised
A shout, while Hector at Idomeneus
Let fly his spear. It missed the chief, but smote
Cœranus, who from pleasant Lyctus came,
The friend and follower of Meriones.
For on that day Idomeneus had come
From his good ships on foot, and great had been

The triumph of the Trojans at his fall,
If Cœranus had not with his swift steeds
Passed near and bid him mount. 'T was thus he came
To save Idomeneus from death, and yield
To the man-queller Hector his own life;
The javelin entered underneath the ear,
By the jaw-bone, where, forcing out the teeth,
It cleft the tongue in twain. He fell to earth,
And dropped the reins. Meriones stooped down
And took them from the dust in his own hands,
And thus bespake Idomeneus: "Ply well
The lash, until thy coursers reach the fleet,
For thou mayst clearly see that victory
To-day is not upon the Grecian side."
  He spake: Idomeneus, fear-smitten, lashed
The long-maned steeds that hurried toward the fleet.
Nor now did Menelaus nor his friend,
The valiant Ajax, fail to see that Jove
Had changed the vantage to the side of Troy.
And thus the son of Telamon began:—
  "Alas! the feeblest mind can now perceive
That Father Jove is with the sons of Troy,
And gives to them the glory of the day.
Their weapons smite, whoever sends them forth,

Coward or brave, for Jove directs them all;
Ours fall to earth in vain. But let us now
Consult how best to bear the corpse away,
And how, returning, we may meet our friends
With joy; for they are grieved as they behold
Our plight, and fear that we may not withstand
The fiery onset and invincible arm
Of the man-queller Hector. Would there were
Some comrade who would bear to Peleus' son
The tidings of the day! for he, I think,
Has not yet heard that his dear friend is slain.
None such can I behold of all the Greeks,
For they are shrouded all—their steeds and they—
In darkness. Father Jove, deliver us
From darkness; clear the heavens and give our eyes
Again to see. Destroy us if thou wilt,
But O destroy us in the light of day!"
  He spake: the All-Father saw him shedding tears,
And pitied him, and bade the shadows flee,
And swept away the cloud. The sun looked forth,
And all the battle lay in light. Then thus
To warlike Menelaus Ajax said:—
  "O Menelaus, foster-child of Jove,
Look round and see if yet Antilochus,

The large-souled son of Nestor, is alive,
And bid him bear the tidings in all haste
To the great son of Peleus, that the one
Of all his friends whom most he loved is slain."
He spake, and Menelaus, great in war,
Complied, and hastened forth, as from a fold
A lion stalks away, that long has kept
In fear the hounds and herdsmen, who all night
Have watched to drive him from their well-fed beeves,
While, eager for his prey, he rushes oft
Against them, but in vain, for many a spear
Is hurled at him, and many a blazing brand,
Which, fierce for ravin as he is, he dreads,
Till sullenly at early morn he goes.
So from Patroclus went unwillingly
The valiant Menelaus, for he feared
Lest, panic-struck, the Greeks should leave his corpse
The enemy's prey. Thus earnestly he prayed
The warriors Ajax and Meriones: —
"Ye warriors Ajax, leaders of the Greeks!
And thou, Meriones! let each of you
Bear well in mind how kindly was the mood
Of poor Patroclus; gentle in his life
Was he to all, and now is with the dead."

The fair-haired Menelaus, speaking thus,
Withdrew. He looked around him as he went,
As looks an eagle, bird of sharpest sight—
So men declare—of all the fowls of air,
From which, though high in heaven, the nimble hare
Beneath the thicket is not hid; he stoops,
And takes the creature's life. Thy piercing eyes,
O Menelaus, thus on every side
Were turned, in eager scrutiny, to find
Among the multitude of Greeks the son
Of Nestor living. Him he soon descried
Upon the battle's left, where manfully
He cheered his fellows on. The fair-haired son
Of Atreus came and stood by him, and said:—

"Stay, foster-child of Jove, Antilochus!
And listen to the sorrowful news I bring
Of what should ne'er have been. Thou must have well
Perceived, I think, that some divinity
Doth heap disaster on our host, and give
The victory to the Trojans. He is dead,—
Patroclus,—the most valiant of the Greeks,
And great their sorrow is. Now hasten thou
To the Greek galleys; let Achilles know
The tidings; he may haply bring the corpse,

Stripped as it is, unmangled to the fleet,
For crested Hector has the arms he wore."
He spake, and at his words Antilochus
Was horror-struck; in grief too great for speech,
Tears filled his eyes, and his clear voice was choked.
Yet heeded he the mandate. Laying off
His arms, he gave them to his blameless friend,
Laodocus, who with his firm-paced steeds
Came toward him. Thus prepared he ran; his feet
Carried him swiftly from the battle-field
To bear the evil news to Peleus' son.
Yet Menelaus, foster-child of Jove,
Thy spirit did not prompt thee to remain
And aid thy hard-pressed comrades at the spot
Whence thou didst send Antilochus, and where
The Pyleans longed to keep him. Yet he sent
The noble Thrasymedes to their aid,
While he returned to where Patroclus lay,
And stood beside the warriors there, and said:—
"I sent to swift Achilles at the fleet
A messenger, yet think he will not come.
Though royal Hector's deed hath roused his rage,
Unarmed he cannot meet the sons of Troy.
Consult we then how we may best convey

The body to the ships, and how ourselves
Escape the doom of death by Trojan hands."
The mighty Ajax, son of Telamon,
Replied: "O Menelaus far-renowned,
Well hast thou spoken. Lift thou now the corse,
Thou and Meriones, and place yourselves
Beneath it, and convey it from the field.
We, following you, will combat with the sons
Of Troy and noble Hector,—we who, named
Alike and one in spirit, oft have borne
The fury of the battle side by side."
He ended, and the warriors in their arms
Raised with main strength the body from the ground.
The Trojans, as they saw it borne away,
Shouted behind them, rushing on like hounds
That spring upon a wounded forest-boar
Before the hunter-youths now pressing close
Upon his flank, to tear him, then again,
Whene'er he turns upon them in his strength,
Retreating in dismay, and put to flight
Hither and thither. Thus, in hot pursuit
And close array, the Trojans following strook
With swords and two-edged spears; but when the twain
Turned and stood firm to meet them, every cheek

Grew pale, and not a single Trojan dared
Draw near the Greeks to combat for the corse.
  Thus rapidly they bore away the dead
Toward their good galleys from the battle-field.
Onward with them the furious battle swept,
As spreads a fire that, kindled suddenly,
Seizes a city, and the dwellings sink
In the consuming blaze, and a strong wind
Roars through the flame. Such fearful din of steeds
And warriors followed the retreating Greeks.
As from a mountain summit strong-backed mules
Drag over the rough ways a ponderous beam
Or mast, till weary with the mighty strain
And streaming sweat, so they with resolute toil
Bore off the dead. Behind them as they went
Their two defenders kept the foe aloof.
As when a river-dike o'ergrown with trees
Crosses a plain, and holds the violent course
Of the swoln stream in check, and, driving back
The waters, spreads them o'er the level fields,
Nor can their fury force a passage through,—
So did the warriors Ajax hold in check
The Trojans; yet they followed close, and two
More closely than the rest,—Æneas, son

Of old Anchises, and the illustrious chief,
Hector. As when a company of daws
Or starlings, startled at a hawk's approach,
The murderous enemy of the smaller birds,
Take wing with piercing cries, so, driven before
The might of Hector and Æneas, fled
The Greeks with clamorous cries, and thought no more
Of combat. In the trench and near it lay
Many fair weapons, which the fugitive Greeks
Had dropped in haste, and still the war went on.

## *BOOK XVIII.*

AS thus they fought with all the rage of fire,
Antilochus, the nimble-footed, came
With tidings to Achilles. Him he found
Before his lofty galleys, deep in thought
Of what he knew had happened. With a sigh
The hero to his mighty spirit said:—
"Ah me! why should the Grecians thus be driven
In utter disarray across the plain?
I tremble lest the gods should bring to pass
What most I dread. My mother told me once
That the most valiant of the Myrmidons,
While yet I live, cut off by Trojan hands,
Shall see the sun no more. It must be so:
The brave son of Menœtius has been slain.
Unhappy! 'Twas my bidding that, when once
The enemy with his firebrands was repulsed,
He should not think to combat gallantly
With Hector, but should hasten to the fleet."

As thus he mused, illustrious Nestor's son
Drew near Achilles, and with eyes that shed
Warm tears he gave his sorrowful message thus:—
"Son of the warlike Peleus, woe is me!
For bitter are the tidings thou must hear
Of what should not have been. Patroclus lies
A naked corpse, and over it the hosts
Are fighting; crested Hector hath his arms."
He spake, and a black cloud of sorrow came
Over the chieftain. Grasping in both hands
The ashes of the hearth, he showered them o'er
His head, and soiled with them his noble face.
They clung in dark lumps to his comely vest.
Prone in the dust of earth, at his full length,
And tearing his disordered hair, he lay.
Then wailed aloud the maidens whom in war
He and Patroclus captured. Forth they came,
And, thronging round him, smote their breasts and swooned.
Antilochus mourned also, and shed tears,
Holding Achilles by the hand, for much
His generous nature dreaded that the chief
Might aim at his own throat the sword he wore.
Loud were the hero's cries, and in the deep
His gracious mother, where she sat beside

Her aged father, heard them. She too raised
A wail of sorrow. All the goddesses,
Daughters of Nereus, dwelling in the depths
Of ocean, gathered to her side. There came
Glaucè, Thaleia, and Cymodocè,
Nesæa, Speio, Halia with large eyes,
And Thoa, and Cymothöè; nor stayed
Actæa, Limnoreia, Melita,
Amphithöè, Iæra, Agavè,
Doto, and Proto, and Dynamenè.
There came Dexamenè, Amphinomè,
Pherusa, Callianira, Panopè,
Doris, and Galateia, the renowned.
With these Nemertes and Apseudes came,
And Callianassa. Clymenè was there,
Janeira and Janassa, and with them
Mæra, and Amatheia with bright hair,
And Orithya, and whoever else,
Children of Nereus, bide within the deep.
The concourse filled the glimmering cave; they beat
Their bosoms, while the sorrowing Thetis spake:—
"Hear, sister Nereids, that ye all may know
The sharpness of my sorrows. Woe is me,
Unhappy! Woe is me! in evil hour,

The mother of a hero,—me who gave
Birth to so noble and so brave a son,
The first among the warriors, saw him grow
Like a green sapling, reared him like a plant
Within a fruitful field, and sent him forth
With his beaked ships to Ilium and the war
Against the Trojans. Never shall I see
That son returning to his home, the halls
Of Peleus. While he lives and sees the light
Of day his lot is sorrow, nor can I
Help him in aught, though at his side; and yet
I go to look on my beloved son,
And learn from him what grief, while he remains
Aloof from war, o'ertakes him in his tent."

She spake, and left the cavern. All the nymphs
Went with her weeping. Round their way the waves
Of ocean parted. When they reached the fields
Of fertile Troas, up the shore they went
In ordered files to where, a numerous fleet,
Drawn from the water, round Achilles lay
The swift ships of the Myrmidons. To him
His goddess mother came, and with a cry
Of grief embraced the head of her dear son,
And, mourning o'er him, spake these wingèd words:—

"Why weepest thou, my son? What sorrow now
O'ercomes thy spirit? Speak, and hide it not.
All thou didst pray for once, with lifted hands,
Has been fulfilled by Jove; the sons of Greece,
Driven to their galleys, and with thy good help
Withdrawn from them, are routed and disgraced."
The swift Achilles, sighing deeply, made
This answer: "O my mother! true it is
Olympian Jove hath done all this for me;
But how can that delight me, since my friend,
My well-beloved Patroclus, is no more?
He whom, of all my fellows in the war,
I prized the most, and loved as my own self,
Is lost to me, and Hector, by whose hand
He was cut off, has spoiled him of his arms, —
His dreaded arms, a wonder to the sight
And glorious, which the gods of heaven bestowed
On Peleus, sumptuous bridal gifts, when thou
Wert led by them to share a mortal's bed.
Yet would that thou hadst evermore remained
Among the immortal dwellers of the deep,
And Peleus had espoused a mortal maid,
Since now thy heart must ache with infinite grief
For thy slain son, whom thou shalt never more

Welcome returning to his home. No wish
Have I to live or to concern myself
In men's affairs, save this: that Hector first,
Pierced by my spear, shall yield his life, and pay
The debt of vengeance for Patroclus slain."
  And Thetis, weeping, answered: "O my son!
Soon must thou die; thou sayest true; that fate
Hangs over thee as soon as Hector dies."
  Again the swift Achilles, sighing, spake:
"Then quickly let me die, since fate denied
That I should aid my friend against the foes
That slew him. Far from his own land he fell,
And longed for me to rescue him. And now,
Since I am never more to see the land
I love, and since I went not to defend
Patroclus, nor the other Greeks, my friends,
Of whom so many have fallen by the hand
Of noble Hector, but beside the fleet
Am sitting here, a useless weight on earth,
Mighty in battle as I am beyond
The other Grecian warriors, though excelled
By other men in council, — would that Strife
Might perish among gods and men, with Wrath,
Which makes even wise men cruel, and, though sweet

At first as dropping honey, growing, fills
The heart with its foul smoke. Such was my rage,
Aroused by Agamemnon, king of men.
Yet now, though great my wrong, let things like these
Rest with the past, and, as the time requires,
Let us subdue the spirit in our breasts.
I go in quest of Hector, by whose hand
My friend was slain. My death will I accept
Whene'er to Jove and to the other gods
It shall seem good to send it. Hercules,
Though mighty and beloved of Jupiter,
The son of Saturn, could not shun his death,
For fate and Juno's cruel wrath prevailed
Against him. I shall lie in death like him,
If a like fate be measured out for me.
Yet now shall I have glory; I shall do
What many a Trojan and Dardanian dame,
Deep-bosomed, wiping with both hands the tears
From their fair cheeks, shall bitterly lament;
And well shall they perceive that, till this hour,
I paused from war. Thou lov'st me; but seek not
To keep me from the field, for that were vain."

The silver-footed Thetis thus rejoined:
"Truly, my son, thy purpose is not ill,

To rescue thy endangered friends from death.
But with the Trojans are thy beautiful arms,
Brazen and dazzling bright; their crested chief,
Hector, exults to wear them: no long space,
I think, will he exult; his death is near.
Yet go not to the battle-field until
Thine eyes shall look upon me yet again.
I come to-morrow with the sun, and bring
Bright arms, the work of Vulcan's royal hand."
So having said, and turning from her son,
She thus bespake her sisters of the sea:
"Return to the broad bosom of the deep,
To its gray Ancient and my father's halls,
And tell him all. I hasten to ascend
The summits of Olympus, there to ask
Of Vulcan, the renowned artificer,
Armor of glorious beauty for my son."
She spake: at once they plunged into the deep,
While Thetis, silver-footed goddess, sought
Olympus, whence it was her hope to bring
New armor for her son. As thus her feet
Bore her toward heaven, the Achaians, fleeing fast,
With infinite clamor, driven before the arm
Of the man-queller Hector, reached the ships

And Hellespont. Nor could the well-armed Greeks
Bear off Patroclus from the shower of darts;
For rushing on them came both foot and horse,
And Hector, son of Priam, like a flame
In fury. Thrice illustrious Hector seized
The body by the heels to drag it off,
And called his Trojans with a mighty shout.
Thrice did the chieftains Ajax, terrible
In resolute valor, drive him from the dead.
Yet kept he to his purpose, confident
In his own might, now charging through the crowd,
Now standing firm and shouting to his men,
And never losing ground. As when, at night,
Herdsmen that watch their cattle strive in vain
To drive a lion, fierce and famine-pinched,
From some slain beast, so the two Ajaxes,
With all their valor, vainly strove to keep
Hector, the son of Priam, from the corpse.
And now would he have dragged it thence, and won
Infinite glory, had not Iris come—
The goddess whose swift feet are like the wind—
To Peleus' son, a messenger from heaven,
In haste, unknown to Jupiter and all
The other gods,—for Juno sent her down,—

To bid the hero arm. She came and stood
Beside him, speaking thus with wingèd words:—
"Pelides, rise, most terrible of men,
In rescue of Patroclus, over whom
They struggle fiercely at the fleet; for there
They slay each other,—these who fight to keep
The dead, and those, the men of Troy, who charge
To drag him off to Ilium's airy heights;
And chief, illustrious Hector longs to seize
The corpse, and from the delicate neck to hew
The head, and fix it on a stake. Arise,
Loiter no longer;—rise, ashamed to leave
Patroclus to be torn by Trojan dogs.
For thine will be the infamy, if yet
The corpse be brought dishonored to thy tent."
The swift Achilles listened and inquired:
"Which of the gods, O Iris, speaks by thee?"
And Iris, whose swift feet are like the wind,
Answered: "The glorious spouse of Jupiter,
Juno, hath sent me. Even Saturn's son,
On his high throne, knows not that I am sent,
Nor any other of the gods who dwell
Upon Olympus overspread with snow."
"But how," the swift Achilles asked again,

"Shall I go forth to war? They have my arms,
And my beloved mother strictly bade
That I should put no armor on until
I saw her face again. She promised me
A suit of glorious mail from Vulcan's hand.
Nor know I any warrior here whose arms
Might serve me, save, perhaps, it were the shield
Of Telamonian Ajax, who, I hope,
Is in the van, and dealing death among
The foe, in vengeance for Patroclus slain."
  Then the swift-footed Iris spake again:
"They have thy glorious armor; that we know.
But go thou to the trench, and show thyself
To them of Troy, that, haply smit with fear,
They may desist from battle, and the host
Of Grecian warriors, overtoiled, may breathe
In a brief respite from the stress of war."
  So the fleet Iris spake, and passed away,
And then arose Achilles, dear to Jove,
While o'er his ample shoulders Pallas held
Her fringèd ægis. The great goddess caused
A golden cloud to gather round his head
And kindled in the cloud a dazzling flame.
And as when smoke, ascending to the sky,

Hangs o'er some city in a distant isle,
Which enemies beleaguer, swarming forth
From their own city, and in hateful strife
Contend all day, but when the sun goes down
Forthwith blaze many bale-fires, sending up
A brightness which the neighboring realms may see,
That haply they may send their ships and drive
The war away,—so from the hero's head
That flame streamed upward to the sky. He came
Without the wall and stood beside the trench,
Nor mingled with the Greeks, for he revered
His mother's words. He stood and called aloud,
And Pallas, from the host, returned his shout,—
A shout that carried infinite dismay
Into the Trojan squadrons. As the sound
Of trumpet rises clear when deadly foes
Lay siege to a walled city, such was heard
The clear shout uttered by Æacides.
The hearts of all who heard that brazen voice
Were troubled, and their steeds with flowing manes
Turned backward with the chariots,—such the dread
Of coming slaughter. When the charioteers
Beheld the terrible flame that played unquenched
Upon the brow of the magnanimous son

Of Peleus, lighted by the blue-eyed maid
Minerva, they were struck with panic fear.
Thrice o'er the trench Achilles shouted; thrice
The men of Troy and their renowned allies
Fell into wild disorder. Then there died,
Entangled midst their chariots, and transfixed
By their own spears, twelve of their bravest chiefs.
The Greeks bore off Patroclus from the field
With eager haste, and placed him on a bier,
And there the friends that loved him gathered round
Lamenting. With them swift Achilles came,
The hot tears on his cheeks, as he beheld
His faithful comrade lying on his bier,
Mangled with many wounds, whom he had sent
With steeds and car to battle, never more
To welcome him alive on his return.

Now Juno, large-eyed and august, bade set
The never-wearied sun; unwillingly
He sank into the ocean streams. Then paused
The noble Greeks from that ferocious strife,
Deadly in equal measure to both hosts.
The Trojans also paused, and from their cars
Unharnessed the fleet steeds, and ere they took
Their evening meal assembled to consult.

Standing they held the council; no man cared
To sit, for all were trembling from the hour
When, long a stranger to the bloody field,
Achilles showed himself again. And now
The son of Panthoüs, wise Polydamas,
Began to speak. Beyond the rest he saw
Things past and things to come, and he had been
Hector's companion, born in the same night,
Mighty in speech as Hector with the spear.
With prudent admonitions thus he spake: —
"Consider well, my friends. My counsel is
That we return, nor wait the holy morn
Here, by the fleet and in the open plain,
Far from our city ramparts. While this man
Was wroth with Agamemnon, we maintained
A strife of far less peril with the Greeks,
And I was ever ready to encamp
By night beside the galleys, which we hoped
To make our prize; but now I fear the might
Of swift Pelides. He will not remain
Content upon the space between the fleet
And town, where Greeks and Trojans wage a war
Of changeful fortune, but will strive to take
The city, and to carry off our wives.

March we then homeward. Let my words prevail,—
It must be so. The gentle Night now keeps
The nimble-footed hero from the war.
But if to-morrow, issuing forth in arms,
He find us here, there are among us those
Who will have cause to know him. Gladly then
Will he find refuge who escapes his arm
In sacred Troy, and many a Trojan corpse
Will feed the dogs and vultures. May mine ear
Hear of it never. But if ye will heed
My words, though sorrowful, ye shall be safe
Assembled in the city squares at night.
The lofty towers and gates, with massive beams
Polished and strongly fitted each to each,
Will keep the town. To-morrow we shall take,
At dawn, our station on the towers, arrayed
In armor, and his difficult task will be,
Far from his ships, to fight us from below;
And after he has tired his high-necked steeds
With coursing round the ramparts to and fro,
Back to his galleys he must go; nor yet
With all his valor can he force his way
Into the town to lay its dwellings waste,—
The dogs will feed upon his carcass first."

And crested Hector answered with a frown:
"The counsel thou hast given, Polydamas,
Pleases me not,—that we return to be
Pent up in Troy. Are ye not weary yet
Of lying long imprisoned within walls
And towers? The time has been that in all lands,
Wherever human speech is heard, the fame
Of Priam's city, for its treasured gold
And brass, was in all mouths. Those treasures now
Have passed away; our dwellings have them not.
Much that we had was sold on Phrygia's coast,
And in Mæonia's pleasant land, for Jove
The mighty was displeased with us. But now,
When politic Saturn's son hath granted me
To win great glory at the fleet, and hold
The Greeks imprisoned by the sea, refrain,
Idler, from laying counsels such as these
Before the people. Not a Trojan here
Will follow them, nor would I suffer it.
Now hearken all, and act as I advise:
First banquet, rank by rank, throughout the host,
And set your guards, and each of you keep watch;
And then, if any Trojan stands in fear
For his possessions, let him bring them all

Into the common stock, to be consumed;
Better that we enjoy them than the Greeks.
To-morrow, with the dawn and all in arms,
We will do battle at the roomy ships
Valiantly. If in truth the noble son
Of Peleus choose to rise and to defend
The ships, so much the worse for him, since I
Shall not for him desert the field, but stand
Firmly against him, whether he obtain
The victory or I. The chance of war
Is equal, and the slayer oft is slain."
So Hector spake: the Trojans shouted forth
Applause, the madmen! Pallas took away
Their reason; all approved the fatal plan
Of Hector; no one ventured to commend
The sober counsel of Polydamas.
And then they banqueted throughout the host;
But all night long the Achaians mourned with tears
Patroclus, while Pelides in the midst,
Leading the ceaseless lamentation, placed
His slaughter-dealing hands upon the breast
Of his companion with continual sighs.
As a maned lion, from whose haunt within
The thick, dark wood a hunter has borne off

The whelps, returning finds them gone, and grieves,
And roams the valleys, tracking as he goes
The robber, bent to find him, for his rage
Is fierce,—with such fierce sorrow Peleus' son
Spake, deeply sighing, to his Myrmidons:—
"O, idle were the words which once I spake,
When in our palace-halls I bade the chief
Menœtius bear a cheerful heart. I said
That I would bring to Opus yet again,
Laden with spoil from Ilium overthrown,
His valiant son. But Jove doth not fulfil
The plans of men. That both of us should stain
Earth with our blood in Troy was the decree
Of fate, and never will the aged knight
Peleus receive me in his palace-halls,
Returning from the war, nor Thetis, she
Who gave me birth; the earth will hold me here.
And now, since after thee I take my place
In earth, Patroclus, I will not perform
Thy funeral rites before I bring to thee
The arms and head of the magnanimous chief
Hector, who slew thee. By thy funeral pile
I will strike off in vengeance for thy death
The heads of twelve illustrious Trojan youths.

Thou meanwhile, lying at the beakèd ships,
Shalt be lamented night and day, with tears,
By many a Trojan and Dardanian maid,
Deep-bosomed, won by our victorious spears
After hard wars and opulent cities sacked."
  Thus having said, the great Achilles bade
Place a huge tripod on the fire in haste,
To cleanse Patroclus from the clotted blood.
They brought and set upon the glowing hearth
A tripod for the bath, and in it poured
Water, and piled the wood beneath. The flame
Crept up the vessel's rounded sides and warmed
The water. When within the murmuring brass
It boiled, they washed the dead, and with rich oil
Anointed him, and filled the open wounds
With ointment nine years old; and laying him
Upon a couch, they spread from head to foot
Fine linen over him, and covered all
With a white mantle. Through the hours of night
The Myrmidons, lamenting their dead chief,
Wept round the swift Achilles. Then did Jove
Thus to his wife and sister Juno speak:—
  "Large-eyed, imperial Juno, thou hast now
Accomplished thy desire, for thou hast roused

The swift Achilles. There is not a doubt
The long-haired Argives owe their birth to thee."
  And large-eyed Juno answered: "What strange words,
Austere Saturnius, hast thou said? A man,
A mortal far less skilled in shaping means
To compass ends, might do what I have done
Against his fellow-man. Then should not I —
Who boast to be the chief of goddesses
By birthright, and because I bear the name
Of wife to thee who rulest o'er the gods —
Plan evil to the Trojans, whom I hate?"
  So talked they. Silver-footed Thetis came
Meanwhile to Vulcan's halls, eternal, gemmed
With stars, a wonder to the immortals, wrought
Of brass by the lame god. She found him there
Sweating and toiling, and with busy hand
Plying the bellows. He was fashioning
Tripods, a score, to stand beside the wall
Of his fair palace. All of these he placed
On wheels of gold, that, of their own accord,
They might roll in among the assembled gods,
And then roll back, a marvel to behold.
So far they all were finished; but not yet
Were added the neat handles, and for these

The god was forging rivets busily.
While thus he labored, with a mind intent
Upon his skilful task, on silver feet
Came Thetis. Charis, of the snowy veil,
The beautiful, whom the great god of fire,
Vulcan, had made his wife, beheld, and came
Forward to meet her, seized her hand, and said:—
"O Thetis of the flowing robe, beloved
And honored, what has brought thee to our home?
Thou dost not often visit us. Come in,
That I may pay the honors due a guest."
So the bright goddess spake, and led the way,
And seated Thetis on a sumptuous throne,
With silver studs divinely wrought, and placed
A footstool, and called out to Vulcan thus:
"Come, Vulcan; Thetis here hath need of thee."
And the great artist, Vulcan, thus replied:
"Then of a truth a goddess is within
Whom I must ever honor and revere;
Who from the danger of my terrible fall
Saved me, what time my shameless mother sought
To cast me from her sight, for I was lame.
Then great had been my misery, had not
Eurynomè and Thetis in their laps

Received me as I fell, — Eurynomè,
Daughter of billowy Ocean. There I dwelt
Nine years, and many ornaments I wrought
Of brass, — clasps, buckles, bracelets, necklaces, —
Within a vaulted cave, round which the tides
Of the vast ocean murmured and flung up
Their foam; nor any of the gods or men
Knew of my hiding-place, save only they
Who saved me, Thetis and Eurynomè.
And now, as she is with us, I must make,
To fair-haired Thetis some thank-offering
For having rescued me. Haste, spread the board
Amply with generous fare, while I shall lay
Aside my bellows and my implements."
   He spake, and from his anvil-block arose,
A mighty bulk; his weak legs under him,
Halting, moved painfully. He laid apart
His bellows from the fire, and gathered up
The scattered implements with which he wrought,
And locked them in a silver chest, and wiped
With a moist sponge his face and both his hands,
Stout neck and hairy chest. He then put on
His tunic, took his massive regal wand
Into his hand, and, tottering, sallied forth.

Two golden statues, like in form and look
To living maidens, aided with firm gait
The monarch's steps. And mind was in their breasts,
And they had speech and strength, and from the gods
Had learned becoming arts. Beside their lord
They walked and tended him. As he drew near,
Halting, to Thetis on the shining throne,
He took the goddess by the hand and said: —
"What cause, O Thetis of the flowing robe,
Honored and dear, has brought thee to our home?
Not often com'st thou hither. Freely say
Whatever lies upon thy mind. My heart
Commands me to obey, if it be aught
That can be done and may be done by me."
And Thetis answered, with a gush of tears:
"O Vulcan! of the goddesses who dwell
Upon Olympus, is there one who bears
Such bitter sorrows as Saturnian Jove
Inflicts on me, distressed above them all?
Me, of the ocean deities, he forced
To take a mortal husband, — Peleus, son
Of Æacus, — and to his bed I came
Unwillingly. Within his palace halls,
Worn with a late old age, my husband lies.

Now I have other woes; for when a son
Was granted me, and I had brought him forth
And reared him, flourishing like a young plant,
A sapling in a fertile field, and great
Among the heroes,—thus maturely trained,
I sent him with his beakèd ships to Troy,
To combat with her sons; but never more
Will it be mine to welcome him returned
Home to the halls of Peleus. While to me
He lives, and sees the sunshine, he endures
Affliction, nor can I, though at his side,
Aid him in aught. The maiden whom the Greeks
Decreed him as his prize, the king of men,
Atrides, took away, and grief for her
Consumes his heart. The Trojans keep the Greeks
Beleaguered by their ships, nor suffer them
To pass beyond their gates. The elder chiefs
Implored him to relent, and offered him
Large presents; he refused to avert the doom
That threatened them himself, but sent instead
Patroclus to the war with his own arms,
And with him sent much people. All the day
They fought before the Scæan gates; and then
Had Ilium fallen, but that Apollo slew

The brave son of Menœtius, who had caused
Vast slaughter,—slew him fighting in the van
Of war, and gave the glory of his death
To Hector. Therefore I approach thy knees,
And ask for him, my son, so soon to die,
Buckler and helm, and beautiful greaves, shut close
With clasps, and all the other arms complete,
Which in the war my son's companion lost.
For now Achilles lies upon the ground
Bitterly grieving in his inmost soul."

And Vulcan, the great artist, answered her:
"Be comforted, and take no further thought
Of this; for would I could as certainly
Shield him from death's dread summons when his hour
Is come at last, as I shall have for him
Beautiful armor ready to put on,
And such as every man, of multitudes
Who look on it hereafter, shall admire."

So speaking he withdrew, and went where lay
The bellows, turned them toward the fire, and bade
The work begin. From twenty bellows came
Their breath into the furnaces,—a blast
Varied in strength as need might be; for now
They blew with violence for a hasty task,

And then with gentler breath, as Vulcan pleased
And as the work required. Upon the fire
He laid impenetrable brass, and tin,
And precious gold and silver; on its block
Placed the huge anvil, took the ponderous sledge,
And held the pincers in the other hand.
  And first he forged the huge and massive shield,
Divinely wrought in every part,—its edge
Clasped with a triple border, white and bright.
A silver belt hung from it, and its folds
Were five; a crowd of figures on its disk
Were fashioned by the artist's passing skill,
For here he placed the earth and heaven, and here
The great deep and the never-resting sun
And the full moon, and here he set the stars
That shine in the round heaven,—the Pleiades,
The Hyades, Orion in his strength,
And the Bear near him, called by some the Wain,
That, wheeling, keeps Orion still in sight,
Yet bathes not in the waters of the sea.
  There placed he two fair cities full of men.
In one were marriages and feasts; they led
The brides with flaming torches from their bowers,
Along the streets, with many a nuptial song.

There the young dancers whirled, and flutes and lyres
Gave forth their sounds, and women at the doors
Stood and admired. Meanwhile a multitude
Was in the forum, where a strife went on,—
Two men contending for a fine, the price
Of one who had been slain. Before the crowd
One claimed that he had paid the fine, and one
Denied that aught had been received, and both
Called for the sentence which should end the strife.
The people clamored for both sides, for both
Had eager friends; the heralds held the crowd
In check; the elders, upon polished stones,
Sat in a sacred circle. Each one took,
In turn, a herald's sceptre in his hand,
And, rising, gave his sentence. In the midst
Two talents lay in gold, to be the meed
Of him whose juster judgment should prevail.
Around the other city sat two hosts
In shining armor, bent to lay it waste,
Unless the dwellers would divide their wealth,—
All that their pleasant homes contained,—and yield
The assailants half. As yet the citizens
Had not complied, but secretly had planned
An ambush. Their beloved wives meanwhile,

And their young children, stood and watched the walls,
With aged men among them, while the youths
Marched on, with Mars and Pallas at their head,
Both wrought in gold, with golden garments on,
Stately and large in form, and over all
Conspicuous, in bright armor, as became
The gods; the rest were of an humbler size.
And when they reached the spot where they should lie
In ambush, by a river's side, a place
For watering herds, they sat them down, all armed
In shining brass. Apart from all the rest
They placed two sentries, on the watch to spy
The approach of sheep and hornèd kine. Soon came
The herds in sight; two shepherds walked with them,
Who, all unweeting of the evil nigh,
Solaced their task with music from their reeds.
The warriors saw and rushed on them, and took
And drave away large prey of beeves, and flocks
Of fair white sheep, whose keepers they had slain.
When the besiegers in their council heard
The sound of tumult at the watering-place,
They sprang upon their nimble-footed steeds,
And overtook the pillagers. Both bands
Arrayed their ranks and fought beside the stream,

And smote each other. There did Discord rage,
And Tumult, and the great Destroyer, Fate.
One wounded warrior she had seized alive,
And one unwounded yet, and through the field
Dragged by the foot another, dead. Her robe
Was reddened o'er the shoulders with the blood
From human veins. Like living men they ranged
The battle-field, and dragged by turns the slain.
  There too he sculptured a broad fallow field
Of soft rich mould, thrice ploughed, and over which
Walked many a ploughman, guiding to and fro
His steers, and when on their return they reached
The border of the field the master came
To meet them, placing in the hands of each
A goblet of rich wine. Then turned they back
Along the furrows, diligent to reach
Their distant end. All dark behind the plough
The ridges lay, a marvel to the sight,
Like real furrows, though engraved in gold.
  There, too, the artist placed a field which lay
Deep in ripe wheat. With sickles in their hands
The laborers reaped it. Here the handfuls fell
Upon the ground; there binders tied them fast
With bands, and made them sheaves. Three binders went

Close to the reapers, and behind them boys,
Bringing the gathered handfuls in their arms,
Ministered to the binders. Staff in hand,
The master stood among them by the side
Of the ranged sheaves and silently rejoiced.
Meanwhile the servants underneath an oak
Prepared a feast apart; they sacrificed
A fatling ox and dressed it, while the maids
Were kneading for the reapers the white meal.
  A vineyard also on the shield he graved,
Beautiful, all of gold, and heavily
Laden with grapes. Black were the clusters all;
The vines were stayed on rows of silver stakes.
He drew a blue trench round it, and a hedge
Of tin. One only path there was by which
The vintagers could go to gather grapes.
Young maids and striplings of a tender age
Bore the sweet fruit in baskets. Midst them all,
A youth from his shrill harp drew pleasant sounds,
And sang with soft voice to the murmuring strings.
They danced around him, beating with quick feet
The ground, and sang and shouted joyously.
  And there the artist wrought a herd of beeves,
High-horned, and sculptured all in gold and tin.

They issued lowing from their stalls to seek
Their pasture, by a murmuring stream, that ran
Rapidly through its reeds. Four herdsmen, graved
In gold, were with the beeves, and nine fleet dogs
Followed. Two lions, seizing on a bull
Among the foremost cattle, dragged him off
Fearfully bellowing; hounds and herdsmen rushed
To rescue him. The lions tore their prey,
And lapped the entrails and the crimson blood.
Vainly the shepherds pressed around and urged
Their dogs, that shrank from fastening with their teeth
Upon the lions, but stood near and bayed.
  There also did illustrious Vulcan grave
A fair, broad pasture, in a pleasant glade,
Full of white sheep, and stalls, and cottages,
And many a shepherd's fold with sheltering roof.
  And there illustrious Vulcan also wrought
A dance,—a maze like that which Dædalus,
In the broad realm of Gnossus once contrived
For fair-haired Ariadne. Blooming youths
And lovely virgins, tripping to light airs,
Held fast each other's wrists. The maidens wore
Fine linen robes; the youths had tunics on
Lustrous as oil, and woven daintily.

The maids wore wreaths of flowers; the young men swords
Of gold in silver belts. They bounded now
In a swift circle,—as a potter whirls
With both his hands a wheel to try its speed,
Sitting before it,—then again they crossed
Each other, darting to their former place.
A multitude around that joyous dance
Gathered, and were amused, while from the crowd
Two tumblers raised their song, and flung themselves
About among the band that trod the dance.
Last on the border of that glorious shield
He graved in all its strength the ocean-stream.
And when that huge and massive shield was done,
He forged a corselet brighter than the blaze
Of fire; he forged a solid helm to fit
The hero's temples, shapely and enchased
With rare designs, and with a crest of gold.
And last he forged him greaves of ductile tin.
When the great artist Vulcan saw his task
Complete, he lifted all that armor up
And laid it at the feet of her who bore
Achilles. Like a falcon in her flight,
Down plunging from Olympus capped with snow,
She bore the shining armor Vulcan gave.

## BOOK XIX.

IN saffron-colored mantle from the tides
Of Ocean rose the Morning to bring light
To gods and men, when Thetis reached the fleet,
Bringing the gift of Vulcan. There she found
Her son, who, bending o'er Patroclus, wept
Aloud, and all around a troop of friends
Lamented bitterly. Beside him stood
The glorious goddess, took his hand, and said:—
"Leave we the dead, my son, since it hath pleased
The gods that he should fall; and now receive
This sumptuous armor, forged by Vulcan's hand,
Beautiful, such as no man ever wore."
The goddess spake, and laid the armor down
Before Achilles; as they touched the earth,
The well-wrought pieces clanked, and terror seized
The Myrmidons. No one among them all
Dared fix his gaze upon them; all shrank back.
Achilles only, as he saw them, felt

His spirit roused within him. In his eyes
A terrible brightness flashed, as if of fire.
He lifted up the god's magnificent gift
Rejoicing, and, when long his eyes had dwelt
Delighted on the marvellous workmanship,
Thus to his mother said, in wingèd words:—
"A god indeed, my mother, must have given
These arms, the work of heavenly hands: no man
Could forge them. Now I arm myself for war.
But for the valiant Menœtiades
I greatly fear that flies will gather round
The wounds inflicted by the spear, and worms
Be bred within them, to pollute the corpse
Now that the life is gone, and taint the whole."
And silver-footed Thetis answered thus:
"Son, have no care for that. The task be mine
To drive away the importunate swarm that feed
On heroes slain in battle. Though it lie
The whole year long, the body shall remain
Even more than uncorrupted. Call thou now
To council all the Achaian chiefs; renounce
Thy feud with Agamemnon, king of men,
And arm for war, and put on all thy might."
She spake, and called a fiery courage up

Within the hero's breast. The goddess then
Infusèd ambrosia and the ruddy juice
Of nectar through the nostrils of the dead
Into the frame, to keep it from decay.
  Along the beach the great Achilles went,
Calling with mighty shouts the Grecian chiefs.
Then even they who till that day remained
Beside the fleet,—the pilots and the men
Who held the helm, the stewards of the ships,
And the purveyors,—all made haste to swell
The assembly, for they knew that he who long
Had borne no part in the disastrous war
Had now come forth. Two ministers of Mars,
The brave Tydides and the nobly born
Ulysses, both supported by their spears,
Came halting, for their wounds were painful yet;
They came and sat among the foremost chiefs.
And last came Agamemnon, king of men,
Wounded, for he had felt in thick of fight
The edge of the sharp spear which Coön bore,
Antenor's son. Now when the Greeks were all
Assembled, swift Achilles rose and said:—
  "Atrides, of a truth it would have been
Better for both of us had we done this

At first, though sorely angered, when we strove
For a girl's sake so fiercely. Would that she
Had perished in my ships, by Dian's shaft,
The day on which I laid Lyrnessus waste!
So many Greeks would then have not been forced,
Slain by the enemy's hand, to bite the dust
Of the great earth, while I was brooding o'er
My wrath. All that was for the good of Troy
And Hector; but the Greeks, I think, will long
Remember our contention. Let us leave
These things among the things that were, and, though
They make us grieve, let us subdue our minds
To what the time requires. Here then my wrath
Shall end; it is not meet that it should burn
Forever. Hasten thou and rouse to war
The long-haired Greeks, that I may yet again
Go forth among the men of Troy, and learn
If they design to encamp another night
Before the fleet. There is among them all
No man, I ween, who will not joyfully
Sit down when he escapes my deadly spear."
He ended, and the Achaians all rejoiced
To hear the brave Pelides thus renounce
His anger. Agamemnon, king of men,

Then rose. He came not forth into the midst,
But stood beside his seat, and thus he spake: —
"O friends, Achaian heroes, ministers
Of Mars! Whoever rises up to speak
'T is well to hear him through, and not break in
Upon his speech, else is the most expert
Confounded. Who amid a clamorous throng
Can listen or can speak? The orator
Of clearest voice must utter it in vain.
Now I address Pelides; for the rest,
Hearken ye all, and ponder what I say.
The Greeks speak often of this feud, and cast
The blame on me. Yet was I not the cause,
But Jupiter and Fate, and she who walks
In darkness, dread Erynnis. It was they
Who filled my mind with fury in the hour
When from Achilles I bore off his prize.
What could I do? A deity prevails
In all things, Atè, mighty to destroy,
Daughter of Jove, and held in awe by all.
Delicate are her feet; she never comes
Near to the ground, but glides above the heads
Of men, to do them harm, and in her net
Entangles one at least of two who strive.

Jove, deemed the mightiest among men and gods,
Once felt her power of mischief. Him his spouse,
Juno, entrapped by cunning, when within
The massive walls of Thebes Alcmena lay
In childbed, and the mighty Hercules
Was near his birth. For Jupiter had said
Boastfully to the immortals: 'Hear, ye gods
And goddesses, what I am moved to speak:
This day shall Ilithyia, who presides
At births, bring into light a prince whose rule
The neighboring tribes shall own; he shall be one
Who bears the blood of my illustrious race.'
"Imperial Juno thus, with words of guile,
Made answer: 'What thou sayest will prove false,
Nor wilt thou keep thy word. Now swear to me,
Olympius, with the irrevocable oath,
That whosoever of thy race shall fall
This day between a woman's feet shall bear
The rule o'er all the neighboring tribes.' She spake,
And Jove, perceiving not her craft, complied,
And took the mighty oath, but afterward
Found himself wronged. For Juno, darting forth,
Shot from the Olympian summit, and at once
Alighted at Achaian Argos. There

She found the noble wife of Sthenelus,
The son of Perseus, pregnant with a son,
In the seventh month. She caused him to be born,
The number of his months yet incomplete,
And kept Alcmena's hour of childbirth back,
And stayed her pangs. The goddess then made haste
To bear the tidings to Saturnian Jove.
"'O Father Jupiter, by whom are hurled
The ruddy lightnings, I have news for thee.
A man-child of a generous stock is born,—
Eurystheus, whom the Argives shall obey,—
Born at this hour to Sthenelus, the son
Of Perseus, who is thine. And well it is
That such a prince should rule the Argive race.'
"She ended: Jupiter was deeply grieved,
And, seizing Atè by her shining locks,
In his great wrath, he swore a mighty oath,—
That Atè, whose delight it is to bring
Mischief to all, should never tread again
Olympus and the starry floor of heaven.
Thus having sworn, he swung her, with raised arm,
On high, and hurled her from the starry heaven
Downward, where soon she reached the haunts of men;
Yet oft in after time because of her

He sighed, beholding his beloved son
Doomed by Eurystheus to unworthy tasks.
So I, while crested Hector in his might
Made havoc at our fleet among the Greeks
Even by their prows, remembered well my fault.
And now since I have borne the penalty,
And Jupiter it was who took away
My reason, I would gladly make amends
With liberal gifts. But rise and join the war;
Inflame the courage of the rest; the gifts
Will I supply,—all that were promised thee
When nobly-born Ulysses yesterday
Went to thy tents. Or, if it please thee, wait,
Though armed for battle, and my train shall bring
The treasures from my ship, that thou mayst see
My presents are peace-offerings indeed."
  The swift of foot, Achilles, answered thus:
"Most glorious son of Atreus, king of men!
Whether, O Agamemnon, thou wilt give
Gifts, as is meet, or keep them, rests with thee.
Now let us think of war; it is not well
To waste the hour in talking, and put off
The mighty work that we have yet to do.
Let every Greek among you, as he sees

Achilles fighting in the foremost ranks,
And slaughtering the Trojan phalanxes,
Take heart and boldly combat with his man."
  And then Ulysses, wise in council, spake,
Answering Achilles: "Nay, thou shouldst not thus,
Brave as thou art, lead on the sons of Greece,
Yet fasting, to the conflict with the men
Of Troy beside their city. No brief space
The struggle will endure when once the foes
Rush on each other, and a god inspires
Both hosts with fury. Bid the Achaians take
In their swift galleys food and wine; in these
Are force and vigor. No man can endure
To combat all the day till set of sun,
Save with the aid of food, however great
The promptings of his valor; for his limbs
Grow heavy, thirst and hunger weaken him,
And his knees fail him as he walks. Not so
The warrior well supplied with food and wine:
He fights the foe all day; a resolute heart
Is in his bosom; nor does weariness
O'ertake him till all others leave the field.
Now let the people be dismissed awhile,
And a repast be ordered. Let the king,

Atrides, bring into the assembly here
His gifts, that all the Greeks may look on them,
And thou rejoice to see them. Let him rise
Among the Greeks, and take a solemn oath
That he has ne'er approached the maiden's bed
To claim a husband's right. Thus let thy heart
Be satisfied. Yet let the monarch spread
A sumptuous banquet in his tent for thee,
That thy redress may be complete. And thou,
Atrides, wilt hereafter be more just
To others. It dishonors not a king
To make amends to one whom he has wronged."

And then King Agamemnon spake in turn:
"Son of Laertes, gladly have I heard
What thou hast said, and well hast thou discoursed
Of all things in their order. I will take
The oath of which thou speakest,—so my heart
Commands me. In the presence of a god
I take it, and commit no perjury.
Now let Achilles, though he longs for war,
Delay awhile; and all assembled here,
Remain ye on the ground till from my ship
The gifts are brought. This charge and this command
I give to thee, Ulysses. Take with thee

A band of youths, the noblest of the host,
And bring the presents promised yesterday
To Peleus' son, and hither let them lead
The women. Meantime let Talthybius haste
To bring from our broad camp a boar, which I
Will offer up to Jove and to the Sun."
  The swift of foot, Achilles, thus replied:
"Most glorious son of Atreus, king of men,
These things are for the time when there shall come
A pause from battle, and this warlike heat
Within my breast shall cool. They whom the spear
Of Hector, son of Priam, has o'ercome
Lie mangled on the earth, since Jupiter
Awarded him the glory of the day:—
And ye propose a banquet. I would call
The sons of Greece to rush into the war
Unfed and fasting, and when this disgrace
Shall be avenged, I would, at sunset, spread
A liberal feast. Be sure that I, till then,
Taste neither food nor drink, while my slain friend
Lies gashed with weapons in my tent, amidst
His sorrowing comrades. Little I regard
The things of which thou speakest, for my thoughts
Are all of bloodshed and of dying groans."

Ulysses, the sagacious, thus rejoined:
"Achilles, son of Peleus, bravest far
Of all the Achaians, mightier with the spear
By no small odds than I, yet do I stand
In prudence much above thee; I have lived
More years, and more have learned. Let then thy mind
Accept what I shall say. Men soon become
Weary of warfare, even when the sword
Lays its most ample harvest on the earth.
But fewer sheaves are reaped when Jupiter,
The arbiter of battles, turns the scale.
It is not well that we of Greece should mourn
The dead with fasting, since from day to day
Our warriors fall in numbers. Where were then
Respite from daily fasts? Lay we our slain
In earth and mourn a day. We who outlive
The cruel combat should refresh ourselves
With food and wine, that we may steadily
Maintain in arms the conflict with the foe.
And then let no man idly wait to hear
A further call to war, — for it will come
Freighted with evil to the man who skulks
Among the ships, — but let us all go forth
To wage fierce battle with the knights of Troy."

He spake, and summoned to his side the sons
Of glorious Nestor, and Meriones,
And Meges, son of Phyleus, and with them
Thoas, and Lycomedes, Creon's son,
And Melanippus. Straight they took their way
To Agamemnon's tent, and there their task
Was done as quickly as the word was given.
They brought seven tripods forth, the promised gifts,
And twenty burnished caldrons, and twelve steeds,
And led away seven graceful women trained
In household arts,—the maid with rosy cheeks,
Briseis, was the eighth. Ulysses came,
Leading the way, and bearing, duly weighed,
Ten talents, all of gold. The Achaian youths
Followed, and placed the presents in the midst
Of that assembly. Agamemnon rose;
And then Talthybius, who was like a god
In power of voice, came near and took his place
Beside the monarch, holding in his hands
A boar. The son of Atreus drew a knife,
Which hung by the great scabbard of his sword,
And, cutting off the forelock of the boar,
Prayed with uplifted hands to Jupiter:
Meantime the Greeks in silence kept their seats,
And, as became them, listened to the king,

Who looked into the sky above, and said:—
  "Now first bear witness, Jove, of all the gods
Greatest and best, and also Earth and Sun,
And Furies dwelling under Earth, who take
Vengeance on men forsworn, that never I
Have laid, for purpose of unchaste desire,
Or other cause, my hand upon the maid
Briseis. She hath dwelt inviolate
Within my tents. If yet in aught I say
Lurk perjury, then may the blessed gods
Heap on my head the many miseries
With which they punish those who falsely swear!"
  He spake, and drew the unrelenting blade
Across the animal's throat. Talthybius took
And swung the carcass round, and cast it forth
Into the gray sea's depths, to be the food
Of fishes. Then again Achilles rose
Among the warlike sons of Greece, and said:—
  "Great sorrows thou dost send, O Father Jove!
Upon mankind; for never would the son
Of Atreus have provoked the wrath that burned
Within my bosom, never would have thought
To bear away the maiden from my tent
In spite of me, had it not been the will

Of Jupiter that many a Greek should die.
But banquet now, and then prepare for war."
So spake Achilles, and at once dissolved
The assembly, each repairing to his ship
Save the large-hearted Myrmidons, who still
Were busy with the gifts, and carried them
Toward their great general's galley. These they laid
Carefully in the tents, and seated there
The women, while the attentive followers drave
The coursers to the stables. When the maid
Briseis, beautiful as Venus, saw
Patroclus lying gashed with wounds, she sprang
And threw herself upon the dead, and tore
Her bosom, her fair cheeks and delicate neck;
And thus the graceful maiden, weeping, said:—
"Patroclus, dear to my unhappy heart!
I left thee in full life, when from this tent
They led me; I return and find thee dead,
O chieftain of the people! Thus it is
That sorrow upon sorrow is my lot.
Him to whose arms my father, in my youth,
And gracious mother gave me as a bride,
I saw before our city pierced and slain,
And the three brothers whom my mother bore

Slain also,—brothers whom I dearly loved.
Yet thou, when swift Achilles struck to earth
My hapless husband, and laid waste the town
Of godlike Mynes, wouldst not suffer me
To weep despairingly; for thou didst give
Thy word to make me yet the wedded wife
Of great Achilles, bear me in the fleet
To Phthia, and prepare the wedding feast
Among the Myrmidons. O ever kind!
I mourn thy death, and cannot be consoled."

  Weeping she spake; the women wept with her,
Seemingly for the dead, but each, in truth,
For her own griefs. Meanwhile the elders came
Around Achilles, praying him to join
The banquet, but the chief, with sighs, refused.

  "Dear comrades, if ye love me, do not thus
Press me to sit and feast. A mighty woe
Weighs down my spirit; it is my resolve
To wait and bear until the setting sun."

  So saying, he dismissed the other kings.
The sons of Atreus, and the high-born chief
Ulysses, Nestor, and Idomeneus,
And Phœnix, aged knight, alone remained,
And anxiously they sought to comfort him

In his great grief; but comfort would he none
Ere entering the red jaws of war. He drew
Deep sighs, and, thinking on Patroclus, spake: —
"The time has been when thou too, hapless one,
Dearest of all my comrades, wouldst have spread
With diligent speed before me in my tent
A genial banquet, while the Greeks prepared
For desperate battle with the knights of Troy.
Thou liest now a mangled corse, and I,
Through grief for thee, refrain from food and drink,
Though they are near. No worse calamity
Could light on me, not even should I hear
News of my father's death, who haply now
Tenderly mourns with tears his absent son
In Phthia, while upon a foreign coast
I wage for hated Helen's sake the war
Against the Trojans; or were I to hear
Tidings that my beloved son had died,
The noble Neoptolemus, who now,
If living, is in Scyros, growing up
To manhood. Once the hope was in my heart
That I alone should perish here at Troy,
Far from the Argive pastures full of steeds,
And thou return to Phthia and bring home

My son from Scyros in thy ship, and show
The youth my wealth, my servants, and my halls,
High-roofed and spacious. For my mind misgives
That Peleus either lives not, or endures
A painful age, and hardly lives, yet waits
To hear the sorrowful news that I am slain."
So spake he weeping, and the elders sighed
To see his tears, as each recalled to mind
Those whom he left at home, while Saturn's son
Beheld their grief with pity, and bespake
His daughter Pallas thus with wingèd words:—
"My child, wilt thou desert that valiant man?
And shall Achilles be no more thy care?
Lo, by his ships, before their lofty prows,
He sits, lamenting his beloved friend.
The rest are at the banquet; he remains
Apart from them, and fasting. Hasten thou;
With nectar and ambrosial sweets refresh
His frame, that hunger overtake him not."
As thus he spake he sent the goddess forth
Eager to do her errand. Plunging down,
In form a shrill-voiced harpy with broad wings,
She cleft the air. The Greeks throughout the camp
Were putting on their armor. She infused

Into the hero's frame ambrosial sweets
And nectar, that his limbs might not grow faint
With hunger. Then the goddess sought again
The stable mansion of Almighty Jove,
While all the Greeks came pouring from the fleet.

As when the flakes of snow fall thick from heaven,
Driven by the north wind sweeping on the clouds
Before it, so from out the galleys came
Helms crowding upon helms that glittered fair,
Strong hauberks, bossy shields, and ashen spears.
The gleam of armor brightened heaven and earth,
And mighty was the sound of trampling feet.
Amidst them all the great Achilles stood,
Putting his armor on; he gnashed his teeth;
His eyes shot fire; a grief too sharp to bear
Was in his heart, as, filled with rage against
The men of Troy, he cased his limbs in mail,
The gift of Vulcan, from whose diligent hand
It came. And first about his legs he clasped
The beautiful greaves, with silver fastenings,
Fitted the corselet to his bosom next,
And from his shoulders hung the brazen sword
With silver studs, and then he took the shield,
Massive and broad, whose brightness streamed as far

As the moon's rays. And as at sea the light
Of beacon, blazing in some lonely spot
By night, upon a mountain summit, shines
To mariners whom the tempest's force has driven
Far from their friends across the fishy deep,
So from that glorious buckler of the son
Of Peleus, nobly wrought, a radiance streamed
Into the sky. And then he raised and placed
Upon his head the impenetrable helm
With horse-hair plume. It glittered like a star,
And all the shining tufts of golden thread,
With which the maker's hand had thickly set
Its cone, were shaken. Next the high-born chief
Tried his new arms, to know if they were well
Adjusted to his shape, and left his limbs
Free play. They seemed like wings, and lifted up
The shepherd of the people. Then he drew
From its ancestral sheath his father's spear,
Heavy and huge and tough. No man of all
The Grecian host could wield that weapon save
Achilles only. 'T was a Pelian ash,
Which Chiron for his father had cut down
On Pelion's highest peak, to be the death
Of heroes. Meantime, busy with the steeds,

Automedon and Alcimus put on
Their trappings and their yoke, and round their necks
Bound the fair collars, thrust into their mouths
The bit, and backward drew the reins to meet
The well-wrought chariot. Then Automedon
Took in his hand the showy lash, and leaped
Into the seat. Behind him, all equipped
For war, Achilles mounted, in a blaze
Of arms that dazzled like the sun, and thus
Called to his father's steeds with terrible voice:—
"Xanthus and Balius, whom Podargè bore,—
A noble stock,—I charge you to bring back
Into the Grecian camp, the battle done,
Him whom ye now are bearing to the field,
Nor leave him, as ye left Patroclus, dead."
Swift-footed Xanthus from beneath the yoke
Answered him with bowed head and drooping mane
That, flowing through the yoke-ring swept the ground,—
For Juno gave him then the power of speech:—
"For this one day, at least, we bear thee safe,
O fiery chief, Achilles! but the hour
Of death draws nigh to thee, nor will the blame
Be ours; a mighty god and cruel fate
Ordain it. Not through our neglect or sloth

Did they of Troy strip off thy glorious arms
From slain Patroclus. That invincible god,
The son of golden-haired Latona, smote
The hero in the foremost ranks, and gave
Glory to Hector. Even though our speed
Were that of Zephyr, fleetest of the winds,
Yet certain is thy doom to be o'ercome
In battle by a god and by a man."

Thus far he spake, and then the Furies checked
His further speech. Achilles, swift of foot,
Replied in anger: "Xanthus, why foretell
My death? It is not needed; well I know
My fate,—that here I perish, far away
From Peleus and my mother. I shall fight
Till I have made the Trojans sick of war."

He spake, and, shouting to his firm-paced steeds,
Drave them, among the foremost, toward the war.

## *BOOK XX.*

THUS, O Pelides, did the sons of Greece,
Impatient for the battle, arm themselves,
By their beaked ships, around thee. Opposite,
Upon a height that rose amidst the plain,
The Trojans waited. Meantime Jupiter
Sent Themis from the Olympian summit, ploughed
With dells, to summon all the immortal ones
To council. Forth she went from place to place,
Bidding them to the palace halls of Jove.
Then none of all the Rivers failed to join
The assembly, save Oceanus, and none
Of all the Nymphs were absent whose abode
Is in the pleasant groves and river-founts
And grassy meadows. When they reached the halls
Of Cloud-compelling Jove they sat them down
On shining thrones, divided each from each
By polished columns, wrought for Father Jove
By Vulcan's skill. Thus all to Jove's abode

Were gathered. Neptune had not disobeyed
The call. He left the sea, and took his seat
Among them, and inquired the will of Jove.
"Why, wielder of the lightning, dost thou call
The gods again to council? Do thy plans
Concern the Greeks and Trojans? For the war
Between their hosts will be rekindled soon."
And thus the Cloud-compeller Jove replied:
"Thou who dost shake the shores, thou knowest well
The purpose of my mind, and for whose sake
I call this council. Though so soon to die,
They are my care. Yet will I keep my place,
Seated upon the Olympian mount, and look
Calmly upon the conflict. All of you
Depart, and aid the Trojans or the Greeks,
As it may list you. For should Peleus' son
Alone do battle with the men of Troy,
Their squadrons could not stand before the assault
Of the swift-footed warrior for an hour.
Beforetime, at the sight of him they fled,
O'ercome with fear, and now, when he is roused
To rage by his companion's death, I fear
Lest, though it be against the will of fate,
He level with the ground the walls of Troy."

Saturnius spake, and moved the hosts to join
In desperate conflict. All the gods went forth
To mingle with the war on different sides.
Juno and Pallas hastened to the fleet
With Neptune, he who makes the earth to shake,
And Hermes, god of useful arts, and shrewd
In forecast. Vulcan also went with them,
Strong and stern-eyed, yet lame, his feeble legs
Moving with labor. To the Trojan side
Went crested Mars, Apollo with his locks
Unshorn, Diana mighty with the bow,
Latona, Xanthus, and the Queen of smiles,
Venus; for while the gods remained apart
From men, the Achaian host was high in hope
Because Achilles, who so long had left
The war, now reappeared upon the field,
And terror shook the limbs of every son
Of Troy when he beheld the swift of foot,
Pelides, terrible as Mars—that curse
Of human-kind—in glittering arms again.
But when the dwellers of Olympus joined
The crowd of mortals, Discord, who makes mad
The nations, rose and raged; Minerva raised
Her war-cry from the trench without the wall,

And then she shouted from the sounding shore;
While, like a cloudy whirlwind, opposite,
Moved Mars, and fiercely yelled, encouraging
The men of Troy, as on the city heights
He stood, or paced with rapid steps the hill
Beside the Simoïs, called the Beautiful.
  Thus, kindling hate between the hosts, the gods
Engaged, and hideous was the strife that rose
Among them. From above, with terrible crash,
Thundered the father of the blessed gods
And mortal men, while Neptune from below
Shook the great earth and lofty mountain peaks.
Then watery Ida's heights and very roots,
The city of Troy, and the Greek galleys, quaked.
Then Pluto, ruler of the nether world,
Leaped from his throne in terror, lest the god
Who makes the earth to tremble, cleaving it
Above him, should lay bare to gods and men
His horrible abodes, the dismal haunts
Which even the gods abhor. Such tumult filled
The field of battle when the immortals joined
The conflict. Then against King Neptune stood
Phœbus Apollo, with his wingèd shafts,
And Pallas, goddess of the azure eyes,

Confronted Mars. Encountering Juno came
The sister of Apollo, archer-queen
And huntress, Dian of the golden bow.
The helpful Hermes, god of useful arts,
Opposed Latona, and the mighty stream
Called Xanthus by the immortals, but by men
Scamander, with his eddies strong and deep,
Stood face to face with Vulcan in the field.

So warred the gods with gods. Meantime the son
Of Peleus, ranging through the thick of fight,
Sought only Hector, Priam's son, whose blood
He meant to pour to greedy Mars, the god
Of carnage. But Apollo, who impels
Warriors to battle, stirred Æneas up
To meet Pelides. First he filled his heart
With resolute valor, and then took the voice
Of Priam's son, Lycaon. In his shape
Thus spake Apollo, son of Jupiter:—

"Æneas, prince of Troy, where now are all
The boasts which thou hast made before the chiefs
Of Troy at banquets, that thou yet wouldst meet
Pelides in the combat hand to hand?"

Æneas made reply: "Priamides,
Why dost thou bid me, when thou knowest me

Unwilling, meet in combat Peleus' son,
The mighty among men? It will not be
For the first time if I confront him now.
He chased me once from Ida with his spear,—
Me and my fellows, when he took our herds
And laid Lyrnessus waste and Pedasus.
But Jove, who gave me strength and nimble feet,
Preserved me; I had else been slain by him
And by Minerva, for the goddess went
Before him, giving him the victory
And moving him to slay the Leleges
And Trojans with the brazen spear he bore.
'T is not for mortal man to fight the son
Of Peleus, at whose side there ever stands
One of the immortal gods, averting harm.
And then his weapon flies right on, nor stops
Until it bites the flesh. Yet were the god
To weigh the victory in an equal scale,
Achilles would not vanquish me with ease,
Though he might boast his frame were all of brass."
 Then spake the king Apollo, son of Jove:
"Pray, warrior, to the eternal gods. They say
That Venus gave thee birth, who has her own
From Jove. His mother is of lower rank

Than thine. Thine is a child of Jove, but his
A daughter of the Ancient of the Deep.
Strike at him with that conquering spear of thine,
Nor let him scare thee with stern words and threats."
  He said, and breathed into the prince's breast
Fresh valor, as, arrayed in glittering arms,
He pressed to where the foremost warriors fought;
Yet not unseen by Juno's eye went forth
The son of old Anchises. She convened
The gods in council, and addressed them thus:—
  "Neptune and Pallas, what shall now be done?
Consider ye. Æneas, all arrayed
In glittering arms, is pressing on to meet
Pelides. Phœbus sends him. Let us join
To turn him back, or let some one of us
Stand near Achilles, fill his limbs with strength,
Nor let his heart grow faint, but let him see
That we, the mightiest of the immortals, look
On him with favor, and that those who strive
Amid the war and bloodshed to protect
The sons of Troy are empty boasters all.
For this we came from heaven to interpose
In battle, that Achilles may endure
No harm from Trojan hands, although, no doubt,

Hereafter he must suffer all that Fate
Spun for him when his mother brought him forth.
But if he hear not, from some heavenly voice,
Of this assurance, fear may fall on him
When, haply, in the battle he shall meet
Some god; for when revealed to human sight
The presence of the gods is terrible."
  And then did Neptune, he who shakes the earth,
Make answer: "Juno, it becomes thee ill
To be so greatly vexed. I cannot wish
A contest with the other gods, though we
In power excel them. Rather let us sit
Apart, where we can look upon the war,
And leave it to mankind. And yet, if Mars
Or Phœbus should begin the fight, or seek
To thwart Achilles or restrain his arm,
There will be cause for us to join the strife
In earnest, and I deem that they full soon,
The contest ended, will return to join
The assembled gods upon the Olympian mount,
Forced to withdraw by our all-potent hands."
  So spake the dark-haired god, and led the way
To the high mound of godlike Hercules,
Raised from the earth by Trojans, with the aid

Of Pallas, that the hero there might find
A refuge when the monster of the deep
Should chase him from the sea-beach to the plain.
With other gods beside him Neptune there
Sat down and drew a shadow, which no sight
Could pierce, around their shoulders. Other gods,
Upon the hill called Beautiful, were grouped
Round thee, Apollo, archer-god, and Mars,
Spoiler of cities. On both sides they sat,
Devising plans, unwilling to begin
The fierce encounter, though Almighty Jove
From where he sat in heaven commanded it.
The warriors thronged into the field, which shone
With brazen armor and caparisons
Of steeds; earth trembled with the sounding tramp
Of marching squadrons. From the opposing ranks
Two chieftains, each the bravest of his host,
Impatient to engage,—Anchises' son,
Æneas, and the great Achilles,—came.
And first Æneas, with defiant mien
And nodding casque, stood forth. He held his shield
Before him, which he wielded right and left,
And shook his brazen spear. On the other side,
Pelides hurried toward him, terrible

As is a lion, which the assembled hinds
Of a whole village chase and seek to slay,
While on he stalks, contemning their assault;
But if the arrow of some strong-armed youth
Have smitten him, he stands, and gathers all
His strength to spring, with open jaws and teeth
Half hid in foam, and uttering fearful growls
From his deep chest; he lashes with his tail
His sides and sinewy thighs to rouse himself
To combat, and then, grimly frowning, leaps
To slay, or by the foremost youths be slain,
So sprang Achilles, moved by his bold heart
To meet the brave Æneas. As the twain
Drew near each other, the swift-footed chief,
The great Achilles, was the first to speak:—
"Why, O Æneas, hast thou come so far
Through this vast crowd to seek me? Does thy heart
Bid thee confront me in the hope to gain
The place which Priam holds, and to bear rule
Over the knights of Troy? Yet shouldst thou take
My life, think not that Priam in thy hand
Will place such large reward. He has his sons,
Nor is he fickle, but of stable mind.
Or will the Trojans, if thou slayest me,

Bestow on thee broad acres, of a soil
Fruitful exceedingly, and suited well
To vines or to the plough, which thou mayst till?
That also, as I hope, thou wilt obtain
With difficulty; for, unless I err,
I forced thee once to flee before my spear.
Dost thou remember, when thou wert alone
Among thy beeves, I drave thee, running fast,
Down Ida's steeps? Then didst thou never turn
To face me, but didst seek a hiding-place
Within Lyrnessus, which I also took
And wasted, with the aid of Father Jove
And Pallas. From the town I led away
The women, never to be free again.
Jove and the other gods protected thee
That day. Yet will they not protect thee now,
As thou dost vainly hope. Withstand me not,
I counsel thee, but hide thyself among
The crowd before thou suffer harm, for he
Who sees past evils only is a fool."
  And then Æneas answered: "Do not think,
Pelides, with such words to frighten me,
As if I were a beardless boy. I too
Might use reproach and taunt; but well we know

Each other's birth and lineage, through report
Of men, although by sight I know not thine,
Nor know'st thou mine. They say that thou art sprung
From Peleus the renowned, and from the nymph
Of ocean, fair-haired Thetis, while I boast
My birth from brave Anchises, and can claim
Venus as mother. Two of these to-day
Must weep the death of a beloved son,
For we are not to part, I think, nor end
The combat after a few childish words;
Yet let me speak, that thou mayst better know
Our lineage, known already far and wide.
Jove was the father, Cloud-compelling Jove,
Of Dardanus, by whom Dardania first
Was peopled, ere our sacred Troy was built
On the great plain,—a populous town; for men
Dwelt still upon the roots of Ida fresh
With many springs. To Dardanus was born
King Erichthonius, richest in his day
Of mortal men, and in his meadows grazed
Three thousand mares, exulting in their brood
Of tender foals. Of some of this vast herd
Boreas became enamored as they fed.
He came to them in likeness of a steed

That wore an azure mane, and they brought forth
Twelve foals, which all were fēmales, of such speed
That when they frolicked on the teeming earth
They flew along the topmost ears of wheat
And broke them not, and when they sported o'er
The mighty bosom of the deep they ran
Along the hoary summits of its waves.
To Erichthonius Tros was born, who ruled
The Trojans, and from Tros there sprang three sons
Of high renown,—Ilus, Assaracus,
And godlike Ganymede, most beautiful
Of men; the gods beheld and caught him up
To heaven, so beautiful was he, to pour
The wine to Jove, and ever dwell with them.
And Ilus had a son, Laomedon,
Of mighty fame, to whom five sons were born,
Tithonus, Priam, Lampus, Clytius,
And Hicetaon, trained to war by Mars.
Assaracus begat my ancestor,
Capys, to whom Anchises owes his birth.
Anchises is my father; Priam's son
Is noble Hector. Such I claim to be
My lineage and my blood; but Jove at will
Gives in large measure, or diminishes,

Men's warlike prowess; and the power of Jove
Is over all. But let us talk no more
Of things like these, as if we were but boys,
While here in the mid-field we stand between
The warring armies. Both of us might cast
Reproaches at each other, many and foul,
Such as no galley of a hundred oars
Could bear and float. Men's tongues are voluble,
And endless are the modes of speech, and far
Extends from side to side the field of words.
Such as thou utterest it will be thy lot
To hear from others. But what profits it
For us to rail and wrangle, in high brawl,
Like women angered to the quick, that rush
Into the middle of the street and scold
With furious words, some true and others false,
As rage may prompt them? Me thou shalt not move
With words from my firm purpose ere thou raise
Thy arm against me. Let us hasten first
To prove the temper of our brazen spears."
He spake, and hurled his brazen spear to smite
The dreadful shield, a terror in men's eyes;
That mighty buckler rang with the strong blow.
Achilles, as it came, held forth his shield

With nervous arm far from him, for he feared
That the long javelin of his valiant foe
Might pierce it. Idle fear; he had not thought
That the bright armor given him by the gods
Not easily would yield to force of man.
Nor could the rapid spear that left the hand
Of brave Æneas pierce the shield; the gold,
The gift of Vulcan, stopped it. Through two folds
It went, but three remained; for Vulcan's skill
Fenced with five folds the disk, — the outer two
Of brass, the inner two of tin; between
Was one of gold, and there the brazen spear
Was stayed. And then in turn Achilles threw
His ponderous spear, and struck the orbèd shield
Borne by Æneas near the upper edge,
Where thinnest was the brass and thinnest lay
The bullock's hide. The Pelian ash broke through;
The buckler crashed; Æneas, stooping low,
Held it above him, terrified; the spear,
Tearing both plate and hide of that huge shield,
Passed over him, and, eager to go on,
Plunged in the earth and stood. He, when he saw
The massive lance which he had just escaped
Fixed in the earth so near him, stood awhile

As struck with fear, and with despairing looks.
Achilles drew his trenchant sword and rushed
With fury on Æneas, uttering
A fearful shout. Æneas lifted up
A stone, a mighty weight, which no two men,
As men are now, could raise, yet easily
He wielded it. Æneas then, to save
His threatened life, had smitten with the stone
His adversary's buckler or his helm,
And with his sword Pelides had laid dead
The Trojan, had not he who shakes the earth,
Neptune, beheld him in that perilous hour,
And instantly addressed the immortal gods:—
"My heart, ye gods, is heavy for the sake
Of the great-souled Æneas, who will sink
To Hades overcome by Peleus' son.
Rash man! he listened to the archer-god
Apollo, who has now no power to save
The chief from death. But, guiltless as he is,
Why should he suffer evil for the wrong
Of others? He has always sought to please
With welcome offerings the gods who dwell
In the broad heaven. Let us withdraw him, then,
From this great peril, lest, if he should fall

Before Achilles, haply Saturn's son
May be displeased. And 't is the will of fate
That he escape; that so the Dardan race,
Beloved by Jove above all others sprung
From him and mortal women, may not yet
Perish from earth and leave no progeny.
For Saturn's son already holds the house
Of Priam in disfavor, and will make
Æneas ruler o'er the men of Troy,
And his sons' sons shall rule them after him."
Imperial Juno with large eyes replied:
"Determine, Neptune, for thyself, and save
Æneas, or, all blameless as he is,
Abandon him to perish by the hand
Of Peleus' son, Achilles. We have sworn—
Minerva and myself—that never we
Would aid in aught the Trojans to escape
Their day of ruin, though the town of Troy
Sink to the dust in the destroying flames,—
Flames kindled by the warlike sons of Greece."
And then did Neptune, shaker of the shores,
Go forth into the battle and amidst
The clash of spears, and come where stood the chiefs,
Æneas and his mighty foe, the son

Of Peleus. Instantly he caused to rise
A darkness round the eyes of Peleus' son,
And from the buckler of Æneas drew
The spear with ashen stem and brazen blade,
And laid it at Achilles' feet, and next
He lifted high Æneas from the ground
And bore him thence. O'er many a warrior's head,
And many a harnessed steed, Æneas flew,
Hurled by the god, until he reached the rear
Of that fierce battle, where the Caucons stood
Arrayed for war. The shaker of the shores
Drew near, and said to him in wingèd words:—
"What god, Æneas, moved thee to defy
Madly the son of Peleus, who in might
Excels thee, and is dearer to the gods?
Whenever he encounters thee in arms
Give way, lest thou, against the will of fate,
Pass down to Hades. When he shall have met
His fate and perished, thou mayst boldly dare
To face the foremost of the enemy;
No other of the Greeks shall take thy life."
He spake, and having thus admonished him
He left Æneas there, and suddenly
Swept off the darkness that so thickly rose

Around Achilles, who, with sight now clear,
Looked forth, and, sighing, said to his great soul:—
"How strange is this! My eyes have seen to-day
A mighty marvel. Here the spear I flung
Is lying on the earth, and him at whom
I cast it, in the hope to take his life,
I see no longer. Well beloved, no doubt,
Is this Æneas by the immortal gods.
Yet that, I thought, was but an empty boast
Of his. Well, let him go; I cannot think
That he who gladly fled from death will find
The courage to encounter me again.
And now will I exhort the Greeks to fight
This battle bravely, while I go to prove
The prowess of the other chiefs of Troy."
He spake, and, cheering on the soldiery,
He sprang into the ranks: "Ye noble Greeks,
Avoid no more the Trojans; press right on.
Let each man single out his man, and fight
With eager heart. 'T is hard for me to chase,
With all my warlike might, so many men,
And fight with all. Not even Mars, the god,
Although immortal, nor Minerva's self,
Could combat with so vast a multitude

Unwearied; yet whatever I can do,
With hands and feet and strength, I give my word
Not to decline, or be remiss in aught.
I go to range the Trojan files, where none,
I think, will gladly stand to meet my spear."
  Such stirring words he uttered, while aloud
Illustrious Hector called, encouraging
The men of Troy, and promising to meet
Achilles: "Valiant Trojans, do not quail
Before Pelides. In the strife of words
I too might bear my part against the gods;
But harder were the combat with the spear,
For greater is their might than ours. The son
Of Peleus cannot make his threatenings good.
A part will he perform and part will leave
Undone. I go to wait him; I would go
Although his hands were like consuming flame, —
His hands like flame, his strength the strength of steel."
  He spake: the Trojans at his stirring words
Lifted their lances, and the adverse hosts
Joined battle with a fearful din. Then came
Apollo and admonished Hector thus: —
  "Hector, encounter not Achilles here
Before the armies, but amidst the throng

And tumult of the battle, lest perchance
He strike thee with the javelin or the sword."
He spake: the Trojan chief, dismayed to hear
The warning of the god, withdrew among
The crowded ranks. Meantime Achilles sprang
Upon the Trojans with a terrible cry,
And slew a leader of the host, the brave
Iphition, whom a Naiad, at the foot
Of snowy Tmolus, in the opulent vale
Of Hyda, bore to the great conqueror
Of towns, Otrynteus. As he came in haste,
The noble son of Peleus with his spear
Smote him upon the forehead in the midst,
And cleft the head in two. He fell; his arms
Clashed, and Achilles boasted o'er him thus:—
"Son of Otrynteus, terrible in arms,
Thou art brought low; thou meetest here thy death,
Though thou wert born by the Gygæan lake
Where lie, by fishy Hyllus and the stream
Of eddying Hermus, thy paternal fields."
Thus boastfully he spake, while darkness came
Over Iphition's eyes, and underneath
The chariots of the Greeks who foremost fought
His corse was mangled. Next Achilles smote

Antenor's son, Demoleon, gallantly
Breasting the onset of the Greeks. He pierced
His temple through the helmet's brazen cheek;
The brass stayed not the blow; the eager spear
Brake through the bone, and crushed the brain within,
And the brave youth lay dead. Achilles next
Struck down Hippodamas; he pierced his back
As, leaping from his car, the Phrygian fled
Before him. With a moan he breathed away
His life, as moans a bull when dragged around
The altar of the Heliconian king
By youths on whom the god that shakes the earth
Looks down well pleased. With such a moaning sound
The fiery spirit left the Phrygian's frame.

Then sprang Achilles with his spear to slay
The godlike Polydorus, Priam's son,
Whose father bade him not to join the war,
For he was younger than the other sons,
And dearest of them all. In speed of foot
He had no peer. Yet, with a boyish pride
To show his swiftness, in the foremost ranks
He ranged the field, until he lost his life.
Him with a javelin the swift-footed son
Of Peleus smote as he was hurrying by.

The weapon pierced the middle of his back,
Where, by its golden rings, the belt was clasped
Above the double corselet; the keen blade
Came forth in front; the Trojan with a cry
Fell forward on his knees, and, bending, clasped
His bowels in his hands. When Hector saw
His brother thus upon the earth, there came
A darkness o'er his eyes, nor could he bear
Longer to stand aloof, but, brandishing
His spear, came forward like a rushing flame
To meet the son of Peleus, who beheld
And bounded toward him, saying boastfully:
"So, he is near whose hand hath given my heart
Its deepest wound, who slew my dearest friend.
No more are we to shun each other now,
Timidly stealing through the paths of war."
  And then he said to Hector with a frown:
"Draw nearer, that thou mayst the sooner die."
  The crested Hector, undismayed, replied:
"Pelides, do not hope with empty words
To frighten me, as if I were a boy.
Insults and taunts I could with ease return.
I know that thou art brave; I know that I
In might am not thy equal; but the event

Rests in the laps of the great gods, and they
May, though I lack thy prowess, give thy life
Into my hands when I shall cast my spear.
The weapon that I bear is keen like thine."
  Thus having spoken, brandishing his spear,
He sent it forth; but with a gentle breath
Minerva turned it from the glorious Greek,
And laid it at the noble Hector's feet.
Then did Achilles, resolute to slay
His enemy, rush against him with a shout
Of fury; but Apollo, with such power
As gods put forth, withdrew him thence, and spread
A darkness round him. Thrice the swift of foot,
Achilles, rushed against him with his spear,
And thrice he smote the cloud. But when once more,
In godlike might, he made the assault, he spake
These wingèd words of menace and reproach: —
  "Hound as thou art, thou hast once more escaped
Thy death; for it was near. Again the hand
Of Phœbus rescues thee; to him thy vows
Are made ere thou dost trust thyself amidst
The clash of javelins. I shall meet thee yet
And end thee utterly, if any god
Favor me also. I will now pursue

And strike the other Trojan warriors down."
He spake, and in the middle of the neck
Smote Dryops with his spear. The Phrygian fell
Before him at his feet. He left him there,
And wounding with his spear Philetor's son,
Demuchus, tall and valiant, in the knee,
Stayed him until he slew him with his sword.
Then from their chariot to the ground he cast
Laogonus and Dardanus, the sons
Of Bias, piercing with a javelin one,
And cutting down the other with his sword.
And Tros, Alastor's son, who came to him
And clasped his knees, in hope that he would spare
A captive,—spare his life, nor slay a youth
Of his own age,—vain hope! he little knew
That not by prayers Achilles could be moved,
Nor was he pitiful, nor mild of mood,
But hard of heart,—while Tros embraced his knees
And passionately sued, Pelides thrust
His sword into his side; the liver came
Forth at the wound; the dark blood gushing filled
The Phrygian's bosom; o'er his eyes there crept
A darkness, and his life was at an end.
Approaching Mulius next, Achilles smote

The warrior at the ear; the brazen point
Passed through the other ear; and then he slew
Agenor's son, Echeclus, letting fall
His heavy-hilted sword upon his head
Just in the midst; the blade grew warm with blood,
And gloomy death and unrelenting fate
Darkened the victim's eyes. Achilles next
Wounded Deucalion, thrusting through his arm
The brazen javelin, where the sinews met
That strung the elbow. While with powerless arm
The wounded Trojan stood awaiting death,
Achilles drave his falchion through his neck.
Far flew the head and helm, the marrow flowed
From out the spine, and stretched upon the ground
Deucalion lay. Pelides still went on,
O'ertaking Rigmus, the renownèd son
Of Peireus, from the fruitful fields of Thrace,
And smote him in the stomach with his lance.
There hung the weapon fixed; the wounded man
Fell from the car. At Areïthoüs
The charioteer, who turned his steeds to flee,
Achilles sent his murderous lance, and pierced
His back, and dashed him from the car, and left
His horses wild with fright. As when, among

The deep dells of an arid mountain-side,
A great fire burns its way, and the thick wood
Before it is consumed, and shifting winds
Hither and thither sweep the flames, so ranged
Achilles in his fury through the field
From side to side, and everywhere o'ertook
His victims, and the earth ran dark with blood.
  As when a yeoman underneath the yoke
Brings his broad-fronted oxen to tread out
White barley on the level threshing-floor,
The sheaves are quickly trodden small beneath
The heavy footsteps of the bellowing beasts,
So did the firm-paced coursers, which the son
Of Peleus guided, trample with their feet
Bucklers and corpses, while beneath the car
Blood steeped the axle, and the chariot-seat
Dripped on its rim with blood, that from below
Was splashed upon them by the horses' hoofs
And by the chariot-wheels. Such havoc made
Pelides in his ardor for renown,
Till his invincible hands were foul with blood.

## BOOK XXI.

NOW when they reached the pleasant banks through which
The eddying Xanthus runs, the river sprung
From deathless Jove, Achilles drave his foes
Asunder. Part he chased across the plain
Townward, along the way by which the Greeks
In terror fled the day before, pursued
By glorious Hector. Panic-struck they ran
Along that way, while, to restrain their flight,
Before them Juno hung a veil of cloud
And darkness. Meanwhile half the flying crowd
Leaped down to that deep stream and rolled among
Its silver eddies. With a mighty noise
They plunged; the torrent dashed; the banks around
Remurmured shrilly to the cries of those
Who floated struggling in the current's whirl,
As when before the fierce, devouring flames
A swarm of locusts, springing into air,

Fly toward a river, while the fire behind
Crackles with sudden fierceness, and in fright
They fall into the waves, the roaring stream
Of the deep-eddied Xanthus thus was filled
Before Achilles with a mingled crowd
Of steeds and men. The Jove-descended man
Left leaning on the tamarisks his spear
Upon the river's border, and leaped in,
Armed only with his sword, intent to deal
Death on the fugitives; on every side
He smote, and from the smitten by the sword
Rose lamentable cries; the waves around
Grew crimson with their blood. As when before
A dolphin of huge bulk the fishes flee
In fear, and crowd the creeks that lie around
The sheltered haven,—for their foe devours
All that he overtakes,—the Trojans thus
Hid from his sight among the hollow rocks
Beside the rushing river. When his hand
Was weary with the work of death, he took
Twelve youths alive, whose blood was yet to pay
The penalty for Menœtiades,
His slaughtered friend. He led them from the stream,
Passive with fear like fawns, and tied their hands

Behind them with the well-twined cords that bound
Their tunics. Then he gave them to his friends,
Who led the captives to the roomy ships.
  Again Achilles rushed upon the foe
Intent on slaughter. One he met who climbed
The river's bank, Dardanian Priam's son,
Lycaon, whom in former days he made
His captive, by surprise, when in the night
He found him lopping with an axe the boughs
Of a wild fig-tree, that the trunk might form
The circle of a wheel. Achilles came,
An unexpected foe, and bore him off
To sea, and sold him in the populous isle
Of Lemnos. He was bought by Jason's son,
The Imbrian prince, Eëtion, who had been
His host, and now redeemed him with large gifts,
And sent him to Arisba's noble town.
Yet thence he stole, and reached his father's house
Again, and there made merry with his friends
Eleven days, but on the twelfth a god
Delivered him again into the hands
Of Peleus' son, who now would send his soul
Repining down to Hades. When the chief,
The swift of foot, beheld him stand unarmed,

With neither helm nor shield nor spear,—for these
He had thrown down,—faint with the sweaty toil
Of clambering up the bank, and every limb
Unstrung with weariness, then wrathfully
Thus said Achilles to his mighty soul:—
"O strange! my eyes behold a miracle.
Sure, the brave sons of Troy whom I have slain
Will rise up from the nether darkness yet,
Since this man, whom I once reprieved from death
And sold in Lemnos the divine, comes back.
Nor could the ocean's gray abyss of brine,
Beyond which many long in vain to pass,
Detain him in that isle. But he shall taste
The sharpness of my spear, that I may prove
Whether he after that will reappear,
And whether the kind earth, which holds so well
The valiant dead, can keep him in her womb."
So pondered he and stood. The Trojan drew
Close to him, with intent to clasp his knees,
Fear-struck, yet hoping to avoid the doom
Of bitter death. The great Achilles raised
His ponderous spear to strike. Lycaon stooped,
And, darting underneath the weapon, seized
The hero's knees; behind him in the ground

The spear stood fixed, though eager yet for blood;
One arm was round his adversary's knees,
The other held—and would not let it go—
The spear, while thus with wingèd words he prayed:—
"I clasp thy knees, Achilles; look on me
Kindly and pity me, O foster-child
Of Jove. I am thy suppliant, and may claim
Thy mercy. I partook with thee the fruits
Of Ceres, when amid my fruitful fields
Thou madest me a captive, carrying me
From friends and kindred to the sacred isle
Of Lemnos. Thou didst sell me there,—my price
A hundred beeves,—and thou shalt now receive,
For ransom, thrice as many. It is yet
But the twelfth morning since I came to Troy
After much hardship, and a pitiless fate
Betrays me to thy hands. I must believe
That Father Jove in wrath delivers me
To thee again. Laothoë brought me forth
To a brief life; that mother was the child
Of aged Altes,—Altes ruling o'er
The warlike Leleges, by whom are tilled
The heights of Pedasus, where Satnio flows,—
And Priam wedded her with other maids.

She bore two children to be slain by thee;
One was the godlike Polydore, whom thou
Didst smite with thy keen spear, in the front rank
Of those who fought on foot. His evil fate
Must overtake me now, for, since a god
Has brought me near thee, there is no escape.
Yet let me tell thee this, and weigh it well,
And let it save my life. I came not forth
From the same womb with Hector, by whose hand
Thy brave and gentle friend, Patroclus, died."

The illustrious son of Priam ended here
His prayer, and heard a merciless reply:—

"Fool! never talk of ransom,—not a word.
Before the evil day on which my friend
Was slain, it pleased me oftentimes to spare
The Trojans. Many a one I took alive
And sold; but now no man of all their race,
Whom any god may bring within my reach,
Shall leave the field alive, and least of all
The sons of Priam. Die thou, then; and why
Shouldst thou, my friend, lament? Patroclus died,
And greatly he excelled thee. Seest thou not
How eminent in stature and in form
Am I, whom to a prince renowned for worth

A goddess mother bore; yet will there come
To me a violent death at morn, at eve,
Or at the midday hour, whenever he
Whose weapon is to take my life shall cast
The spear or send an arrow from the string."
  He spake: the Trojan's heart and knees grew faint;
His hand let go the spear; he sat and cowered
With outstretched arms. Achilles drew his sword,
And smote his neck just at the collar-bone;
The two-edged blade was buried deep. He fell
Prone on the earth; the black blood spouted forth
And steeped the soil. Achilles by the foot
Flung him to float among the river-waves,
And uttered, boastfully, these wingèd words:—
  "Lie there among the fishes, who shall feed
Upon thy blood unscared. No mother there
Shall weep thee lying on thy bier; thy corpse
Scamander shall bear down to the broad sea,
Where, as he sees thee darkening its face,
Some fish shall hasten, darting through the waves,
To feed upon Lycaon's fair white limbs.
So perish ye, till sacred Troy be ours,
You fleeing, while I follow close and slay.
This river cannot aid you,—this fair stream

With silver eddies, to whose deity
Ye offer many beeves in sacrifice,
And fling into its gulfs your firm-paced steeds;
But thus ye all shall perish, till I take
Full vengeance for Patroclus of the Greeks,
Whom, while I stood aloof from war, ye slew."
He spake: and, deeply moved with inward wrath,
The River pondered how to render vain
The prowess of Achilles, and avert
Destruction from the Trojans. Now the son
Of Peleus rushed, his ponderous spear in hand,
To slay Asteropæus, who was sprung
From Pelegon, and Pelegon was born
To the broad river Axius, of a maid,
The eldest-born of Acessamenus,
Named Peribœa; for the river-god
Was joined with her in love. Achilles sprang
To meet the youth, as, rising from the stream,
Armed with two spears, he stood, his heart made strong
And resolute by Xanthus, who had seen
Indignantly so many Trojans die,—
Youths whom Achilles slaughtered in his stream,
And had no pity on them. When the twain
Were near each other, standing face to face,

The swift Achilles was the first to speak:—
"Who and whence art thou that dost venture thus
To meet me? They who seek to measure strength
With me are sons of most unhappy men."
And thus the illustrious son of Pelegon
Made answer: "Brave Pelides, why inquire
My lineage? I am from a distant coast,—
Pæonia's fertile fields; I lead to war
Pæonia's warriors with long spears, and this
Is now the eleventh morning since I came
To join the war at Troy. I claim descent
From Axius, the broad Axius, who pours forth
The fairest river on the earth. His son
Was Pelegon, expert to wield the spear,
And I was born to Pelegon. And now,
Illustrious son of Peleus, let us fight."
He spake: Achilles raised the Pelian ash
To smite; Asteropæus aimed at him
Both lances, for he used both hands alike.
One struck the Grecian's shield, yet passed not through,
Stopped by the god-given gold; the other gashed
Lightly the elbow of his dexter arm;
The black blood spouted forth, the spear passed on
Beyond him, and, still eager for its prey,

Stood fixed in earth. Achilles then, intent
To slay Asteropæus, hurled at him
His trusty spear. The weapon missed its mark,
And, striking the high bank, was buried there
Up to the middle of its ashen staff.
Achilles drew the keen sword from his thigh,
And flew with fury toward his foe, who toiled
In vain with sinewy arm to pluck that spear
From out the bank; and thrice he shook the beam
Fiercely, and thrice desisted, lacking strength,
And last he sought, by bending it, to break
The ashen weapon of Æacides.
But ere it snapped Achilles took his life,
Smiting him at the navel with the sword.
Forth gushed the entrails to the ground, and o'er
His dying eyes the darkness came; and then
Achilles, leaping on his breast, tore off
The armor, and exultingly exclaimed: —
"Lie there! a perilous task it was for thee
To combat with a son of Jove, though born
Thyself to a great River. I can boast
Descent from sovereign Jove. I owe my birth
To Peleus, ruler of the Myrmidons.
His father was Æacus, who was born

To Jupiter, a god more potent far
Than all the rivers flowing to the sea.
And mightier is the race of Jupiter
Than that of any stream. Here close at hand
Is a great river, if such aid can aught
Avail thee; but to strive with Jupiter
Is not permitted. Acheloüs, king
Of rivers, cannot vie with him, nor yet
The great and mighty deep from which proceed
All streams and seas and founts and watery depths.
He trembles at the bolt of mighty Jove
And his hoarse thunder crashing in the sky."
As thus he spake he plucked from out the bank
His brazen spear, and left the lifeless chief
Stretched in the sand, where the dark water steeped
His limbs, and eels and fishes came and gnawed
The warrior's reins. Achilles hastened on,
Pursuing the Pæonian knights, who now,
When they beheld their bravest overthrown
In desperate battle by the mighty arm
And falchion of Pelides, took to flight
Along the eddying river. There he slew
Mydon, Thersilochus, Astypylus,
Mnesus, and Thrasius, and struck down in death

Ænius and Ophelestes. Many more
Of the Pæonians the swift-footed Greek
Had slain, had not the eddying River, roused
To anger, put a human semblance on,
And uttered from its whirling deeps a voice:—
"O son of Peleus! thou who dost excel
All other men in might and dreadful deeds,—
For the gods aid thee ever,—if the son
Of Saturn gives thee to destroy the race
Of Trojans, drive them from me to the plain,
And there perform thy terrible exploits.
For now my pleasant waters, in their flow,
Are choked with heaps of dead, and I no more
Can pour them into the great deep, so thick
The corpses clog my bed, while thou dost slay
And sparest not. Now then, withhold thy hand,
Prince of the people! I am horror-struck."
Achilles the swift-footed made reply:
"Be it as thou commandest, foster-child
Of Jove, Scamander! Yet I shall not cease
To slay these treaty-breakers till at length
I shut them up within their town, and force
Hector to meet me, that we may decide
Which shall o'ercome the other,—he or I."

He spake, and rushed upon the men of Troy,
Terrible as a god, while from his bed
The eddying River called to Phœbus thus:—
"Why this, thou bearer of the silver bow,
Thou son of Jove? Thou heedest not the will
Of Saturn's son, who strictly bade that thou
Shouldst aid the Trojans till the latest gleam
Of sunset, and till night is on the fields."
And then Achilles, mighty with the spear,
From the steep bank leaped into the mid-stream,
While, foul with ooze, the angry River raised
His waves, and pushed along the heaps of dead
Slain by Achilles. These, with mighty roar
As of a bellowing ox, Scamander cast
Aground; the living with his whirling gulfs
He hid, and saved them in his friendly streams.
In tumult terribly the surges rose
Around Achilles, beating on his shield,
And made his feet to stagger, till he grasped
A tall, fair-growing elm upon the bank.
Down came the tree, and in its loosened roots
Brought the earth with it; the fair stream was checked
By the thick branches, and the prostrate trunk
Bridged it from side to side. Achilles sprang

From the deep pool, and fled with rapid feet
Across the plain in terror. Nor did then
The mighty river-god refrain, but rose
Against him with a darker crest, to drive
The noble son of Peleus from the field,
And so deliver Troy. Pelides sprang
A spear's cast backward,—sprang with all the speed
Of the black eagle's wing, the hunter-bird,
Fleetest and strongest of the fowls of air.
Like him he darted; clashing round his breast,
The brazen mail rang fearfully. Askance
He fled; the water with a mighty roar
Followed him close. As, when a husbandman
Leads forth, from some dark spring of earth, a rill
Among his planted garden-beds, and clears
Its channel, spade in hand, the pebbles there
Move with the current, which runs murmuring down
The sloping surface and outstrips its guide,—
So rushed the waves where'er Achilles ran,
Swift as he was; for mightier are the gods
Than men. As often as the noble son
Of Peleus made a stand in hope to know
Whether the deathless gods of the great heaven
Conspired to make him flee, so often came

A mighty billow of the Jove-born stream
And drenched his shoulders. Then again he sprang
Away; the rapid torrent made his knees
To tremble, while it swept, where'er he trod,
The earth from underneath his feet. He looked
To the broad heaven above him, and complained:—
"Will not some god, O Father Jove, put forth
His power to save me in my hour of need
From this fierce river? Any fate but this
I am resigned to suffer. None of all
The immortal ones is more in fault than she
To whom I owe my birth; her treacherous words
Deluded me to think that I should fall
Beneath the walls of Troy by the swift shafts
Of Phœbus. Would that Hector, the most brave
Of warriors reared upon the Trojan soil,
Had slain me; he had slain a brave man then,
And a brave man had stripped me of my arms.
But now it is my fate to perish, caught
In this great river, like a swineherd's boy,
Who in the time of rains attempts to pass
A torrent, and is overwhelmed and drowned."
He spake, and Neptune and Minerva came
Quickly and stood beside him. In the form

Of men they came, and took his hand, and cheered
His spirit with their words. And thus the god
Neptune, who makes the earth to tremble, said:—
"Fear not, Pelides, neither let thy heart
Be troubled, since thou hast among the gods,
By Jove's consent, auxiliars such as I
And Pallas. It is not thy doom to be
Thus vanquished by a river. Soon its rage
Will cease, as thou shalt see. Meantime we give
This counsel; heed it well: let not thy hand
Refrain from slaughter till the Trojan host
Are all shut up—all that escape thy arm—
Within the lofty walls of Troy. Then take
The life of Hector, and return on board
Thy galleys; we will make that glory thine."
Thus having spoken, they withdrew and joined
The immortals, while Achilles hastened on,
Encouraged by the mandate of the gods,
Across the plain. The plain was overflowed
With water; sumptuous arms were floating round,
And bodies of slain youths. Achilles leaped,
And stemmed with powerful limbs the stream, and still
Went forward; for Minerva mightily
Had strengthened him. Nor did Scamander fail

To put forth all his power, enraged the more
Against the son of Peleus; higher still
His torrent swelled and tossed with all its waves,
And thus he called to Simoïs with a shout:—
"O brother, join with me to hold in check
This man, who threatens soon to overthrow
King Priam's noble city; for no more
The Trojan host resist him. Come at once
And aid me; fill thy channel from its springs,
And summon all thy brooks, and lift on high
A mighty wave, and roll along thy bed,
Mingled in one great torrent, trees and stones,
That we may tame this savage man, who now
In triumph walks the field, and bears himself
As if he were a god. His strength, I deem,
Will not avail him, nor his noble form,
Nor those resplendent arms, which yet shall lie
Scattered along the bottom of my gulfs,
And foul with ooze. Himself too I shall wrap
In sand, and pile the rubbish of my bed
In heaps around him. Never shall the Greeks
Know where to gather up his bones, o'erspread
By me with river-slime, for there shall be
His burial-place; no other tomb the Greeks

Will need when they perform his funeral rites."
  He spake, and wrathfully he rose against
Achilles,—rose with turbid waves, and noise,
And foam, and blood and bodies of the dead.
One purple billow of the Jove-born stream
Swelled high and whelmed Achilles. Juno saw,
And trembled lest the hero should be whirled
Downward by the great river, and in haste
She called to Vulcan, her beloved son:—
  "Vulcan, my son, arise! We deemed that thou
And eddying Xanthus were of equal might
In battle. Come with instant aid, and bring
Thy vast array of flames, while from the deep
I call a tempest of the winds,—the West
And the swift South,—and they shall sweep along
A fiery torrent to consume the foe,
Warriors and weapons. Thou meantime lay waste
The groves along the Xanthus; hurl at him
Thy fires, nor let him with soft words or threats
Avert thy fury. Pause not from the work
Of ruin till I shout and give the sign,
And then shalt thou restrain thy restless fires."
  She spake, and Vulcan at her word sent forth
His fierce, devouring flames. Upon the plain

They first were kindled, and consumed the dead
That strewed it, where Achilles struck them down.
The ground was dried; the glimmering flood was stayed.
As when the autumnal north-wind, breathing o'er
A newly watered garden, quickly dries
The clammy mould, and makes the tiller glad,
So did the spacious plain grow dry on which
The dead were turned to ashes. Then the god
Seized on the river with his glittering fires.
The elms, the willows, and the tamarisks
Fell, scorched to cinders, and the lotus-herbs,
Rushes, and reeds that richly fringed the banks
Of that fair-flowing current were consumed.
The eels and fishes, that were wont to glide
Hither and thither through the pleasant depths
And eddies, languished in the fiery breath
Of Vulcan, mighty artisan. The strength
Of the great River withered, and he spake:—
"O Vulcan, there is none of all the gods
Who may contend with thee. I combat not
With fires like thine. Cease then. With my consent
The noble son of Peleus may drive out
The Trojans from their city. What have I
To do with war,—the attack or the defence?"

Thus in that fiery glow he spake, while seethed
His pleasant streams. As over a strong fire
A caldron filled with fat of pampered swine
Glows bubbling on all sides, while underneath
Burns the dry fuel, thus were his fair streams
Scorched by the heat, and simmered, while the blast
Sent forth by Vulcan, the great artisan,
Tormented him, and he besought the aid
Of Juno with these supplicating words:—
"Why should thy son, O Juno, wreak on me
His fury, more than on the other gods?
My fault is less than theirs who give their aid
To Troy; and I will cease, if thou command.
Bid him desist, and here I pledge my oath
Not to attempt to save the Trojan race
From ruin, though their city sink in flames
Before the torches of the warlike Greeks."
This when the white-armed goddess Juno heard,
She said to Vulcan, her beloved son:—
"Dear son, refrain; it is not well that thus
A god should suffer for the sake of men."
She spake, and Vulcan quenched his dreadful fires,
And back the pleasant waters to their bed
Went gliding. Xanthus had been made to yield,

And the two combatants no longer strove
Since Juno, though offended, bade them cease.
Yet was the conflict terrible among
The other gods, as zeal for different sides
Impelled them. With a loud uproar they met
Each other in the field; the spacious earth
Rebellowed to the noise, and the great heaven
Returned it. To the ear of Jove it rose,
Who, sitting on Olympus, laughed within
His secret heart as he beheld the gods
Contending, for not long they stood apart.
Shield-breaking Mars began the assault; he rushed
Toward Pallas, brandishing his brazen spear,
And thus accosted her with insolent words:—
"Thou shameless one, thou whose effrontery
Is boundless, why wilt thou provoke the gods
To strife? Thy temper is most arrogant.
Rememberest thou the time when thou didst prompt
Tydides Diomed to strike at me?
It was thy hand that held his shining spear,
And aimed it well, and gave the wound; but now
Will I take vengeance on thee for that wrong."
He spake, and smote Minerva's fringèd shield,
The dreadful ægis, which not even Jove

Could pierce with thunderbolts. The murderous Mars
Smote it with his huge spear. She only stepped
Backward a space, and with her powerful hand
Lifted a stone that lay upon the plain,
Black, huge, and jagged, which the men of old
Had placed there for a landmark. This she hurled
At Mars, and struck him on the neck; he fell
With nerveless limbs, and covered, as he lay,
Seven acres of the field: his armor clashed
Around him in his fall; his locks all soiled
Lay in the trodden dust. The goddess stood
O'er him, and boasted thus with wingèd words:—

"Fool that thou art, hast thou not learned how much
The might I boast excels thine own, that thus
Thou measurest strength with me? Now dost thou feel
Thy mother's curse fulfilled, who meditates
Thy chastisement, since thou hast left the Greeks
And joined the treaty-breaking sons of Troy."

She spake, and turned away her glorious eyes.
Jove's daughter, Venus, took the hand of Mars,
And led him groaning thence, while hardly yet
His strength came back. The white-armed Juno saw,
And spake to Pallas thus, with wingèd words:—

"See, daughter of the Ægis-bearer, Jove,

Unconquerable maid! that shameless one,
Through all the tumult, from the thick of fight,
Leads hence the murderous Mars; but follow her."
She spake, and Pallas gladly hastened forth,
And, overtaking Venus, dealt at her
A mighty buffet on the breast; her heart
Fainted, her knees gave way; and, as she lay
Prostrate with Mars upon the fruitful earth,
Exulting Pallas spake these wingèd words:—
"Would that all those who aid the cause of Troy
And combat with the mailèd Greeks were thus!
Would that they were as hardy and as brave
As Venus here, who ventured to the help
Of Mars, and met the force of my right arm!
Then had the stately Ilium been o'erthrown
Long since, and we had rested from the war."
She spake: the white-armed Juno gently smiled,
And then King Neptune to Apollo said:—
"Why, Phœbus, stand we thus aloof? it ill
Becomes us, while the other gods engage
In conflict. 'T were a shame should we return
Up to Olympus and the brazen halls
Of Jove with no blow struck. Begin, for thou
Art younger born, and I, who both in years

And knowledge am before thee, must not make
The assault. O silly god, and slow of thought!
Hast thou indeed forgotten all the wrongs
We suffered once in Troy, and only we
Of all the gods, when, sent to earth by Jove,
We served a twelvemonth for a certain hire
The proud Laomedon, by whom our tasks
Were set? I built a city and a wall
Of broad extent, and beautiful, and strong
To stand assault; and, Phœbus, thou didst feed
His stamping oxen, with curved horns, among
The lawns of woody Ida seamed with glens.
But when the welcome hours had brought the day
Of our reward, the ruffian king refused
The promised wages, and dismissed us both
With menaces; to bind thee hand and foot
He threatened, and to sell thee as a slave
In distant isles, and to cut off the ears
Of both of us. So we returned to heaven,
Incensed at him who thus withheld the hire
He promised. Dost thou favor Troy for this?
Wilt thou not rather act with us until
These treaty-breakers, with their children all
And their chaste matrons, perish utterly?"

Then thus the archer-king, Apollo, spake:
"Thou wouldst not deem me wise, should I contend
With thee, O Neptune, for the sake of men,
Who flourish like the forest-leaves awhile,
And feed upon the fruits of earth, and then
Decay and perish. Let us quit the field,
And leave the combat to the warring hosts."
He spake, and turned, afraid to meet in arms
His uncle; but the sylvan Dian heard,—
His sister, mistress of the beasts that range
The wilds,—and harshly thus upbraided him:—
"O mighty Archer, dost thou flee and yield
The victory to Neptune, who bears off
A glory cheaply earned? Why dost thou bear
That idle bow, thou coxcomb? I shall hope
No more to hear thee in our father's halls,
And in the presence of the immortals, boast
That thou wilt fight with Neptune hand to hand."
The archer-god, Apollo, answered not;
But thus the imperial wife of Jupiter,
Indignantly and with reproachful words,
Rebuked the quivered goddess of the chase:—
"How is it that thou darest, shameless one,
Resist me? Thou wilt find it hard, though trained

In archery, to match thy strength with mine,
Though Jove has made thee among womankind
A lioness, and though he gives thee power
To slay whomever of thy sex thou wilt;
Yet wilt thou find it easier to strike down
The mountain beasts of prey, and forest deer,
Than combat with thy betters. If thou choose
To try the event of battle, then put forth
Thy strength against me, and thou shalt be taught
How greatly I excel in might of arm."
  Thus Juno spake, and grasped in her left hand
Both Dian's wrists, and, plucking with her right
The quiver from her shoulders, beat with it
Her ears, and smiled as under her quick blows
The sufferer writhed. To earth the arrows fell,
And Dian weeping fled. As when a dove,
Not fated to be overtaken yet,
Flees from a hawk to find her hiding-place,
The hollow rock, so Dian fled in tears,
And left her arrows. To Latona, then,
Heaven's messenger, the Argus-queller, spake:—
  "Far be it from me to contend with thee,
Latona; perilous it were to meet
A consort of the Cloud-compeller, Jove,

In combat. Go and freely make thy boast
Among the gods that thou hast vanquished me."
He spake: Latona gathered from the ground
The bow and shafts which in that whirl of dust
Had fallen here and there, and, bearing them,
Followed her daughter, who meantime had reached
Olympus and the brazen halls of Jove.
And there, a daughter at her father's knees,
She sat her down, while, as she wept, her robe
Of heavenly texture trembled. Graciously
Jove smiled, and drew her toward him and inquired:
"What dweller of the sky has dared do this,
Dear child, as though some flagrant guilt were thine?
And thus replied the mistress of the chase
Crowned with the crescent: "Father, 't was thy queen,
The white-armed Juno; she who causes strife
And wrath among the gods has done me wrong."
So talked they, while to sacred Ilium came
Phœbus Apollo; 't was his charge to watch
The well-built city's ramparts, lest the Greeks
That day should lay it waste against the will
Of fate. The other gods went back to heaven,
Some angry, some exulting. They sat down
Beside the All-Father, him who darkens heaven

With gathered clouds. Meantime Achilles chased
And slew the Trojans and their firm-paced steeds.
As, when the smoke rolls heavenward from a town
Given by the angry gods a prey to fire,
Toil is the lot of all, and bitter woe
The fate of many, such the woe and toil
Caused by Achilles to the sons of Troy.
The aged Priam from a lofty tower
Beheld the large-limbed son of Peleus range
The field, and all the Trojans helplessly
Fleeing in tumult. With a cry of grief
He came from that high station to the ground,
And gave commandment to the sturdy men
Who stood to watch the gates along the wall:—
"Hold the gates open while the flying host
Enter the city; for Achilles comes,
Routing them, near at hand, and we may see
Terrible havoc. But when all our troops
Are once within the walls, and breathe again,
Shut the close-fitting portals; for I dread
Lest that fierce warrior rush into our streets."
He spake: they drew the bolts and opened wide
The gates, and gave a refuge to the host.
Then leaped Apollo forth to meet their flight

And rescue them. All faint with burning thirst,
And grimed with dust, they hurried o'er the plain,
And toward the city and its lofty walls,
While eagerly Achilles on their track
Pressed with his spear; his heart was full of rage;
And all on fire his spirit with desire
For glory. Then the Greeks had overthrown
The towery Troy, if Phœbus had not moved
Agenor, a young hero, nobly born,
Blameless, and brave, Antenor's son, to meet
Achilles. Phœbus breathed into his heart
Courage, as, standing by the youth, he leaned
Against a beechen tree, and, wrapped from sight
In darkness, watched to rescue him from death.
Agenor stood as he beheld approach
The mighty spoiler, and, perplexed in mind,
Sighed heavily, and said to his great soul: —
"Ah me! if with the routed troops I flee
From fierce Achilles, he will overtake
And slay me; I shall die as cowards die.
But if I leave the host to be pursued
By Peleus' son, and by another way
Flee from the wall across the plain, until
I reach the lawns of Ida, and am hid

Among its thickets, then I may at eve
Bathe in the river and return refreshed
To Troy. But why give way to thoughts like these?
For he may yet observe me as I haste
From Ilium o'er the plain, and his swift feet
May follow; there will then be no escape
From death and fate, since he in might of arm
Excels all other men. If now I here
Confront him before Troy, I cannot think
That he is weapon-proof; one life alone
Dwells in him, though Saturnian Jupiter
Bestows on him the glory of the day."

He spake, and firmly waited for the son
Of Peleus; eagerly his fearless heart
Longed for the combat. As a panther leaves
The covert of the wood and comes to meet
A huntsman, nor is scared nor put to flight
By noise of baying hounds, not even though
A spear's thrust or a javelin flung from far
Have wounded him, yet, wounded, he fights on,
Until he grapples with his enemy
Or perishes,—thus did the noble son
Of the renowned Antenor press to try
His prowess with Achilles, and disdained

To flee before him. Holding his round shield
Before his face, and with his lifted spear
Aimed at the Greek, he shouted thus aloud: —
"Renowned Achilles! thou dost fondly hope
That thou to-day wilt overthrow the town
Of the magnanimous Trojans. Many toils,
Thou fool! must be endured ere that can be;
For we are many and are brave who dwell
Within it, and shall well defend the town
For our beloved parents and our wives
And little ones. Here shalt thou meet thy doom,
Brave as thou art, and terrible in war."
As thus he spake, his powerful hand dismissed
The keen-edged spear, nor missed his aim; it struck
The son of Peleus just below the knee.
The tin of which the greave was newly forged
Rang shrilly, and sent back the brazen point;
It could not pierce the armor which a god
Had given. And then the son of Peleus aimed
His weapon at Agenor. Phœbus came
And snatched away his triumph, bearing off
The godlike youth, Agenor, in a veil
Of darkness from the perils of the war.
Then he decoyed Achilles from the host

Of Troy; the archer of the skies put on
Agenor's perfect semblance, and appeared
Before the Greek, and fled; his hasty flight
Was followed close. Achilles chased the god
Ever before him, yet still near, across
The fruitful fields, to the deep-eddied stream
Of Xanthus; for Apollo artfully
Made it to seem that he should soon o'ertake
His flying foe, and thus beguiled him on.
Meantime the routed Trojans gladly thronged
Into the city, filled the streets, and closed
The portals. None now dared without the walls
To wait for others, or remain to know
Who had escaped with life, and who were slain
In battle; eagerly they flung themselves
Into the city, — every one whose feet
And knees had borne him from the field alive.

## *BOOK XXII.*

THUS were they driven within the city walls
Like frighted fawns, and there dispersing cooled
Their sweaty limbs, and quenched their eager thirst,
And rested on the battlements. The Greeks,
Bearing their shields upon their shoulders, came
Close to the ramparts. Hector's adverse fate
Detained him still without the walls of Troy,
And near the Scæan gates. Meantime the god
Apollo to the son of Peleus said:—
"O son of Peleus! why pursue me thus
With thy swift feet,—a mortal man in chase
Of an immortal? That I am a god
Thou seest not yet, but turnest all thy rage
On me, and, having put the host of Troy
To rout, dost think of them no more. They find
A refuge in their town, while far astray
Thou wanderest hither. Thou hast not the power
To slay me; I am not of mortal birth."

The swift Achilles angrily replied:
"O archer-god, thou most unjust of all
The immortals! thou hast wronged me, luring me
Aside; since many a warrior I had forced
To bite the dust before they reached the gates
Of Ilium but for thee, who from my grasp
Hast snatched the glory and hast rescued them.
Thou didst not fear my vengeance; yet if power
Were given me, I would punish thee for this."
He spake, and with heroic purpose turned
Toward Ilium. As a steed that wins the race
Flies at his utmost speed across the plain,
And whirls along the chariot, with such speed
The son of Peleus moved his rapid feet.
The aged monarch Priam was the first
To see him as he scoured the plain, and shone
Like to the star which in the autumn time
Rises and glows among the lights of heaven
With eminent lustre at the dead of night,—
Orion's Hound they call it,—bright indeed,
And yet of baleful omen, for it brings
Distressing heat to miserable men.
So shone the brass upon the warrior's breast
As on he flew. The aged Priam groaned,

And smote his head with lifted hands, and called
Aloud, imploring his beloved son,
Who eagerly before the city gate
Waited his foe Achilles. Priam thus,
With outstretched hands, besought him piteously:—
"O wait not, Hector, my beloved son,
To combat with Pelides, thus alone
And far from succor, lest thou meet thy death
Slain by his hand, for he is mightier far
Than thou art. Would that he, the cruel one,
Were but as much the favorite of the gods
As he is mine! then should the birds of prey
And dogs devour his carcass, and the grief
That weighs upon my spirit would depart.
I have been robbed by him of many sons,—
Brave youths, whom he has slain or sold as slaves
In distant isles; and now I see no more
Among our host on whom the gates are closed
My Polydorus and Lycaon, whom
The peerless dame Laothoë bore to me.
If yet they are within the Grecian camp,
I will redeem their lives with brass and gold;
For I have store, which Altes, the renowned
And aged, gave his daughter. If they live

No longer, but have passed to the abode
Of Hades, bitter will our sorrow be,—
Mine and their mother's,—but the popular grief
Will sooner be consoled if thou fall not,
Slain by Achilles. Come within the walls,
My son, that thou mayst still be the defence
Of Ilium's sons and daughters, nor increase
The glory of Pelides with the loss
Of thine own life. Have pity upon me,
Who only live to suffer,—whom the son
Of Saturn, on the threshold of my age,
Hath destined to endure a thousand griefs,
And then to be destroyed,—to see my sons
Slain by the sword, my daughters dragged away
Into captivity, their chambers made
A spoil, our infants dashed against the ground
By cruel hands, the consorts of my sons
Borne off by the ferocious Greeks; and last,
Perchance the very dogs which I have fed
Here in my palaces and at my board,
The guardians of my doors, when, by the spear
Or sword, some enemy shall take my life,
And at my threshold leave me stretched a corpse,
Will rend me, and, with savage greediness,

Will lap my blood, and in the porch lie down.
When one in prime of youth lies slain in war,
Gashed with the spear, his wounds become him well,
And honor him in all men's eyes; but when
An aged man is slain, and his white head
And his white beard and limbs are foully torn
By ravening dogs, there is no sadder sight."
  So the old monarch spake, and with his hands
Tore his gray hair, but moved not Hector thus.
Then came, with lamentations and in tears,
The warrior's mother forward. One hand laid
Her bosom bare; she pressed the other hand
Beneath it, sobbed, and spake these wingèd words:—
  "Revere this bosom, Hector, and on me
Have pity. If when thou wert but a babe
I ever on this bosom stilled thy cries,
Think of it now, beloved child; avoid
That dreadful chief; withdraw within the walls,
Nor madly think to encounter him alone,
Son of my love and of my womb! If he
Should slay thee, I shall not lament thy death
Above thy bier,—I, nor thy noble wife,—
But far from us the greedy dogs will throng
To mangle thee beside the Grecian fleet."

Thus, weeping bitterly, the aged pair
Entreated their dear son, yet moved him not.
He stood and waited for his mighty foe
Achilles, as a serpent at his den,
Fed on the poisons of the wild, awaits
The traveller, and, fierce with hate of man,
And glaring fearfully, lies coiled within.
So waited Hector with a resolute heart,
And kept his ground, and, leaning his bright shield
Against a tower that jutted from the walls,
Conferred with his great soul impatiently:—
"Ah me! if I should pass within the walls,
Then will Polydamas be first to cast
Reproach upon me; for he counselled me
To lead the Trojans back into the town
That fatal night which saw Achilles rise
To join the war again. I yielded not
To his advice; far better if I had.
Now, since my fatal stubbornness has brought
This ruin on my people, I most dread
The censure of the men and long-robed dames
Of Ilium. Men less brave than I will say,
'Foolhardy Hector in his pride has thrown
His people's lives away.' So will they speak,

And better were it for me to return,
Achilles slain, or, slain myself by him,
To perish for my country gloriously.
But should I lay aside this bossy shield
And this stout helm, and lean against the wall
This spear, and go to meet the gallant son
Of Peleus, with a promise to restore
Helen and all the treasure brought with her
To Troy by Paris, in his roomy ships,—
All that the war was waged for,—that the sons
Of Atreus may convey it hence, besides
Wealth drawn from all the hoards within the town,
And to be shared among the Greeks; for I
Would bind the Trojans by a solemn oath
To keep back nothing, but divide the whole—
Whate'er of riches this fair town contains—
Into two parts— But why should I waste thought
On plans like these? I must not act the part
Of suppliant to a man who may not show
Regard or mercy, but may hew me down
Defenceless, with my armor laid aside
As if I were a woman. Not with him
May I hold parley from a tree or rock,
As youths and maidens with each other hold

Light converse. Better 't were to rush at once
To combat, and the sooner learn to whom
Olympian Jove decrees the victory."
  Such were his thoughts. Achilles now drew near.
Like crested Mars, the warrior-god, he came.
On his right shoulder quivered fearfully
The Pelian ash, and from his burnished mail
There streamed a light as of a blazing fire,
Or of the rising sun. When Hector saw,
He trembled, nor could venture to remain,
But left the gates and fled away in fear.
Pelides, trusting to his rapid feet,
Pursued him. As, among the mountain wilds,
A falcon, fleetest of the birds of air,
Darts toward a timid dove that wheels away
To shun him by a sidelong flight, while he
Springs after her again and yet again,
And screaming follows, certain of his prey, —
Thus onward flew Achilles, while as fast
Fled Hector in dismay, with hurrying feet,
Beside the wall. They passed the Mount of View,
And the wind-beaten fig-tree, and they ran
Along the public way by which the wall
Was skirted, till they came where from the ground

The two fair springs of eddying Xanthus rise, —
One pouring a warm stream from which ascends
And spreads a vapor like a smoke from fire;
The other, even in summer, sending forth
A current cold as hail, or snow, or ice.
And there were broad stone basins, fairly wrought,
At which, in time of peace, before the Greeks
Had landed on the plain, the Trojan dames
And their fair daughters washed their sumptuous robes.
Past these they swept; one fled, and one pursued, —
A brave man fled, a braver followed close,
And swiftly both. Not for a common prize,
A victim from the herd, a bullock's hide,
Such as reward the fleet of foot, they ran, —
The race was for the knightly Hector's life.
As firm-paced coursers, that are wont to win,
Fly toward the goal, when some magnificent prize,
A tripod or a damsel, is proposed
In honor of some hero's obsequies,
So these flew thrice on rapid feet around
The city of Priam. All the gods of heaven
Looked on, and thus the Almighty Father spake: —
"Alas! I see a hero dear to me
Pursued around the wall. My heart is grieved

For Hector, who has brought so many thighs
Of bullocks to my altar on the side
Of Ida ploughed with glens, or on the heights
Of Ilium. The renowned Achilles now
Is chasing him with rapid feet around
The city of Priam. Now bethink yourselves,
And answer. Shall we rescue him from death?
Or shall we doom him, valiant as he is,
To perish by the hand of Peleus' son?"
 Minerva, blue-eyed goddess, answered thus:
"O Father, who dost hurl the thunderbolt,
And hide the sky in clouds, what hast thou said?
Wouldst thou reprieve from death a mortal man,
Whose doom is fixed? Then do it; but know this,
That all the other gods will not approve."
 Then spake again the Cloud-compeller Jove:
"Tritonia, my dear child, be calm. I spake
Of no design. I would be kind to thee.
Do as thou wilt, and be there no delay."
 He spake; and Pallas from the Olympian peaks,
Encouraged by his words in what her thought
Had planned already, downward shot to earth.
Still, with quick steps, the fleet Achilles pressed
On Hector's flight. As when a hound has roused

A fawn from its retreat among the hills,
And chases it through glen and forest ground,
And to close thickets, where it skulks in fear
Until he overtake it, Hector thus
Sought vainly to elude the fleet pursuit
Of Peleus' son. As often as he thought,
By springing toward the gates of Troy, to gain
Aid from the weapons of his friends who stood
On the tall towers, so often was the Greek
Before him, forcing him to turn away
From Ilium toward the plain. Achilles thus
Kept nearest to the city. As in dreams
The fleet pursuer cannot overtake,
Nor the pursued escape, so was it now;
One followed but in vain, the other fled
As fruitlessly. But how could Hector thus
Have put aside the imminent doom of death,
Had not Apollo met him once again,
For the last time, and given him strength and speed?
  The great Achilles nodded to his host
A sign that no man should presume to strike
At Hector with his weapon, lest perchance
Another, wounding him, should bear away
The glory, and Pelides only wear

The second honors. When the twain had come
For the fourth time beside Scamander's springs,
The All-Father raised the golden balance high,
And, placing in the scales two lots which bring
Death's long dark sleep,—one lot for Peleus' son,
And one for knightly Hector,—by the midst
He poised the balance. Hector's fate sank down
To Hades, and Apollo left the field.

The blue-eyed goddess Pallas then approached
The son of Peleus with these wingèd words:—

"Renowned Achilles, dear to Jupiter!
Now may we, as I hope, at last return
To the Achaian army and the fleet
With glory, Hector slain, the terrible
In war. Escape he cannot, even though
The archer-god Apollo fling himself
With passionate entreaty at the feet
Of Jove the Ægis-bearer. Stay thou here
And breathe a moment, while I go to him
And lure him hither to encounter thee."

She spake, and he obeyed, and gladly stood
Propped on the ashen stem of his keen spear;
While, passing on, Minerva overtook
The noble Hector. In the outward form,

And with the strong voice of Deiphobus,
She stood by him and spake these wingèd words:—
"Hard pressed I find thee, brother, by the swift
Achilles, who, with feet that never rest,
Pursues thee round the walls of Priam's town.
But let us make a stand and beat him back."
And then the crested Hector spake in turn:
"Deiphobus, thou ever hast been dear
To me beyond my other brethren, sons
Of Hecuba and Priam. Now still more
I honor thee, since thou hast seen my plight,
And for my sake hast ventured forth without
The gates, while all the rest remain within."
And then the blue-eyed Pallas spake again:
"Brother! 't is true, my father, and the queen,
My mother, and my comrades, clasped my knees
In turn, and earnestly entreated me
That I would not go forth, such fear had fallen
On all of them; but I was grieved for thee.
Now let us combat valiantly, nor spare
The weapons that we bear, and we shall learn
Whether Achilles, having slain us both,
Will carry to the fleet our bloody spoil,
Or die himself, the victim of thy spear."

The treacherous goddess spake, and led the way;
And when the advancing chiefs stood face to face,
The crested hero, Hector, thus began:—
"No longer I avoid thee as of late,
O son of Peleus! Thrice around the walls
Of Priam's mighty city have I fled,
Nor dared to wait thy coming. Now my heart
Bids me encounter thee; my time is come
To slay or to be slain. Now let us call
The gods to witness, who attest and guard
The covenants of men. Should Jove bestow
On me the victory, and I take thy life,
Thou shalt meet no dishonor at my hands;
But, stripping off the armor, I will send
The Greeks thy body. Do the like by me."
The swift Achilles answered with a frown:
"Accursed Hector, never talk to me
Of covenants. Men and lions plight no faith,
Nor wolves agree with lambs, but each must plan
Evil against the other. So between
Thyself and me no compact can exist,
Or understood intent. First, one of us
Must fall and yield his life-blood to the god
Of battles. Summon all thy valor now.

A skilful spearman thou hast need to be,
And a bold warrior. There is no escape,
For now doth Pallas doom thee to be slain
By my good spear. Thou shalt repay to me
The evil thou hast done my countrymen,—
My friends whom thou hast slaughtered in thy rage."
He spake, and, brandishing his massive spear,
Hurled it at Hector, who beheld its aim
From where he stood. He stooped, and over him
The brazen weapon passed, and plunged to earth.
Unseen by royal Hector, Pallas went
And plucked it from the ground, and brought it back
And gave it to the hands of Peleus' son,
While Hector said to his illustrious foe:—
"Godlike Achilles, thou hast missed thy mark;
Nor hast thou learned my doom from Jupiter,
As thou pretendest. Thou art glib of tongue,
And cunningly thou orderest thy speech,
In hope that I who hear thee may forget
My might and valor. Think not I shall flee,
That thou mayst pierce my back; for thou shalt send
Thy spear, if God permit thee, through my breast
As I rush on thee. Now avoid in turn
My brazen weapon. Would that it might pass

Clean through thee, all its length! The tasks of war
For us of Troy were lighter for thy death,
Thou pest and deadly foe of all our race!"
He spake, and, brandishing his massive spear,
Hurled it, nor missed, but in the centre smote
The buckler of Pelides. Far away
It bounded from the brass, and he was vexed
To see that the swift weapon from his hand
Had flown in vain. He stood perplexed and sad;
No second spear had he. He called aloud
On the white-bucklered chief, Deiphobus,
To bring another; but that chief was far,
And Hector saw that it was so, and said: —
"Ah me! the gods have summoned me to die.
I thought my warrior-friend, Deiphobus,
Was by my side; but he is still in Troy,
And Pallas has deceived me. Now my death
Cannot be far, — is near; there is no hope
Of my escape, for so it pleases Jove
And Jove's great archer-son, who have till now
Delivered me. My hour at last is come;
Yet not ingloriously or passively
I die, but first will do some valiant deed,
Of which mankind shall hear in after time."

He spake, and drew the keen-edged sword that hung,
Massive and finely tempered, at his side,
And sprang — as when an eagle high in heaven,
Through the thick cloud, darts downward to the plain
To clutch some tender lamb or timid hare,
So Hector, brandishing that keen-edged sword,
Sprang forward, while Achilles opposite
Leaped toward him, all on fire with savage hate,
And holding his bright buckler, nobly wrought,
Before him. On his shining helmet waved
The fourfold crest; there tossed the golden tufts
With which the hand of Vulcan lavishly
Had decked it. As in the still hours of night
Hesper goes forth among the host of stars,
The fairest light of heaven, so brightly shone,
Brandished in the right hand of Peleus' son,
The spear's keen blade, as, confident to slay
The noble Hector, o'er his glorious form
His quick eye ran, exploring where to plant
The surest wound. The glittering mail of brass
Won from the slain Patroclus guarded well
Each part, save only where the collar-bones
Divide the shoulder from the neck, and there
Appeared the throat, the spot where life is most

In peril. Through that part the noble son
Of Peleus drave his spear; it went quite through
The tender neck, and yet the brazen blade
Cleft not the windpipe, and the power to speak
Remained. The Trojan fell amid the dust,
And thus Achilles boasted o'er his fall: —
"Hector, when from the slain Patroclus thou
Didst strip his armor, little didst thou think
Of danger. Thou hadst then no fear of me,
Who was not near thee to avenge his death.
Fool! there was left within the roomy ships
A mightier one than he, who should come forth,
The avenger of his blood, to take thy life.
Foul dogs and birds of prey shall tear thy flesh;
The Greeks shall honor him with funeral rites."
And then the crested Hector faintly said:
"I pray thee by thy life, and by thy knees,
And by thy parents, suffer not the dogs
To tear me at the galleys of the Greeks.
Accept abundant store of brass and gold,
Which gladly will my father and the queen,
My mother, give in ransom. Send to them
My body, that the warriors and the dames
Of Troy may light for me the funeral pile."

The swift Achilles answered with a frown:
"Nay, by my knees entreat me not, thou cur,
Nor by my parents. I could even wish
My fury prompted me to cut thy flesh
In fragments, and devour it, such the wrong
That I have had from thee. There will be none
To drive away the dogs about thy head,
Not though thy Trojan friends should bring to me
Tenfold and twenty-fold the offered gifts,
And promise others, — not though Priam, sprung
From Dardanus, should send thy weight in gold.
Thy mother shall not lay thee on thy bier,
To sorrow over thee whom she brought forth;
But dogs and birds of prey shall mangle thee."
And then the crested Hector, dying, said:
"I know thee, and too clearly I foresaw
I should not move thee, for thou hast a heart
Of iron. Yet reflect that for my sake
The anger of the gods may fall on thee,
When Paris and Apollo strike thee down,
Strong as thou art, before the Scæan gates."
Thus Hector spake, and straightway o'er him closed
The night of death; the soul forsook his limbs,
And flew to Hades, grieving for its fate, —

So soon divorced from youth and youthful might.
Then said the great Achilles to the dead:—
"Die thou; and I, whenever it shall please
Jove and the other gods will meet my fate."
He spake, and, plucking forth his brazen lance,
He laid it by, and from the body stripped
The bloody mail. The thronging Greeks beheld
With wonder Hector's tall and stately form,
And no one came who did not add a wound;
And, looking to each other, thus they said:—
"How much more tamely Hector now endures
Our touch than when he set the fleet on fire!"
Such were the words of those who smote the dead;
But now, when swift Achilles from the corpse
Had stripped the armor, he stood forth among
The Achaian host, and spake these wingèd words:—
"Leaders and princes of the Grecian host!
Since we, my friends, by favor of the gods,
Have overcome the chief who wrought more harm
To us than all the rest, let us assault
The town, and learn what they of Troy intend,—
Whether their troops will leave the citadel
Since he is slain, or hold it with strong hand,
Though Hector is no more. But why give thought

To plans like these while yet Patroclus lies
A corse unwept, unburied, at the fleet?
I never will forget him while I live
And while these limbs have motion. Though below
In Hades they forget the dead, yet I
Will there remember my beloved friend.
Now then, ye youths of Greece, move on and chant
A pæan, while, returning to the fleet,
We bring great glory with us; we have slain
The noble Hector, whom, throughout their town,
The Trojans ever worshipped like a god."

He spake, and, planning in his mind to treat
The noble Hector shamefully, he bored
The sinews of his feet between the heel
And ankle; drawing through them leathern thongs
He bound them to the car, but left the head
To trail in dust. And then he climbed the car,
Took in the shining mail, and lashed to speed
The coursers. Not unwillingly they flew.
Around the dead, as he was dragged along,
The dust arose; his dark locks swept the ground.
That head, of late so noble in men's eyes,
Lay deep amid the dust, for Jove that day
Suffered the foes of Hector to insult

His corse in his own land. His mother saw,
And tore her hair, and flung her lustrous veil
Away, and uttered piercing shrieks. No less
His father, who so loved him, piteously
Bewailed him; and in all the streets of Troy
The people wept aloud, with such lament
As if the towery Ilium were in flames
Even to its loftiest roofs. They scarce could keep
The aged king within, who, wild with grief,
Struggled to rush through the Dardanian gates,
And, rolling in the dust, entreated all
Who stood around him, calling them by name:—
"Refrain, my friends, though kind be your intent.
Let me go forth alone, and at the fleet
Of Greece will I entreat this man of blood
And violence. He may perchance be moved
With reverence for my age, and pity me
In my gray hairs; for such a one as I
Is Peleus, his own father, by whose care
This Greek was reared to be a scourge to Troy,
And, more than all, a cause of grief to me,
So many sons of mine in life's fresh prime
Have fallen by his hand. I mourn for them,
But not with such keen anguish as I mourn

For Hector. Sorrow for his death will bring
My soul to Hades. Would that he had died
Here in my arms! this solace had been ours, —
His most unhappy mother and myself
Had stooped to shed these tears upon his bier."
  He spake, and wept, and all the citizens
Wept with him. Hecuba among the dames
Took up the lamentation, and began: —
  "Why do I live, my son, when thou art dead,
And I so wretched? — thou who wert my boast
Ever, by night and day, where'er I went,
And whom the Trojan men and matrons called
Their bulwark, honoring thee as if thou wert
A god. They glory in thy might no more,
Since Fate and Death have overtaken thee."
  Weeping she spake. Meantime Andromache
Had heard no tidings of her husband yet.
No messenger had even come to say
That he was still without the gates. She sat
In a recess of those magnificent halls,
And wove a twofold web of brilliant hues,
On which were scattered flowers of rare device;
And she had given her bright-haired maidens charge
To place an ample caldron on the fire,

That Hector, coming from the battle-field,
Might find the warm bath ready. Thoughtless one!
She knew not that the blue-eyed archer-queen,
Far from the bath prepared for him, had slain
Her husband by the hand of Peleus' son.
She heard the shrieks, the wail upon the tower,
Trembled in every limb, and quickly dropped
The shuttle, saying to her bright-haired maids:—
"Come with me, two of you, that I may learn
What now has happened. 'T is my mother's voice
That I have heard. My heart leaps to my mouth;
My limbs fail under me. Some deadly harm
Hangs over Priam's sons; far be the hour
When I shall hear of it. And yet I fear
Lest that Achilles, having got between
The daring Hector and the city gates,
May drive him to the plain alone, and quell
The desperate valor that was ever his;
For never would he keep the ranks, but ranged
Beyond them, and gave way to no man's might."
She spake, and from the royal mansion rushed
Distractedly, and with a beating heart.
Her maids went with her. When she reached the tower
And throng of men, and, standing on the wall,

Looked forth, she saw her husband dragged away
Before the city. Toward the Grecian fleet
The swift steeds drew him. Sudden darkness came
Over her eyes, and in a breathless swoon
She sank away and fell. The ornaments
Dropped from her brow, — the wreath, the woven band,
The net, the veil which golden Venus gave
That day when crested Hector wedded her,
Dowered with large gifts, and led her from her home,
Eëtion's palace. Round her in a throng
Her sisters of the house of Priam pressed,
And gently raised her in that deathlike swoon.
But when she breathed again, and to its seat
The conscious mind returned, as in their arms
She lay, with sobs and broken speech she said: —

"Hector, — O wretched me! — we both were born
To sorrow; thou at Troy, in Priam's house,
And I at Thebè in Eëtion's halls,
By woody Placos. From a little child
He reared me there, — unhappy he, and I
Unhappy! O that I had ne'er been born!
Thou goest down to Hades and the depths
Of earth, and leavest me in thine abode,
Widowed, and never to be comforted.

Thy son, a speechless babe, to whom we two
Gave being,—hapless parents!—cannot have
Thy loving guardianship now thou art dead,
Nor be a joy to thee. Though he survive
The cruel warfare which the sons of Greece
Are waging, hard and evil yet will be
His lot hereafter; others will remove
His landmarks and will make his fields their own.
The day in which a boy is fatherless
Makes him companionless; with downcast eyes
He wanders, and his cheeks are stained with tears.
Unfed he goes where sit his father's friends,
And plucks one by the cloak, and by the robe
Another. One who pities him shall give
A scanty draught, which only wets his lips,
But not his palate; while another boy,
Whose parents both are living, thrusts him thence
With blows and vulgar clamor: 'Get thee gone!
Thy father is not with us at the feast.'
Then to his widowed mother shall return
Astyanax in tears, who not long since
Was fed, while sitting in his father's lap,
On marrow and the delicate fat of lambs.
And ever when his childish sports had tired

The boy, and sleep came stealing over him,
He slumbered, softly cushioned, on a couch
And in his nurse's arms, his heart at ease
And satiate with delights. But now thy son
Astyanax,—whom so the Trojans name
Because thy valor guarded gate and tower,—
Thy care withdrawn, shall suffer many things.
While far from those who gave thee birth, beside
The roomy ships of Greece, the restless worms
Shall make thy flesh their banquet when the dogs
Have gorged themselves. Thy garments yet remain
Within the palace, delicately wrought
And graceful, woven by the women's hands;
And these, since thou shalt put them on no more,
Nor wear them in thy death, I burn with fire
Before the Trojan men and dames; and all
Shall see how gloriously thou wert arrayed."
Weeping she spake, and with her wept her maids.

## BOOK XXIII.

SO mourned they in the city; but the Greeks,
When they had reached the fleet and Hellespont,
Dispersed, repairing each one to his ship,
Save that Achilles suffered not his band
Of Myrmidons to part in disarray.
And thus the chief enjoined his warrior friends: —
"Myrmidons, gallant knights, my cherished friends!
Let us not yet unyoke our firm-paced steeds,
But bring them with the chariots, and bewail
Patroclus with the honors due the dead,
And, when we have indulged in grief, release
Our steeds and take our evening banquet here."
He spake, and led by him the host broke forth
In lamentation. Thrice around the dead,
Weeping, they drave their steeds with stately manes,
While Thetis in their hearts awoke the sense
Of hopeless loss; their tears bedewed the sands,
And dropped upon their arms, so brave was he

For whom they sorrowed. Peleus' son began
The mourning; on the breast of his dead friend
He placed his homicidal hands, and said:—
"Hail thou, Patroclus, even amid the shades!
For now shall I perform what once I vowed:
That, dragging Hector hither, I will give
His corse to dogs, and they shall rend his flesh;
And at thy funeral pile there shall be slain
Twelve noble Trojan youths, to avenge thy death."
So spake he, meditating outrages
To noble Hector's corse, which he had flung
Beside the bier of Menœtiades,
Amid the dust. The Myrmidons unbraced
Their shining brazen armor, and unyoked
Their neighing steeds, and sat in thick array
Beside the ship of swift Æacides,
While he set forth a sumptuous funeral feast.
Many a white ox, that day, beneath the axe
Fell to the earth, and many bleating goats
And sheep were slain, and many fattened swine,
White-toothed, were stretched to roast before the flame
Of Vulcan, and around the corse the earth
Floated with blood. Meantime the Grecian chiefs
To noble Agamemnon's royal tent

Led the swift son of Peleus, though he went
Unwillingly, such anger for the death
Of his companion burned within his heart.
As soon as they had reached his tent, the king
Bade the clear-throated heralds o'er the fire
Place a huge tripod, that Pelides there
Might wash away the bloody stains he bore.
Yet would he not, and with an oath replied:—
"No! by the greatest and the best of gods,
By Jupiter, I may not plunge my head
Into the bath before I lay my friend
Patroclus on the fire, and heap his mound,
And till my hair is shorn; for never more
In life will be so great a sorrow mine.
But now attend we to this mournful feast.
And with the morn, O king of men, command
That wood be brought, and all things duly done
Which may beseem a warrior who goes down
Into the lower darkness. Let the flames
Seize fiercely and consume him from our sight,
And leave the people to the tasks of war."
He spake; they hearkened and obeyed, and all
Prepared with diligent hands the meal, and each
Sat down and took his portion of the feast.

And when their thirst and hunger were allayed,
Most to their tents betook them and to rest.
But Peleus' son, lamenting bitterly,
Lay down among his Myrmidons, beside
The murmuring ocean, in the open space,
Where plashed the billows on the beach. And there,
When slumber, bringing respite from his cares,
Came softly and enfolded him,—for much
His shapely limbs were wearied with the chase
Of Hector round the windy Ilium's walls,—
The soul of his poor friend Patroclus came,
Like him in all things,—stature, beautiful eyes,
And voice, and garments which he wore in life.
Beside his head the vision stood and spake:—
"Achilles, sleepest thou, forgetting me?
Never of me unmindful in my life,
Thou dost neglect me dead. O, bury me
Quickly, and give me entrance through the gates
Of Hades; for the souls, the forms of those
Who live no more, repulse me, suffering not
That I should join their company beyond
The river, and I now must wander round
The spacious portals of the House of Death.
Give me thy hand, I pray; for never more

Shall I return to earth when once the fire
Shall have consumed me. Never shall we take
Counsel together, living, as we sit
Apart from our companions; the hard fate
Appointed me at birth hath drawn me down.
Thou too, O godlike man, wilt fall beneath
The ramparts of the noble sons of Troy.
Yet this I ask, and if thou wilt obey,
This I command thee,—not to let my bones
Be laid apart from thine. As we were reared
Under thy roof together, from the time
When first Menœtius brought thee, yet a boy,
From Opus, where I caused a sorrowful death;—
For by my hand, when wrangling at the dice,
Another boy, son of Amphidamas,
Was slain without design,—and Peleus made
His halls my home, and reared me tenderly,
And made me thy companion;—so at last
May one receptacle, the golden vase
Given by thy gracious mother, hold our bones."
The swift Achilles answered: "O most loved
And honored, wherefore art thou come, and why
Dost thou command me thus? I shall fulfil
Obediently thy wish; yet draw thou near,

And let us give at least a brief embrace,
And so indulge our grief." He said, and stretched
His longing arms to clasp the shade. In vain;
Away like smoke it went, with gibbering cry,
Down to the earth. Achilles sprang upright,
Astonished, clapped his hands, and sadly said: —
"Surely there dwell within the realm below
Both soul and form, though bodiless. All night
Hath stood the spirit of my hapless friend
Patroclus near me, sad and sorrowful,
And asking many duties at my hands,
A marvellous semblance of the living man."
He spake, and moved the hearts of all to grief
And lamentation. Rosy-fingered Morn
Dawned on them as around the hapless dead
They stood and wept. Then Agamemnon sent
In haste from all the tents the mules and men
To gather wood, and summoned to the task
Meriones, himself a gallant chief,
Attendant on the brave Idomeneus.
These went with woodmen's axes and with ropes
Well twisted, and before them went the mules.
O'er steep, o'er glen, by straight, by winding ways,
They journeyed till they reached the woodland wilds

Of Ida fresh with springs, and quickly felled
With the keen steel the towering oaks that came
Crashing to earth. Then, splitting the great trunks,
They bound them on the mules, that beat the earth
With hasty footsteps through the tangled wood,
Impatient for the plain. Each woodcutter
Shouldered a tree, for so Meriones,
Companion of the brave Idomeneus,
Commanded, and at last they laid them down
In order on the shore, where Peleus' son
Planned that a mighty sepulchre should rise
Both for his friend Patroclus and himself.

So brought they to the spot vast heaps of wood,
And sat them down, a numerous crowd. But then
Achilles bade his valiant Myrmidons
Put on their brazen mail and yoke their steeds.
At once they rose, and put their harness on,
And they who fought from chariots climbed their seats
With those who reined the steeds. These led the van,
And after them a cloud of men on foot
By thousands followed. In the midst was borne
Patróclus by his comrades. Cutting off
Their hair, they strewed it, covering the dead.
Behind the corpse, Achilles in his hands

Sustained the head, and wept, for on that day
He gave to Hades his most cherished friend.
Now when they reached the spot which Peleus' son
Had chosen, they laid down the dead, and piled
The wood around him, while the swift of foot,
The great Achilles, bent on other thoughts,
Standing apart, cut off his amber hair,
Which for the river Sperchius he had long
Nourished to ample growth, and, sighing, turned
His eyes upon the dark-blue sea, and said: —
"Sperchius, in vain my father made a vow
That I, returning to my native shore,
Should bring my hair, an offering to thee,
And slay a consecrated hecatomb,
And burn a sacrifice of fifty rams,
Beside the springs where in a sacred field
Thy fragrant altar stands. Such was the vow
Made by the aged man, yet hast thou not
Fulfilled his wish. And now, since I no more
Shall see my native land, the land I love,
Let the slain hero bear these locks away."
He spake, and in his dear companion's hands
He placed the hair, and all around were moved
To deeper grief; the setting sun had left

The host lamenting, had not Peleus' son
Addressed Atrides, standing at his side:—
"Atrides, thou whose word the Greeks obey
Most readily, all mourning has an end.
Dismiss the people from the pyre to take
Their evening meal, while we with whom it rests
To pay these mournful duties to the dead
Will close the rites; but let the chiefs remain."
This when the monarch Agamemnon heard,
Instantly he dismissed to their good ships
The people. They who had the dead in charge
Remained, and heaped the wood, and built a pyre
A hundred feet each way from side to side.
With sorrowful hearts they raised and laid the corse
Upon the summit. Then they flayed and dressed
Before it many fatlings of the flock,
And oxen with curved feet and crooked horns.
From these magnanimous Achilles took
The fat, and covered with it carefully
The dead from head to foot. Beside the bier,
And leaning toward it, jars of honey and oil
He placed, and flung, with many a deep-drawn sigh,
Twelve high-necked steeds upon the pile. Nine hounds
There were, which from the table of the prince

Were daily fed; of these Achilles struck
The heads from two, and laid them on the wood,
And after these, and last, twelve gallant sons
Of the brave Trojans, butchered by the sword;
For he was bent on evil. To the pile
He put the iron violence of fire,
And, wailing, called by name the friend he loved:—
"Rejoice, Patroclus, even in the land
Of souls. Lo! I perform the vow I made;
Twelve gallant sons of the brave men of Troy
The fire consumes with thee. For Hector's corse,
The flames shall not devour it, but the dogs."
Such was his threat; but Hector was not made
The prey of dogs, for Venus, born to Jove,
Drave off by night and day the ravenous tribe,
And with a rosy and ambrosial oil
Anointed him, that he might not be torn
When dragged along the earth. Above the spot,
And all around it, where the body lay,
Phœbus Apollo drew a veil of clouds
Reaching from heaven, that on his limbs the flesh
And sinews might not stiffen in the sun.
The flame seized not upon the funeral pile
Of the dead chief. Pelides, swift of foot,

Bethought him of another rite. He stood
Apart, and offered vows to the two winds,
Boreas and Zephyr. Promising to bring
Fair offerings to their shrines, and pouring out
Libations from a golden cup, he prayed
That they would haste and wrap the pile in flames,
And burn the dead to ashes. At his prayer
Fleet Iris on a message to the Winds
Took instant wing. They sat within the halls
Of murmuring Zephyr, at a solemn feast.
There Iris lighted on the threshold-stone.
As soon as they beheld her, each arose
And bade her sit beside him. She refused
To seat her at the banquet, and replied: —
  "Not now; for I again must take my way
Over the ocean currents to the land
Where dwell the Æthiopians, who adore
The gods with hecatombs, to take my share
Of sacrifice. Achilles supplicates,
With promise of munificent offerings,
Boreas and sounding Zephyrus to come
And blow the funeral structure into flames
On which, bewailed by all the Grecian host,
Patroclus lies, and waits to be consumed."

So spake she, and departed. Suddenly
Arose the Winds with tumult, driving on
The clouds before them. Soon they reached the deep;
Beneath the violence of their sounding breath
The billows heaved. They swept the fertile fields
Of Troas, and descended on the pyre,
And mightily it blazed with fearful roar.
All night they howled and tossed the flames. All night
Stood swift Achilles, holding in his hand
A double beaker; from a golden jar
He dipped the wine, and poured it forth, and steeped
The earth around, and called upon the soul
Of his unhappy friend. As one laments
A newly married son upon whose corse
The flames are feeding, and whose death has made
His parents wretched, so did Peleus' son,
Burning the body of his comrade, mourn,
As round the pyre he moved with frequent sighs.

Now when the star that ushers in the day
Appeared, and after it the morning, clad
In saffron robes, had overspread the sea,
The pyre sank wasted, and the flames arose
No longer, and the winds, departing, flew
Homeward across the Thracian sea, which tossed

And roared with swollen billows as they went.
And now Pelides from the pyre apart
Weary lay down, and gentle slumber soon
Came stealing over him. Meantime the Greeks
Gathered round Agamemnon, and the stir
And bustle of their coming woke the chief,
Who sat upright and thus addressed his friends:—
"Atrides, and all ye who lead the hosts
Of Greece! our task is, first to quench the pyre
With dark red wine where'er the flames have spread,
And next to gather, with discerning care,
The bones of Menœtiades. And these
May well be known; for in the middle space
He lay, and round about him, and apart
Upon the border, were the rest consumed,—
The bodies of the captives and the steeds.
Be his enclosed within a golden vase,
And wrapped around with caul, a double fold,
Till I too pass into the realm of Death.
And be a tomb not over-spacious reared,
But of becoming size, which afterward
Ye whom we leave behind in our good ships,
When we are gone, will build more broad and high."
So spake the swift Pelides, and the chiefs

Complied; and first they quenched with dark red wine
The pyre, where'er the flames had spread, and where
Lay the deep ashes; then, with many tears,
Gathered the white bones of their gentle friend,
And laid them in a golden vase, wrapped round
With caul, a double fold. Within the tents
They placed them softly, wrapped in delicate lawn,
Then drew a circle for the sepulchre,
And, laying its foundations to enclose
The pyre, they heaped the earth, and, having reared
A mound, withdrew. Achilles yet detained
The multitude, and made them all sit down,
A vast assembly. From the ships he brought
The prizes,—caldrons, tripods, steeds, and mules,
Oxen in sturdy pairs, and graceful maids,
And shining steel. Then for the swiftest steeds
A princely prize he offered first,—a maid
Of peerless form, and skilled in household arts,
And a two-handled tripod of a size
For two-and-twenty measures. He gave out
The second prize,—a mare unbroken yet,
Of six years old, and pregnant with a mule.
For the third winner in the race he staked
A caldron that had never felt the fire,

Holding four measures, beautiful, and yet
Untarnished. For the fourth, he offered gold,
Two talents. For the fifth, and last, remained
A double vessel never touched by fire.
He rose and stood, and thus addressed the Greeks:—
"Atrides, and ye other well-armed Greeks,
These prizes lie within the chariot-course,
And wait the charioteers. Were but these games
In honor of another, then would I
Contend, and win and carry to my tent
The first among these prizes. For my steeds,
Ye know, surpass the rest in speed, since they
Are of immortal birth, by Neptune given
To Peleus, and by him in turn bestowed
On me his son. But I and they will keep
Aloof; they miss their skilful charioteer,
Who washed in limpid water from the fount
Their manes, and moistened them with softening oil.
And now they mourn their friend, and sadly stand
With drooping heads and manes that touch the ground.
Let such of you as trust in their swift steeds
And their strong cars prepare to join the games."
Pelides spake: the abler charioteers
Arose, and, first of all, the king of men,

Eumelus, eminent in horsemanship,
The dear son of Admetus. Then arose
The valiant son of Tydeus, Diomed,
And led beneath the yoke the Trojan steeds
Won from Æneas when Apollo saved
That chief from death. The son of Atreus next,
The noble Menelaus, yellow-haired,
Brought two swift coursers underneath the yoke,
King Agamemnon's Æthè, and with her
His own Podargus. Echepolus once,
Anchises' son, sent Æthè as a gift
To Agamemnon, that he might be free
From following with the army to the heights
Of Ilium, and enjoy the ease he loved;
For Jove had given him wealth, and he abode
On Sicyon's plains. Now, eager for the race,
She took the yoke. Antilochus, the fourth,
The gallant son of the magnanimous king,
Neleian Nestor, harnessed next his steeds
With stately manes. Swift coursers that were foaled
At Pylus drew his chariot. To his side
His father came and stood, and spake and gave
Wise counsels, though the youth himself was wise:—
"Antilochus, I cannot doubt that Jove

And Neptune both have loved thee, teaching thee,
Young as thou art, all feats of horsemanship.
Small is the need to instruct thee. Thou dost know
Well how to turn the goal, and yet thy steeds
Are slow, and ill for thee may be the event.
Their steeds are swift, yet have they never learned
To govern them with greater skill than thou.
Now then, dear son, bethink thee heedfully
Of all precautions, lest thou miss the prize.
By skill the woodman, rather than by strength,
Brings down the oak; by skill the pilot guides
His wind-tossed galley over the dark sea;
And thus by skill the charioteer o'ercomes
His rival. He who trusts too much his steeds
And chariot lets them veer from side to side
Along the course, nor keeps a steady rein
Straight on, while one expert in horsemanship,
Though drawn by slower horses, carefully
Observes the goal, and closely passes it,
Nor fails to know how soon to turn his course,
Drawing the leathern reins, and steadily
Keeps on, and watches him who goes before.
Now must I show the goal which, easily
Discerned, will not escape thine eye. It stands

An ell above the ground, a sapless post,
Of oak or larch,—a wood of slow decay
By rain, and at its foot on either side
Lies a white stone; there narrow is the way,
But level is the race-course all around.
The monument it is of one long dead,
Or haply it has been in former days
A goal, as the swift-footed Peleus' son
Has now appointed it. Approach it near,
Driving thy chariot close upon its foot,
Then in thy seat lean gently to the left
And cheer the right-hand horse, and ply the lash,
And give him a loose rein, yet firmly keep
The left-hand courser close beside the goal,—
So close that the wheel's nave may seem to touch
The summit of the post; yet strike thou not
The stone beside it, lest thou lame thy steeds
And break the chariot, to thy own disgrace
And laughter of the others. My dear son,
Be on thy guard; for if thou pass the goal
Before the rest, no man in the pursuit
Can overtake or pass thee, though he drave
The noble courser of Adrastus, named
Arion the swift-footed, which a god

Bade spring to life, or those of matchless speed
Reared here in Ilium by Laomedon."
  Neleian Nestor spake, and, having thus
Given all the needful cautions, took his seat
In his own place. Meriones, the fifth,
Harnessed his steeds with stately manes, and all
Mounted their chariots. Lots were cast; the son
Of Peleus shook the helmet, and the lot
Of Nestor's son, Antilochus, leaped forth;
And next the lot of King Eumelus came;
And Menelaus, mighty with the spear,
Had the third lot; Meriones was next;
And to the bravest of them all, the son
Of Tydeus, fell the final lot and place.
They stood in order, while Achilles showed
The goal far off upon the level plain,
And near it, as the umpire of the race,
He placed the godlike Phœnix, who had been
His father's armor-bearer, to observe
With judging eye, and bring a true report.
  All raised at once the lash above their steeds,
And smote them with the reins, and cheered them on
With vehement cries. Across the plain they swept,
Far from the fleet; beneath them rose the dust,

A cloud, a tempest, and their tossing manes
Were lifted by the wind. And now the cars
Touched earth, and now were flung into the air.
Erect the drivers stood, with beating hearts,
Eager for victory, each encouraging
His steeds, that flew beneath the shroud of dust.

But when they turned their course, and swiftly ran
Back to the hoary deep to close the course,
Well did the skill of every chief appear.
They put their horses to the utmost speed,
And then did the quick-footed steeds that drew
Eumelus bear him on beyond the rest.
But with his Trojan coursers Diomed
Came next, so near it seemed that they would mount
The car before them, and upon the back
And ample shoulders of Eumelus smote
Their steaming breath; for as they ran their heads
Leaned over him. And then would Diomed
Have passed him by, or would at least have made
The victory doubtful, had not Phœbus struck,
In his displeasure, from the hero's hand
The shining scourge. It fell, and to his eyes
Started indignant tears; for now he saw
The others gaining on him, while the speed

Of his own steeds, which feared the lash no more,
Was slackened. Yet Apollo's stratagem
Was not unseen by Pallas, who o'ertook
The shepherd of the people, and restored
The scourge he dropped, and put into his steeds
New spirit. In her anger she approached
Eumelus, snapped his yoke, and caused his mares
To start asunder from the track; the pole
Was dashed into the ground, and from the seat
The chief was flung beside the wheel, his mouth,
Elbows, and nostrils torn, his forehead bruised.
Grief filled his eyes with tears and choked his voice,
While Diomed drave by his firm-paced steeds,
Outstripping all the rest; for Pallas nerved
Their limbs with vigor, and bestowed on him
Abundant glory. After him the son
Of Atreus, fair-haired Menelaus, came,
While Nestor's son cheered on his father's steeds:—
"On, on! press onward with your utmost speed!
Not that I bid you strive against the steeds
Of warlike Diomed, for Pallas gives
Swiftness to them and glory to the man
Who holds the reins; but let us overtake
The horses of Atrides, nor submit

To be thus distanced, lest the victory
Of the mare Æthè cover you with shame.
Fleet as ye are, why linger? This at least
I tell you, and my words will be fulfilled:
Look not for kindly care at Nestor's hands,
That shepherd of the people, but for death
With the sharp steel, if through your fault we take
A meaner prize. Then onward and away,
With all your strength, for this is my design,—
To pass by Menelaus where the way
Is narrow, and he cannot thwart my plan."

He spake, and they who feared their master's threat
Mended their speed awhile. The warlike son
Of Nestor saw just then the narrow pass
Within the hollow way, a furrow ploughed
By winter floods, which there had torn the course
And deepened it. Atrides, to avoid
The clash of wheels, drave thither; thither too
Antilochus—who turned his firm-paced steeds
A little from the track in which they ran—
Followed him close. Atrides saw with fear,
And shouted to Antilochus aloud:—

"Antilochus, thou drivest rashly; rein
Thy horses in. The way is narrow here,

But soon will broaden, and thou then canst pass.
Beware lest with thy chariot-wheels thou dash
Against my own, and harm befall us both."
He spake; but all the more Antilochus
Urged on his coursers with the lash, as if
He had not heard. As far as flies a quoit
Thrown from the shoulder of a vigorous youth
Who tries his strength, so far they ran abreast.
The horses of Atrides then fell back;
He slacked the reins; for much he feared the steeds
Would dash against each other in the way,
And overturn the sumptuous cars, and fling
The charioteers contending for the prize
Upon the dusty track. With angry words
The fair-haired Menelaus chided thus:—
"Antilochus, there is no man so prone
As thou to mischief, and we greatly err,
We Greeks, who call thee wise. Go now, and yet
Thou shalt not take the prize without an oath."
Again he spake, encouraging his steeds:
"Check not your speed, nor sorrowfully stand:
Their feet and knees will fail with weariness
Before your own; they are no longer young."
He spake; the coursers, honoring his voice,

Ran with fresh speed, and soon were near to those
Of Nestor's son. Meantime the assembled Greeks
Sat looking where the horses scoured the plain
And filled the air with dust. Idomeneus,
The lord of Crete, descried the coursers first,
For on a height he sat above the crowd.
He heard the chief encouraging his steeds,
And knew him, and he marked before the rest
A courser, chestnut-colored save a spot
Upon the middle of the forehead, white,
And round as the full moon. And then he stood
Upright, and from his place harangued the Greeks:—
"O friends, the chiefs and leaders of the Greeks,
Am I the sole one that descries the steeds,
Or do ye also? Those who lead the race,
I think, are not the same, and with them comes
A different charioteer. The mares, which late
Were foremost, may have somewhere come to harm.
I saw them first to turn the goal, and now
I can no more discern them, though my sight
Sweeps the whole Trojan plain from side to side.
Either the charioteer has dropped the reins,
And could not duly round the goal, or else
Met with disaster at the turn, o'erthrown,

His chariot broken, and the affrighted mares
Darting, unmastered, madly from the way.
But rise: look forth yourselves. I cannot well
Discern, but think the charioteer is one
Who, born of an Ætolian stock, commands
Among the Argives,—valiant Diomed,
A son of Tydeus, tamer of wild steeds."
  And Ajax, swift of foot, Oïleus' son,
Answered with bitter words: "Idomeneus,
Why this perpetual prating? Far away
The mares with rapid hoofs are traversing
The plain, and thou art not the youngest here
Among the Argives, nor hast such sharp eyes
Beneath thy brows, yet must thou chatter still.
Among thy betters here it ill becomes
A man like thee to be so free of tongue.
The coursers of Eumelus, which at first
Outran the rest, are yet before them all,
And he is drawing near and holds the reins."
  The Cretan leader angrily rejoined:
"Ajax, thou railer, first in brawls, yet known
As in all else below the other Greeks,
A man of brutal mood, come, let us stake
A tripod or a caldron, and appoint

As umpire Agamemnon, to decide
Which horses are the foremost in the race,
That when thou losest thou mayst be convinced."
He spake: Oïlean Ajax, swift of foot,
Started in anger from his seat, to cast
Reproaches back, and long and fierce had been
The quarrel if Achilles had not risen,
And said: "No longer let this strife go on,
Idomeneus and Ajax! Ill such words
Become you; ye would blame in other men
What now ye do. Sit then among the rest,
And watch the race; for soon the charioteers
Contending for the victory will be here,
And each of you—for well ye know the steeds
Of the Greek chieftains—for himself will see
Whose hold the second place, and whose are first."
He spake: Tydides rapidly drew near,
Lashing the shoulders of his steeds, and they
Seemed in the air as, to complete the course,
They flew along, and flung the dust they trod
Back on the charioteer. All bright with tin
And gold, the car rolled after them; its tires
Made but a slender trace in the light dust,
So rapidly they ran. And now he stopped

Within the circle, while his steeds were steeped
In sweat, that fell in drops from neck and breast.
Then from his shining seat he leaped, and laid
His scourge against the yoke. Brave Sthenelus
Came forward, and at once received the prize
For Diomed, and bade his comrades lead
The maid away, and in their arms bear off
The tripod, while himself unyoked the steeds.
  Next the Neleian chief, Antilochus,
Came with his coursers. More by fraud than speed
He distanced Menelaus, yet that chief
Drave his fleet horses near him. Just so far
As runs the wheel behind a steed that draws
His master swiftly o'er the plain, his tail
Touching the tire with its long hairs, and small
The space between them as the spacious plain
Is traversed, Menelaus just so far
Was distanced by renowned Antilochus.
For though at first he fell as far behind
As a quoit's cast, yet was he gaining ground
Rapidly, now that Agamemnon's mare,
Æthè the stately-maned, increased her speed,
And Menelaus, had the race for both
Been longer, would have passed his rival by,

Nor left the victory doubtful. After him,
A spear's throw distant, came Meriones,
The gallant comrade of Idomeneus,
Whose full-maned steeds were slower than the rest,
And he unskilled in contests such as these.
And last of all Eumelus came. He drew
His showy chariot after him, and drave
His steeds before him. Great Achilles saw
With pity, and from where he stood among
The Greeks addressed him thus with wingèd words:—
"The ablest horseman brings his steeds the last,
But let us, as is just, confer on him
The second prize; Tydides takes the first."
He spake, and all approved his words; and now
The mare, to please the Greeks, had been bestowed
Upon Eumelus, if Antilochus,
Son of magnanimous Nestor, had not risen
To plead for justice with Achilles thus:—
"Achilles, I shall deem it grave offence
If thou fulfil thy word; for thou wilt take
My prize, because thou seest that this man's car
And his fleet steeds have suffered injury,
Though he be skilful. Yet he should have prayed
To the good gods; then had he not been seen

Bringing his steeds the last. But if thou feel
Compassion for him, and if so thou please,
Large store of brass and gold is in thy tent,
And thine are cattle, and handmaidens thine,
And firm-paced steeds; hereafter give of these
A nobler largess, or bestow it now,
And hear the Greeks applaud thee. But this prize
I yield not; let the warrior who may claim
To take it try with me his strength of arm."
He ceased: the noble son of Peleus smiled,
And, pleased to see Antilochus succeed,—
For he was a beloved friend,—he spake
These wingèd words: "Since, then, Antilochus,
Thou wilt that I bestow some recompense
Upon Eumelus from my store, I give
The brazen corselet which my arm in war
Took from Asteropæus, edged around
With shining tin,—a gift of no mean price."
He ceased, and sent his friend Automedon
To bring it from the tent. He went and brought
The corselet, and Eumelus joyfully
Received it from Achilles. Then arose,
Among them Menelaus, ill at ease,
And angry with Antilochus. He took

The sceptre from a herald's hand, who hushed
The crowd to silence, and the hero spake:—
"Antilochus, who wert till now discreet,
What hast thou done? Thou hast disgraced my skill
And wronged my steeds by thrusting in thine own,
Which were less fleet, before them. Now, ye chiefs
And leaders of the Achaians, judge between
This man and me, and judge impartially,
Lest that some warrior of the Greeks should say
That Menelaus, having overcome
Antilochus by falsehood, led away
The mare a prize; for his were slower steeds,
But he the mightier man in feats of arms.
Nay, I myself will judge; and none of all
The Greeks will censure me, for what I do
Will be but just. Antilochus, step forth,
Illustrious as thou art, and in due form,
Standing before thy horses and thy car,
And taking in thy hand the pliant scourge
Which thou just now hast wielded, touch thy steeds,
And swear by Neptune, whose embrace surrounds
The earth, that thou hast wittingly employed
No stratagem to break my chariot's speed."
And thus discreet Antilochus replied:

"Have patience with me: I am younger far
Than thou, King Menelaus; thou art both
My elder and my better. Thou dost know
The faults to which the young are ever prone;
The will is quick to act, the judgment weak.
Bear with me then. The mare which I received
I cheerfully make over to thy hands.
And if thou wilt yet more of what I have,
I give it willingly and instantly,
Rather, O loved of Jove, than lose a place
In thy good-will, and sin against the gods."
The son of large-souled Nestor, speaking thus,
Led forth the mare, and gave her to the hand
Of Menelaus, o'er whose spirit came
A gladness. As upon a field of wheat
Bristling with ears gathers the freshening dew,
So was his spirit gladdened in his breast,
And he bespake the youth with wingèd words:—
"Antilochus, now shall my anger cease,
For hitherto thou hast not shown thyself
Foolish or fickle, though the heat of youth
Just now hath led thee wrong. In time to come,
Beware to practise stealthy arts on men
Of higher rank than thou. No other Greek

Would easily have made his peace with me.
But thou hast suffered much, and much hast done,—
Thou, and thy worthy father, and his son,
Thy brother,—for my sake. I therefore yield
To thy petition; yet I give to thee
The mare, though mine she be, that these who stand
Around us may perceive that I am not
Of unforgiving or unyielding mood."

He spake, and to Noëmon gave the mare,—
Noëmon, comrade of Antilochus,—
To lead her thence, while for himself he took
The shining caldron. Then Meriones,
Fourth in the race, received the prize of gold,—
Two talents. But the fifth prize and the last,
The double goblet, still was left unclaimed;
And this Achilles carried through the crowd
Of Greeks, and placed in Nestor's hands, and said:—

"Receive thou this, O ancient man, to keep
In memory of the funeral honors paid
Patroclus, whom thou never more shalt see
Among the Greeks. I give this prize, which thou
Hast not contended for, since thou wilt wield
No more the cestus, nor wilt wrestle more,
Nor hurl the javelin at the mark, nor join

The foot-race; age lies heavy on thy limbs."
He spake, and gave the prize, which Nestor took,
Well pleased, and thus with wingèd words replied: —
"Son, thou hast spoken rightly, for these limbs
Are strong no longer; neither feet nor hands
Move on each side with vigor as of yore.
Would I were but as young, with strength as great,
As when the Epeians in Buprasium laid
King Amarynceus in the sepulchre,
And funeral games were offered by his sons!
Then of the Epeians there was none like me,
Nor of the Pylian youths, nor yet among
The brave Ætolians. In the boxing match
I took the prize from Clytomedes, son
Of Enops, and in wrestling overcame
Ancæus the Pleuronian, who rose up
Against me. In the foot-race I outstripped,
Fleet as he was, Iphiclus, and beyond
Phyleus and Polydore I threw the spear.
Only the sons of Actor won the race
Against me with their chariot, and they won
Through force of numbers. Much they envied me,
And feared lest I should bear away the prize;
For largest in that contest of the steeds

Was the reward, and they were two,—one held,
Steadily held, the reins, the other swung
The lash. Such was I once. Now feats like these
Belong to other, younger men, and I,
Though eminent among the heroes once,
Must do as sad old age admonishes.
Go thou, and honor thy friend's funeral
With games. Thy gift I willingly accept,
Rejoicing that thy thoughts revert to one
Who loves thee, and that thou forgettest not
To pay the honor due to me among
The Greeks. The gods will give thee thy reward."
  He ceased. The son of Peleus, having heard
This praise from Nestor, left him, and passed through
The mighty concourse of the Greeks. He laid
Before them prizes for the difficult strife
Between the boxers. To the middle space
He led a mule, and bound him, six years old
And strong for toil, unbroken and most hard
To break, while to the vanquished he assigned
A goblet. Rising, he addressed the host:—
  "Ye sons of Atreus and ye well-armed Greeks,
We call for two of the most skilled to strive
For these, by striking with the lifted fist;

And he to whom Apollo shall decree
The victory, acknowledged by you all,
Shall have this sturdy mule to lead away.
The vanquished takes this goblet as his meed."
He spake. A warrior strong and huge of limb,
Skilled in the cestus, named Epeius, son
Of Panopeus, rose at the word, and laid
His hand upon the sturdy mule, and said:—
"Let him appear whose lot will be to take
The goblet. No man of the Grecian host
Will get the mule by overcoming me
In combat with the cestus,—so I deem.
In that I claim to be the best man here.
And should it not suffice that in the war
Others surpass me? All cannot excel
In everything alike. I promise this,
And shall fulfil my word,—that I will crush
His body, and will break his bones. His friends
Should all remain upon the ground to bear
Their comrade off when beaten by my hand."
He spake, and all were silent. Only rose
Euryalus, whose father was the king
Mecisteus of Talaïon's line, the same
Who went to Thebes and overcame, of old,

In all the funeral games of Œdipus,
The sons of Cadmus. To Euryalus
Came Diomed, the spearman, bidding him
Expect the victory which he greatly wished
His friend might gain. Around his waist he drew
A girdle, adding straps that from the hide
Of a wild bull were cut with dextrous care.
And, fully now arrayed, the twain stepped forth
Into the middle space, and both began
The combat. Lifting their strong arms, they brought
Their heavy hands together. Fearfully
Was heard the crash of jaws; from every limb
The sweat was streaming. As Euryalus
Looked round, his noble adversary sprang
And smote him on the cheek,—too rude a blow
To be withstood; his shapely limbs gave way
Beneath him. As upon the weedy shore,
When the fresh north-wind stirs the water's face,
A fish leaps forth to light, and then again
The dark wave covers it, so sprang and fell
The chief. Magnanimous Epeius gave
His hands and raised him up; his friends came round
And led him thence with dragging feet, and head
That drooped from side to side, while from his mouth

Came clotted blood. They placed him in the midst,
Unconscious still, and sent and took the cup.
Then, third in order, for the wrestling-match
The son of Peleus brought and showed the Greeks
Yet other prizes. To the conqueror
A tripod for the hearth, of ample size,
He offered; twice six oxen, as the Greeks
Esteemed it, were its price. And next he placed
In view a damsel for the vanquished, trained
In household arts; four beeves were deemed her price.
Then rose Achilles, and addressed the Greeks:
"Ye who would try your fortune in this strife,
Arise." He spake, and mighty Ajax rose,
The son of Telamon, and after him
The wise Ulysses, trained to stratagems.
They, girding up their loins, came forth and stood
In the mid space, and there with vigorous arms
They clasped each other, locked like rafters framed
By some wise builder for the lofty roof
Of a great mansion proof against the winds.
Then their backs creaked beneath the powerful strain
Of their strong hands; the sweat ran down their limbs;
Large whelks upon their sides and shoulders rose,
Crimson with blood. Still eagerly they strove

For victory and the tripod. Yet in vain
Ulysses labored to supplant his foe,
And throw him to the ground, and equally
Did Ajax strive in vain, for with sheer strength
Ulysses foiled his efforts. When they saw
That the Greeks wearied of the spectacle,
The mighty Telamonian Ajax said:—
"Son of Laertes, nobly born and trained
To wise expedients, lift me up, or I
Will lift up thee; and leave the rest to Jove."
He spake, and raised Ulysses from the ground,
Who dealt, with ready stratagem, a blow
Upon the ham of Ajax, and the limb
Gave way; the hero fell upon his back,
And on his breast Ulysses, while the host
Stood wondering and amazed. Ulysses strove,
In turn, to lift his rival, but prevailed
Only to move him from his place; he caught
The knee of Ajax in his own, and both
Came to the ground together, soiled with dust.
They rose to wrestle still, but from his seat
Achilles started, and forbade them thus:—
"Contend no longer, nor exhaust your strength
With struggling; there is victory for both,

And equal prizes. Now depart, and leave
The field of contest to the other Greeks."

He spake: they listened and obeyed, and wiped
The dust away, and put their garments on.
And then the son of Peleus placed in sight
Prizes of swiftness, — a wrought silver cup
That held six measures, and in beauty far
Excelled all others known; the cunning hands
Of the Sidonian artisans had given
Its graceful shape, and over the dark sea
Men of Phœnicia brought it, with their wares,
To the Greek harbors; they bestowed it there
On Thoas. Afterward Euneüs, son
Of Jason, gave it to the hero-chief,
Patroclus, to redeem a captive friend,
Lycaon, Priam's son. Achilles now
Brought it before the assembly as a prize,
For which, in honor of the friend he loved,
The swiftest runners of the host should strive.
Next, for the second in the race, he showed
A noble fatling ox; and for the last,
Gold, half a talent. Then he stood and said
To the Achaians: "Those who would contend
For these rewards, rise up." And then arose

Oïlean Ajax, fleet of foot; and next
Ulysses the sagacious; last upstood
Antilochus, the son of Nestor, known
As swiftest of the youths. In due array
They stood; Achilles showed the goal. At once
Forward they sprang. Oïlean Ajax soon
Gained on the rest, but close behind him ran
The great Ulysses. As a shapely maid
Flinging the shuttle draws with careful hand
The thread that fills the warp, and so brings near
The shuttle to her bosom, just so near
To Ajax ran Ulysses, in the prints
Made by his rival's feet, before the dust
Fell back upon them. As he ran, his breath
Smote on the head of Ajax. All the Greeks
Shouted applause to him, encouraging
His ardor for the victory; but when now
They neared the goal, Ulysses silently
Prayed thus to Pallas: "Goddess, hear my prayer,
And help these feet to win." The goddess heard,
And lightened all his limbs, his feet, his hands;
And just as they were rushing on the prize,
Ajax, in running, slipped and fell—the work
Of Pallas—where in heaps the refuse lay

From entrails of the bellowing oxen slain
In honor of Patroclus by the hand
Of swift Achilles. Mouth and nostrils both
Were choked with filth. The much-enduring man
Ulysses, coming first, received the cup,
While Ajax took the ox, and as he stood
Holding the animal's horn and spitting forth
The dirt, he said to those around: "'T is plain
The goddess caused my feet to slide; she aids
Ulysses like a mother." So he said,
And the Greeks laughed. And then Antilochus
Received the third reward, and with a smile
Said to the Greeks: "I tell you all, my friends,
What you must know already, that the gods
Honor the aged ever. Ajax stands
Somewhat in years above me, but this chief
Who takes the prize is of a former age
And earlier race of men; they call him old,
But hard it were for any Greek to vie
With him in swiftness, save Achilles here."

Such praise he gave Pelides, fleet of foot,
Who answered: "Thy good word, Antilochus,
Shall not be vainly spoken. I will add
Yet half a talent to thy gold." He said,

And gave the gold; Antilochus, well pleased,
Received it. Then Pelides brought a spear
Of ponderous length into the middle space,
And laid it down, and placed a buckler near
And helmet, which had been Sarpedon's arms,
And which Patroclus won of him in war.
Then stood Achilles and addressed the Greeks:—
"I call on two, the bravest of the host,
To arm themselves and take their spears in hand,
And in a contest for these weapons put
Each other to the proof. Whoever first
Shall wound his adversary, piercing through
The armor to the delicate skin beneath,
And draw the crimson blood, to him I give
This beautiful sword of Thrace, with silver studs,
Won from Asteropæus. And let both
Bear off these arms, a common gift, and both
Shall sit and banquet nobly in my tent."
He spake, and Telamonian Ajax rose,
The large of limb; Tydides Diomed,
The strong, rose also. When they had put on
Their arms apart from all the host, they came,
All eager for the combat, to the lists,
And fearful was their aspect. All the Greeks

Looked on with dread and wonder, and when now
Stood face to face the warriors, thrice they rushed
Against each other; thrice they dealt their blows.
Then Ajax thrust through Diomed's round shield
His weapon, but it wounded not; the mail
Beyond it stopped the stroke. Tydides aimed
Over his adversary's mighty shield
A blow to reach his neck. The Greeks, alarmed
For Ajax, shouted that the strife should cease,
And both divide the prize. Achilles heard,
But gave to Diomed the ponderous sword,
Its sheath, and the fair belt from which it hung.
  Again Pelides placed before the host
A mass of iron, shapeless from the forge,
Which once the strong Eëtion used to hurl;
But swift Achilles, when he took his life,
Brought it with other booty in his ships
To Troas. Rising, he addressed the Greeks:—
  "Stand forth, whoever will contend for this,
And if broad fields and rich be his, this mass
Will last him many years. The man who tends
His flocks, or guides his plough, need not be sent
To town for iron; he will have it here."
  He spake, and warlike Polypœtes rose.

Uprose the strong Leonteus, who in form
Was like a god. The son of Telamon
Rose also, and Epeius nobly born;
Each took his place. Epeius seized the mass,
And sent it whirling. All the Achaians laughed.
The loved of Mars, Leonteus, flung it next,
And after him the son of Telamon,
The large-limbed Ajax, from his vigorous arm
Sent it beyond the mark of both. But when
The sturdy warrior Polypœtes took
The mass in hand, as far as o'er his beeves
A herdsman sends his whirling staff, so far
This cast outdid the rest. A shout arose;
The friends of sturdy Polypœtes took
The prize, and bore it to the hollow ships.
  Achilles for the archers brought forth steel,
Tempered for arrow-heads,—ten axes, each
With double edge, and single axes ten,—
And from a galley's azure prow took off
A mast, and reared it on the sands afar,
And, tying to its summit by the foot
A timorous dove, he bade them aim at her:
"Whoever strikes the bird shall bear away
The double axes to his tent; while he

Who hits the cord, but not the bird, shall take
The single axes, as the humbler prize."
  He ceased, and then arose the stalwart king,
Teucer; then also rose Meriones,
The valiant comrade of Idomeneus.
The lots were shaken in a brazen helm,
And Teucer's lot was first. He straightway sent
A shaft with all his strength, but made no vow
Of a choice hecatomb of firstling lambs
To Phœbus, monarch-god. He missed the bird,
Such was the will of Phœbus, but he struck,
Close to her foot, the cord that made her fast.
The keen shaft severed it; the dove flew up
Into the heavens; the fillet dropped to earth
Amid the loud applauses of the Greeks.
And then Meriones made haste to take
The bow from Teucer's hand. Long time he held
The arrow aimed, the while he made a vow
To Phœbus, the great archer, promising
A chosen hecatomb of firstling lambs;
Then, looking toward the dove, as high in air
She wheeled beneath the clouds, he pierced her breast
Beneath the wing; the shaft went through and fell,
Fixed in the ground, beside Meriones,

While the bird settled on the galley's mast
With drooping head and open wings. The breath
Forsook her soon, and down from that high perch
She fell to earth. The people all looked on,
Admiring and amazed. Meriones
Took up the double axes as his prize,
While Teucer bore the others to the fleet.
  And then Pelides brought into the midst
A ponderous spear, and laid a caldron down
Which never felt the fire, inwrought with flowers,
Its price an ox. And then the spearmen rose.
Atrides Agamemnon, mighty king,
First rose, and after him Meriones,
The brave companion of Idomeneus;
And thus to both the swift Achilles said:—
  "O son of Atreus, for we know how far
Thou dost excel all others, and dost cast
The spear with passing strength and skill, bear thou
This prize, as victor, to the roomy ships,
And if it please thee, let us, as I wish,
Give to our brave Meriones the spear."
  He spake, and Agamemnon, king of men,
Complied, and gave Meriones in hand
The brazen spear, while to Talthybius,
The herald, he consigned the greater prize.

## *BOOK XXIV.*

THE assembly was dissolved, the people all
Dispersed to their swift galleys, and prepared
With food and gentle slumber to refresh
Their wearied frames. But still Achilles wept,
Remembering his dear comrade. Sleep, whose sway
Is over all, came not; he turned and tossed,
Still yearning for his strong and valiant friend
Patroclus. All that they had ever done
Together, all the hardships they had borne,
The battles fought with heroes, the wild seas
O'erpassed, came thronging on his memory.
He shed warm tears, as now upon his sides,
Now on his back, now on his face he lay.
Then, starting from his couch, he wandered forth
In sorrow by the margin of the deep.
Nor did the morn that rose o'er sea and shore
Dawn unperceived by him; for then he yoked
His fleet steeds to the chariot, and made fast

The corse of Hector, that it might be dragged
After the wheels. Three times around the tomb
Of Menœtiades he dragged the slain,
Then turned and sought his tent, again to rest,
And left him there stretched out amid the dust
With the face downward. Yet Apollo, moved
With pity for the hero, kept him free
From soil or stain, though dead, and o'er him held
The golden ægis, lest, when roughly dragged
Along the ground, the body might be torn.
  So in his anger did Achilles treat
Unworthily the noble Hector's corse.
The blessed gods themselves with pity looked
Upon the slain, and bade the vigilant one,
The Argus-queller, bear him thence by stealth.
This counsel pleased the immortals all, except
Juno and Neptune and the blue-eyed maid,
And these persisted in their wrath. To them
Ilium, the hallowed city, and its king,
Priam, and all his people, from the first
Were hateful; 't was for Alexander's fault,
Affronting the two goddesses what time
They sought his cottage, and preferring her
Who ministered to his calamitous love.

But now, when the twelfth morning from that day
Arose, Apollo spake among the gods:—
"Cruel are ye, O gods, and prone to wrong.
For was not Hector wont before your shrines
To burn the thighs of chosen bulls and goats?
And now that he is dead ye venture not
To rescue him, and let his wife and son
And mother and King Priam look again
Upon his face. Soon would they light the pile,
And burn the dead, and pay the funeral rite.
Ye seek to favor, O ye gods, that pest,
Achilles, in whose breast there dwells no love
Of justice, nor a temper to be moved
By prayers, but who delights in savage deeds.
And as a lion, conscious of vast strength
And scornful of resistance, falls upon
The shepherd's flock, and slays for his repast,
Thus with Achilles neither mercy dwells
Nor shame, which often profits, often harms
Mankind. For when another man has met
A greater grief than he,—has lost, perchance,
A brother or a son,—he dries at length
His tears, and ceases to lament; for fate
Bestows the power to suffer patiently.

But this Achilles, after he has spoiled
The godlike Hector of his life in war,
Hath bound him to his chariot, and hath dragged
The corse around his dear companion's tomb.
Unseemly is the deed, and small will be
The good it brings him. Brave although he be,
We may be angry with him when he thus
Insults a portion of insensible earth."

The white-armed Juno was incensed, and spake:
"So mightst thou say, God of the silver bow,
Were equal honor to Achilles due
And Hector. Hector is a mortal man,
And suckled at a woman's breast. Not so
Achilles; he was born of one of us,
A goddess whom I nurtured and brought up
And gave to Peleus. Ye were present all,
Ye gods, when they were wedded. Thou wert there
To share the marriage banquet, harp in hand,
Thou plotter with the vile, thou faithless one!"

Then answered cloud-compelling Jove, and said:
"Let not thy anger rise against the gods,
O Juno, for the honor of the chiefs
Shall not be equal. Yet of all the race
Of mortals dwelling in the city of Troy

Was Hector dearest to the gods; to me
He ever was; and never did he fail
To offer welcome gifts. My altar ne'er
Lacked fitting feast, libation, and the fume
Of incense,—hallowed rites which are our due.
Yet seek we not to steal away the corse
Of valiant Hector; that we could not do
Without his slayer's knowledge, who by night
And day is ever near to him and keeps
Watch o'er him like a mother. Let some god
Call hither Thetis. I will counsel her
Prudently, that Achilles may receive
Ransom from Priam, and restore his son."
  He ceased, and with the swiftness of the storm
Rose Iris up, to be his messenger.
Half-way 'twixt Samos and the rugged coast
Of Imbrus down she plunged to the dark sea,
Entering the deep with noise. Far down she sank
As sinks the ball of lead, that, sliding o'er
A wild bull's horn, bears into ocean's depths
Death to the greedy fishes. There she found
Thetis within her roomy cave, among
The goddesses of ocean, seated round
In full assembly. Thetis in the midst

Bewailed the fate of her own blameless son,
About to perish on the fertile soil
Of Troy, and far from Greece. The swift of wing,
Iris, approached her and addressed her thus:—
"Arise, O Thetis. Father Jupiter,
Whose counsel stands forever, sends for thee."
And silver-footed Thetis answered him:
"Why should that potent deity require
My presence, who have many griefs, and shrink
From mingling with immortals? Yet I go,
Perforce, for never doth he speak in vain."
So spake the goddess-queen, and, speaking, took
Her mantle,—darker web was never worn,—
And onward went. Wind-footed Iris led
The way; the waters of the sea withdrew
On either side. They climbed the steepy shore,
And took their way to heaven. They found the son
Of Saturn, him of the far-sounding voice,
With all the blessed, ever-living gods
Assembled round him. Close to Father Jove
She took her seat, for Pallas yielded it,
And Juno put a beautiful cup of gold
Into her hand, and spake consoling words.
She drank and gave it back, and thus began

The father of immortals and of men:—
"Thou comest to Olympus, though in grief,
O goddess Thetis, and I know the cause
That makes thee sad and will not from thy thoughts;
Yet let me now declare why I have called
Thee hither. For nine days the immortal gods
Have been at strife concerning Hector's corse
And Peleus' son, the spoiler. They have asked
The vigilant Argus-queller to remove
The dead by stealth. But I must yet bestow
Fresh honor on Achilles, and thus keep
Thy love and reverence. Now descend at once
Into the camp and carry to thy son
My message: say that it offends the gods,
And me the most, that in his spite he keeps
The corse of Hector at the beakèd ships,
Refusing to restore it. He perchance
Will listen, and, revering me, give back
The slain. And I will send a messenger,
Iris, to large-souled Priam, bidding him
Hasten in person to the Grecian fleet,
To ransom his beloved son, and bring
Achilles gifts that shall appease his rage."
He spake: the goddess of the silver feet,

Thetis, obeyed, and with precipitate flight
Descended from the mountain-peaks. She came
To her son's tent, and found him uttering moans
Continually, while his beloved friends
Were busy round him; they prepared a feast,
And had just slain within the tent a ewe
Of ample size and fleece. She took her seat
Beside her son, and smoothed his brow, and said:—
"How long, my son, wilt thou lament and grieve
And pine at heart, abstaining from the feast
And from thy couch? Yet well it is to seek
A woman's love. Thy life will not be spared
Long time to me, for death and cruel fate
Stand near thee. Listen to me; I am come
A messenger from Jove, who bids me say
The immortals are offended, and himself
The most, that thou shouldst in thy spite detain
The corse of Hector at the beakèd ships,
Refusing its release. Comply thou then,
And take the ransom and restore the dead."
And thus Achilles, swift of foot, replied:
"Let him who brings the ransom come and take
The body, if it be the will of Jove."
Thus did the mother and the son confer

Among the galleys, and between them passed
Full many a wingèd word, while Saturn's son
Bade Iris go with speed to sacred Troy: —
"Fleet Iris, haste thee. Leave the Olympian seats,
And send magnanimous Priam to the fleet,
To ransom his dear son, and bear him back
To Ilium. Let him carry gifts to calm
The anger of Achilles. He should go
Alone, no Trojan with him, save a man
In years, a herald, who may guide the mules
And strong-wheeled chariot, harnessed to bear back
Him whom the great Achilles has o'erthrown;
And let him fear not death nor other harm,
For we will send a guide to lead him safe,
The Argus-queller, till he stand beside
Achilles; and when once he comes within
The warrior's tent, Achilles will not raise
His hand to slay, but will restrain the rest.
Nor mad, nor rash, nor criminal is he,
And will humanely spare a suppliant man."
He spake, and Iris, the swift messenger,
Whose feet are like the wind, went forth with speed,
And came to Priam's palace, where she found
Sorrow and wailing. Round the father sat

His sons within the hall, and steeped with tears
Their garments. In the midst the aged man
Sat with a cloak wrapped round him, and much dust
Strewn on his head and neck, which, when he rolled
Upon the earth, he gathered with his hands.
His daughters and the consorts of his sons
Filled with their cries the mansion, sorrowing
For those, the many and brave, who now lay slain
By Grecian hands. The ambassadress of Jove
Stood beside Priam, and in soft, low tones,
While his limbs shook with fear, addressed him thus:—
"Be comforted, and have no fear; for I
Am come, Dardanian Priam, not to bring
Mischief, but blessing. I am sent to thee
A messenger from Jove, who, though afar,
Pities thee and will aid thee. He who rules
Olympus bids thee ransom thy slain son,
The noble Hector, carrying gifts to calm
The anger of Achilles. Thou shouldst go
Alone, no Trojan with thee, save a man
In years, a herald, who shall guide the mules
And strong-wheeled chariot, harnessed to bring back
Him whom the great Achilles has o'erthrown.
And have no fear of death or other harm;

A guide shall go with thee to lead thee safe,
The Argus-queller, till thou stand beside
Achilles, and when once thou art within
The warrior's tent, Achilles will not raise
His hand to slay, but will restrain the rest.
He is not mad, nor rash, nor prone to crime,
And will humanely spare a suppliant man."
  Thus the swift-footed Iris spake, and then
Departed. Priam bade his sons prepare
The strong-wheeled chariot, drawn by mules, and bind
A coffer on it. He descended next
Into a fragrant chamber, cedar-lined,
High-roofed, and stored with many things of price,
And calling Hecuba, his wife, he said:—
  "Dear wife, a message from Olympian Jove
Commands that I betake me to the fleet,
And thence redeem my slaughtered son with gifts
That may appease Achilles. Tell me now
How this may seem to thee? for I am moved
By a strong impulse to approach the ships,
And venture into the great Grecian camp."
  He spake: his consort wept, and answered thus:
"Ah me! the prudence which was once so praised
By strangers and by those who own thy sway,

Where is it now? Why wouldst thou go alone
To the Greek fleet, to meet the eye of him
Who slew so many of thy gallant sons?
An iron heart is thine. If that false man,
Remorseless as he is, should see thee there
And seize thee, neither pity nor respect
Hast thou to hope from him. Let us lament
Our Hector in these halls. A cruel fate
Spun, when I brought him forth, his thread of life,—
That far from us his corse should feed the hounds
Near that fierce man, whose liver I could tear
From out his bosom. Then the indignities
Done to my son would be repaid, for he
Was slain, not shunning combat, coward-like,
But fighting to defend the men of Troy
And the deep-bosomed Trojan dames. He fell
Without a thought of flight or of retreat."

And thus the aged, godlike king rejoined:
"Keep me not back from going, nor be thou
A bird of evil omen in these halls,
For thou shalt not persuade me. This I say:
If any of the dwellers of the earth,
Soothsayer, seer, or priest, had said to me
What I have heard, I well might deem the words

A lie, and heed them not. But since I heard
Myself the mandate from a deity,
And saw her face to face, I certainly
Will go, nor shall the message be in vain.
And should it be my fate to perish there
Beside the galleys of the mail-clad Greeks,
So be it; for Achilles will forthwith
Put me to death embracing my poor son,
And satisfying my desire to weep."
He spake, and, raising the fair coffer-lids,
Took out twelve robes of state most beautiful,
Twelve single cloaks, as many tapestried mats,
And tunics next and mantles twelve of each,
And ten whole talents of pure gold, which first
He weighed. Two burnished tripods from his store
He added, and four goblets and a cup
Of eminent beauty, which the men of Thrace
Gave him when, as an envoy to their coast,
He came from Troy,—a sumptuous gift, and yet
The aged king reserved not even this
To deck his palace, such was his desire
To ransom his dear son. And then he drave
Away the Trojans hovering round his porch,
Rebuking them with sharp and bitter words:—

"Hence with you, worthless wretches! have ye not
Sorrow enough at home, that ye are come
To vex me thus? Or doth it seem to you
Of little moment, that Saturnian Jove
Hath sent such grief upon me in the loss
Of my most valiant son? Ye yet will know
How great that loss has been; for it will be
A lighter task for the beleaguering Greeks
To work our ruin, now that he is dead.
But I shall sink to Hades ere mine eyes
Behold the city sacked and made a spoil."
He spake, and with his staff he chased away
The loiterers; forth before the aged man
They went. With like harsh words he chid his sons.
Helenus, Paris, noble Agathon,
Pammon, Antiphonus, Deiphobus,
Polites, great in war, Hippothoüs,
And gallant Dios, nine in all he called,
And thus bespake them with reproachful words:—
"Make haste, ye idle fellows, my disgrace!
Would ye had all been slain beside the fleet
Instead of Hector! Woe is me! the most
Unhappy of mankind am I, who had
The bravest sons in all the town of Troy,

And none of them, I think, are left to me.
Mestor, divine in presence, Troïlus,
The gallant knight, and Hector, he who looked
A god among his countrymen,—no son
Of man he seemed, but of immortal birth,—
Those Mars has slain, but these who are my shame
Remain,—these liars, dancers, excellent
In choirs, whose trade is public robbery
Of lambs and kids. Why haste ye not to get
My chariot ready, and bestow these things
Within it, that my journey may begin?"
He spake, and they, in fear of his rebuke,
Lifted from out its place the strong-wheeled car,
Framed to be drawn by mules, and beautiful,
And newly built, and on it they made fast
The coffer. From its pin they next took down
The boxwood mule-yoke, fitted well with rings,
And carved with a smooth boss. With this they brought
A yoke-band nine ells long, which carefully
Adjusting to the polished pole's far end,
They cast the ring upon the bolt, and thrice
Wound the long band on each side of the bolt
Around the yoke, and made it fast, and turned
The loose ends under. Then they carried forth

The treasures that should ransom Hector's corse;
And having piled them in the polished car,
They yoked the hardy, strong-hoofed mules which once
The Mysians gave to Priam, princely gifts.
To bear the yoke of Priam they led forth
The horses which the aged man himself
Fed at the polished manger. These the king
Yoked, aided by the herald, while in mind,
Within the palace court, they both revolved
Their prudent counsels. Hecuba, the queen,
Came to them in deep sorrow. In her hand
She bore a golden cup of delicate wine,
That they might make libations and depart.
She stood before the steeds, and thus she spake:—
"Take this, and pour to Father Jove, and pray
That thou mayst safely leave the enemy's camp
For home, since 't is thy will, though I dissuade,
To go among the ships. Implore thou then
The god of Ida and the gatherer
Of the black tempest, Saturn's son, who looks
Down on all Troy, to send his messenger,
His swift and favorite bird, of matchless strength,
On thy right hand, that, with thine eye on him,
Thou mayst with courage journey to the ships

Of the Greek horsemen. But if Jupiter
All-seeing should withhold his messenger,
I cannot bid thee, eager as thou art,
Adventure near the galleys of the Greeks."
  And thus the godlike Priam made reply:
"Dear wife, indeed, I will not disobey
Thy counsel; meet it is to raise our hands
To Jove, and ask him to be merciful."
  He spake, and bade the attendant handmaid pour
Pure water on his hands, for near him stood
A maid who came and held a basin forth
And ewer. When his hands were washed, he took
The goblet from the queen, and then, in prayer,
Stood in the middle of the court, and poured
The wine, and, looking heavenward, spake aloud:—
  "O Father Jove, most glorious and most great,
Who rulest all from Ida, let me find
Favor and pity with Achilles. Send
A messenger, thy own swift, favorite bird,
Of matchless strength, on my right hand, that I,
Beholding him, may confidently pass
To where the fleet of the Greek horsemen lies!"
  Thus in his prayer he spake, and Jupiter,
The All-disposer, hearkened, and sent forth

An eagle, bird of surest augury,
Named the Black Chaser, and by others called
Percnos, with wings as broad as is the door
Skilfully fashioned for the lofty hall
Of some rich man, and fastened with a bolt.
Such ample wings he spread on either side
As townward on the right they saw him fly.
They saw and they rejoiced; their hearts grew light
Within their bosoms. Then the aged king
Hastened to mount the polished car, and drave
Through vestibule and echoing porch. The mules,
Harnessed to draw the four-wheeled car, went first,
Driven by the sage Idæus; after them,
The horses, urged by Priam with the lash
Rapidly through the city. All his friends
Followed lamenting, as for one who went
To meet his death. And now when they had reached
The plain descending from the town, the sons
And sons-in-law of Priam all returned
To Ilium, and the twain proceeded on,
Yet not unmarked by all-beholding Jove,
Who, moved with pity for the aged man,
Turned to his well-beloved son and said:—

"Hermes, who more than any other god

Delightest to consort with human-kind,
And willingly dost listen to their prayers,
Haste, guide King Priam to the Grecian fleet,
Yet so that none may see him, and no Greek
Know of his coming, till he stand before
Pelides." Thus he spake: the messenger
Who slew the Argus hearkened and obeyed;
And hastily beneath his feet he bound
The fair, ambrosial, golden sandals worn
To bear him over ocean like the wind,
And o'er the boundless land. His wand he took
Wherewith he seals in sleep the eyes of men,
And opens them at will. With this in hand,
The mighty Argus-queller flew, and soon
Was at the Troad and the Hellespont.
Like to some royal stripling seemed the god,
In youth's first prime, when youth has most of grace.
And there the Trojans twain, when they had passed
The tomb of Ilus, halted with their mules
And horses, that the beasts might drink the stream;
For twilight now was creeping o'er the earth.
The herald looked, and saw that Mercury
Was near, and thus, addressing Priam, said:—
"Be on thy guard, O son of Dardanus,

For here is cause for wariness. I see
A warrior, and I think he seeks our lives.
Now let us urge our steeds and fly, or else
Descend and clasp his knees, and sue for grace."
He spake, and greatly was the aged king
Bewildered by his words; with hair erect
He stood, and motionless, while Mercury
Drew near, and took the old man's hand, and asked:—
"Whither, O father, guidest thou thy mules
And steeds in the dim night, while others sleep?
Fearest thou nothing from the warlike Greeks,
Thy foes, who hate thee, and are near at hand?
Should one of them behold thee bearing off
These treasures in the swiftly darkening night,
What wouldst thou do? Thou art not young, and he
Who comes with thee is old; ye could not make
Defence against the foe. Fear nought from me,
And I will save thee, since thou art so like
To my own father, from all other harm."
Priam, the godlike ancient, answered thus:
"Thou sayest true, dear son; but sure some god
Holds over me his kind, protecting hand,
Who sends a guide like thee to join me here,
So noble art thou both in form and air,

And gracious are thy thoughts, and blessed they
Who gave thee birth." With that the messenger,
The Argus-queller, spake again, and said:
"Most wisely hast thou spoken, aged man.
But tell, and truly, why thou bearest hence
This store of treasures among stranger men?
Is it that they may be preserved for thee?
Or are ye all deserting in alarm
Your hallowed Troy? for such a man of might
Was thy brave son who died, that I may say
The Greeks in battle had no braver man."
  And Priam, godlike ancient, spake in turn:
"Who then art thou, and of what parents born,
Excellent youth, who dost in such kind words
Speak of the death of my unhappy son?"
  The herald, Argus-queller, answered him:
"I see that thou wouldst prove me, aged man,
By questions touching Hector, whom I oft
Have seen with mine own eyes in glorious fight,
Putting the Greeks to rout and slaying them
By their swift ships with that sharp spear of his.
We stood and marvelled, for Achilles, wroth
With Agamemnon, would not suffer us
To join the combat. I attend on him;

The same good galley brought us to this shore,
And I am one among his Myrmidons.
Polyctor is my father, who is rich,
And now as old as thou. Six are his sons
Beside me, I the seventh. In casting lots
With them, it fell to me that I should come
To Ilium with Achilles. I am here
In coming from the fleet, for with the dawn
The dark-eyed Greeks are planning to renew
The war around the city. They have grown
Impatient of long idleness; their chiefs
Seek vainly to restrain their warlike rage."
  Then spake the godlike ancient, Priam, thus:
"If thou indeed dost serve Pelides, tell,
And truly tell me, whether yet my son
Is at the fleet, or has Achilles cast,
Torn limb from limb, his body to the hounds?"
  The herald, Argus-queller, thus replied:
"O aged monarch, neither have the hounds
Devoured thy son, nor yet the birds of prey;
But near the galleys of Achilles still
He lies neglected and among the tents.
Twelve mornings have beheld him lying there,
Nor hath corruption touched him, nor the worms

That make the slain their feast begun to feed.
'T is true that, when the holy morning dawns
Achilles drags him fiercely round the tomb
Of his dear friend; yet that disfigures not
The dead. Shouldst thou approach him, thou wouldst see
With marvelling eyes how fresh and dewy still
The body lies, the blood all cleansed away,
Unsoiled in every part, and all the wounds
Closed up wherever made; for many a spear
Was thrust into his sides. Thus tenderly
The blessed gods regard thy son, though dead,
For dearly was he loved by them in life."
He spake; the aged man was comforted,
And said: "'T is meet, O son, that we should pay
Oblations to the immortals; for my son
While yet alive neglected not within
His palace the due worship of the gods
Who dwell upon Olympus; therefore they
Are mindful of him, even after death.
Take this magnificent goblet; be my guard,
And guide me, by the favor of the gods,
Until I reach Pelides in his tent."
Again the herald, Argus-queller, spake:
"Thou seekest yet to try me, aged man,

Who younger am than thou. Yet think thou not
That I, without the knowledge of my chief,
Will take thy gifts; for in my heart I fear
Achilles, nor would wrong him in the least,
Lest evil come upon me. Yet I go
Willingly with thee, as thy faithful guide.
Were it as far as Argos the renowned,
In a swift galley, or on foot by land,
Yet none would dare to harm thee while with me."

So Hermes spake, and leaped into the car,
And took into his hands the lash and reins,
And breathed into the horses and the mules
Fresh vigor. Coming to the wall and trench
About the ships, they found the guard engaged
With their night-meal. The herald Argicide
Poured sleep upon them all, and quickly flung
The gates apart, and pushed aside the bars,
And led in Priam, with the costly gifts
Heaped on the car. They went until they reached
The lofty tent in which Achilles sat,
Reared by the Myrmidons to lodge their king,
With timbers of hewn fir, and over-roofed
With thatch, for which the meadows had been mown,
And fenced for safety round with rows of stakes.

One fir-tree bar made fast its gate, which three
Strong Greeks were wont to raise aloft, and three
Were needed to take down the massive beam.
Achilles wielded the vast weight alone;
Beneficent Hermes opened it before
The aged man, and brought the treasures in,
Designed for swift Achilles. Then he left
The car and stood upon the ground, and said:—
"O aged monarch, I am Mercury,
An ever-living god; my father, Jove,
Bade me attend thy journey. I shall now
Return, nor must Achilles look on me;
It is not meet that an immortal god
Should openly befriend a mortal man.
Enter, approach Pelides, clasp his knees;
Entreat him by his father, and his son,
And fair-haired mother; so shall he be moved."
Thus having spoken, Hermes took his way
Back to the Olympian summit. Priam then
Sprang from the chariot to the ground. He left
Idæus there to guard the steeds and mules,
And, hastening to the tent where, dear to Jove,
Achilles lodged, he found the chief within,
While his companions sat apart, save two,—

Automedon the brave, and Alcimus,
Who claimed descent from Mars. These stood near by,
And ministered to Peleus' son, who then
Was closing a repast, and had just left
The food and wine, and still the table stood.
Unmarked the royal Priam entered in,
And, coming to Achilles, clasped his knees,
And kissed those fearful slaughter-dealing hands,
By which so many of his sons had died.
And as, when some blood-guilty man, whose hand
In his own land has slain a fellow-man,
Flees to another country, and the abode
Of some great chieftain, all men look on him
Astonished,—so, when godlike Priam first
Was seen, Achilles was amazed, and all
Looked on each other, wondering at the sight.
And thus King Priam supplicating spake:—
"Think of thy father, an old man like me,
Godlike Achilles! On the dreary verge
Of closing life he stands, and even now
Haply is fiercely pressed by those who dwell
Around him, and has none to shield his age
From war and its disasters. Yet his heart
Rejoices when he hears thou yet dost live,

And every day he hopes that his dear son
Will come again from Troy. My lot is hard,
For I was father of the bravest sons
In all wide Troy, and none are left me now.
Fifty were with me when the men of Greece
Arrived upon our coast; nineteen of these
Owned the same mother, and the rest were born
Within my palaces. Remorseless Mars
Already had laid lifeless most of these,
And Hector, whom I cherished most, whose arm
Defended both our city and ourselves,
Him didst thou lately slay while combating
For his dear country. For his sake I come
To the Greek fleet, and to redeem his corse
I bring uncounted ransom. O, revere
The gods, Achilles, and be merciful,
Calling to mind thy father! happier he
Than I; for I have borne what no man else
That dwells on earth could bear,—have laid my lips
Upon the hand of him who slew my son."

He spake: Achilles sorrowfully thought
Of his own father. By the hand he took
The suppliant, and with gentle force removed
The old man from him. Both in memory

Of those they loved were weeping. The old king,
With many tears, and rolling in the dust
Before Achilles, mourned his gallant son.
Achilles sorrowed for his father's sake,
And then bewailed Patroclus, and the sound
Of lamentation filled the tent. At last
Achilles, when he felt his heart relieved
By tears, and that strong grief had spent its force,
Sprang from his seat; then lifting by the hand
The aged man, and pitying his white head
And his white chin, he spake these wingèd words:—

"Great have thy sufferings been, unhappy king!
How couldst thou venture to approach alone
The Grecian fleet, and show thyself to him
Who slew so many of thy valiant sons?
An iron heart is thine. But seat thyself,
And let us, though afflicted grievously,
Allow our woes to sleep awhile, for grief
Indulged can bring no good. The gods ordain
The lot of man to suffer, while themselves
Are free from care. Beside Jove's threshold stand
Two casks of gifts for man. One cask contains
The evil, one the good, and he to whom
The Thunderer gives them mingled sometimes falls

Into misfortune, and is sometimes crowned
With blessings. But the man to whom he gives
The evil only stands a mark exposed
To wrong, and, chased by grim calamity,
Wanders the teeming earth, alike unloved
By gods and men. So did the gods bestow
Munificent gifts on Peleus from his birth,
For eminent was he among mankind
For wealth and plenty; o'er the Myrmidons
He ruled, and, though a mortal, he was given
A goddess for a wife. Yet did the gods
Add evil to the good, for not to him
Was born a family of kingly sons
Within his house, successors to his reign.
One short-lived son is his, nor am I there
To cherish him in his old age; but here
Do I remain, far from my native land,
In Troy, and causing grief to thee and thine.
Of thee too, aged king, they speak, as one
Whose wealth was large in former days, when all
That Lesbos, seat of Macar, owns was thine,
And all in Phrygia and the shores that bound
The Hellespont; men said thou didst excel
All others in thy riches and thy sons.

But since the gods have brought this strife on thee,
War and perpetual slaughter of brave men
Are round thy city. Yet be firm of heart,
Nor grieve forever. Sorrow for thy son
Will profit nought; it cannot bring the dead
To life again, and while thou dost afflict
Thyself for him fresh woes may fall on thee."
  And thus the godlike Priam, aged king,
Made answer: "Bid me not be seated here,
Nursling of Jove, while Hector lies among
Thy tents unburied. Let me ransom him
At once, that I may look on him once more
With my own eyes. Receive the many gifts
We bring thee, and mayst thou possess them long,
And reach thy native shore, since by thy grace
I live and yet behold the light of day."
  Achilles heard, and, frowning, thus rejoined:
"Anger me not, old man; 't was in my thought
To let thee ransom Hector. To my tent
The mother came who bore me, sent from Jove,
The daughter of the Ancient of the Sea,
And I perceive, nor can it be concealed,
O Priam, that some god hath guided thee
To our swift galleys; for no mortal man,

Though in his prime of youthful strength, would dare
To come into the camp; he could not pass
The guard, nor move the beams that bar our gates.
So then remind me of my griefs no more,
Lest, suppliant as thou art, I leave thee not
Unharmed, and thus transgress the laws of Jove."
He spake: the aged man in fear obeyed.
And then Pelides like a lion leaped
Forth from the door, yet not alone he went;
For of his comrades two — Automedon,
The hero, and his comrade Alcimus,
He whom Achilles held in most esteem
After the slain Patroclus — followed him.
The mules and horses they unyoked, and led
The aged monarch's clear-voiced herald in,
And bade him sit. Then from the polished car
They took the costly ransom of the corse
Of Hector, save two cloaks, which back they laid
With a fair tunic, that their chief might give
The body shrouded to be borne to Troy.
And then he called the maidens, bidding them
Wash and anoint the dead, yet far apart
From Priam, lest, with looking on his son,
The grief within his heart might rise uncurbed

To anger, and Achilles in his rage
Might stay him and transgress the laws of Jove.
And when the handmaids finished, having washed
The body and anointed it with oil,
And wrapped a sumptuous cloak and tunic round
The limbs, Achilles lifted it himself
And placed it on a bier. His comrades gave
Their aid, and raised it to the polished car.
When all was done, Achilles groaned, and called
By name the friend he dearly loved, and said:—
"O my Patroclus, be not wroth with me
Shouldst thou in Hades hear that I restore
Hector to his dear father, since I take
A ransom not unworthy; but of this
I yield to thee the portion justly thine."
So spake the godlike warrior, and withdrew
Into his tent, and took the princely seat
From which he had arisen, opposite
To that of Priam, whom he thus bespake:—
"Behold thy son is ransomed, aged man,
As thou hast asked, and lies upon his bier.
Thou shalt behold him with the early dawn,
And bear him hence. Now let us break our fast,
For even Niobe, the golden-haired,

Refrained not from her food, though children twelve
Perished within her palace,—six young sons
And six fair daughters. Phœbus slew the sons
With arrows from his silver bow, incensed
At Niobe, while Dian, archer-queen,
Struck down the daughters; for the mother dared
To make herself the peer of rosy-cheeked
Latona, who, she boastfully proclaimed,
Had borne two children only, while herself
Had brought forth many. Yet, though only two,
The children of Latona took the lives
Of all her own. Nine days the corses lay
In blood, and there was none to bury them,
For Jove had changed the dwellers of the place
To stone; but on the tenth the gods of heaven
Gave burial to the dead. Yet Niobe,
Though spent with weeping long, did not refrain
From food. And now forever mid the rocks
And desert hills of Sipylus, where lie,
Fame says, the couches of the goddess-nymphs,
Who lead the dance where Acheloüs flows,
Although she be transformed to stone, she broods
Over the woes inflicted by the gods.
But now, O noble Ancient, let us sit

At our repast, and thou mayst afterward
Mourn thy beloved son, while bearing him
Homeward, to be bewailed with many tears."
  Achilles, the swift-footed, spake, and left
His seat, and, slaying a white sheep, he bade
His comrades flay and dress it. Then they carved
The flesh in portions which they fixed on spits,
And roasted carefully, and drew them back.
And then Automedon distributed
The bread in shapely canisters around
The table, while Achilles served the flesh,
And all put forth their hands and shared the feast.
But when their thirst and hunger were appeased,
Dardanian Priam fixed a wondering look
Upon Achilles, who in nobleness
Of form was like the gods. Achilles fixed
A look of equal wonder on his guest,
Dardanian Priam, for he much admired
His gracious aspect and his pleasant speech.
And when at length they both withdrew their gaze,
Priam, the godlike Ancient, spake, and said:—
  "Nursling of Jove, dismiss me speedily
To rest, that we may lie, and be refreshed
With gentle slumbers. Never have these eyes

Been closed beneath their lids, since by thy hand
My Hector lost his life; and evermore
I mourn and cherish all my griefs, and writhe
Upon the ground within my palace courts;
But I have taken food at last, and drunk
Draughts of red wine, untasted till this hour."

Achilles bade the attending men and maids
Place couches in the porch, and over them
Draw sumptuous purple mats on which to lay
Embroidered tapestries, and on each of these
Spread a broad, fleecy mantle, covering all.
Forth went the train with torches in their hands,
And quickly spread two couches. Then the swift
Achilles pleasantly to Priam said:—

"Sleep, excellent old man, without the tent,
Lest some one of our counsellors arrive,
Such as oft come within my tent to sit
And talk of warlike matters. Seeing thee
In the dark hours of night, he might relate
The tale to Agamemnon, king of men,
And hinder thus the ransom of thy son.
But say, and truly say, how many days
Requirest thou to pay the funeral rites
To noble Hector, so that I may rest
As many, and restrain the troops from war."

Then answered godlike Priam, aged king:
"Since, then, thou wilt, Achilles, that we pay
The rites of burial to my noble son,
I own the favor. Well thou knowest how
We Trojans are constrained to keep within
The city walls, for it is far to bring
Wood from the mountains, and we fear to dare
The journey. Nine days would we mourn the dead
Within our dwellings, and upon the tenth
Would bury him, and make a solemn feast,
And the next day would rear his monument,
And on the twelfth, if needful, fight again."
And swift Achilles, godlike chief, rejoined:
"Be it, O reverend Priam, as thou wilt,
And for that space will I delay the war."
He spake, and that the aged king might feel
No fear, he grasped his right hand at the wrist;
And then King Priam and the herald went
To sleep within the porch, but wary still.
Achilles slumbered in his stately tent,
The rosy-cheeked Briseis at his side,
And all the other gods and men who fought
In chariots gave themselves to slumber, save
Beneficent Hermes; sleep came not to him,

For still he meditated how to bring
King Priam back from the Achaian fleet
Unnoticed by the watchers at the gate.
So at the monarch's head he stood, and spake:—
"O aged king, thou givest little heed
To danger, sleeping thus amid thy foes,
Because Achilles spares thee. Thou hast paid
Large ransom for thy well-beloved son,
And yet the sons whom thou hast left in Troy
Would pay three times that ransom for thy life,
Should Agamemnon, son of Atreus, learn—
Or any of the Greeks—that thou art here."
He spake: the aged king in fear awaked
The herald. Hermes yoked the steeds and mules,
And drave them quickly through the camp unmarked
By any there. But when they reached the ford
Where Xanthus, progeny of Jupiter,
Rolls the smooth eddies of his stream, the god
Departed for the Olympian height, and Morn
In saffron robes o'erspread the Earth with light.
Townward they urged the steeds, and as they went
Sorrowed and wailed: the mules conveyed the dead,
And they were seen by none of all the men
And graceful dames of Troy save one alone.

Cassandra, beautiful as Venus, stood
On Pergamus, and from its height discerned
Her father, standing on the chariot-seat,
And knew the herald, him whose voice so oft
Summoned the citizens, and knew the dead
Stretched on a litter drawn by mules. She raised
Her voice, and called to all the city thus:—
"O Trojan men and women, hasten forth
To look on Hector, if ye e'er rejoiced
To see him coming from the field alive,
The pride of Troy, and all who dwell in her."
She spake, and suddenly was neither man
Nor woman left within the city bounds.
Deep grief was on them all; they went to meet,
Near to the gates, the monarch bringing home
The dead. And first the wife whom Hector loved
Rushed with his reverend mother to the car
As it rolled on, and, plucking out their hair,
Touched with their hands the forehead of the dead,
While round it pressed the multitude, and wept,
And would have wept before the gates all day,
Even to the set of sun, in bitter grief
For Hector's loss, had not the aged man
Addressed the people from his chariot-seat:

"Give place to me, and let the mules pass on,
And ye may weep your fill when once the dead
Is laid within the palace." As he spake,
The throng gave way and let the chariot pass;
And having brought it to the royal halls,
On a fair couch they laid the corse, and placed
Singers beside it, leaders of the dirge,
Who sang a sorrowful, lamenting strain,
And all the women answered it with sobs.
White-armed Andromache in both her hands
Took warlike Hector's head, and over it
Began the lamentation midst them all: —
"Thou hast died young, my husband, leaving me
In this thy home a widow, and one son,
An infant yet. To an unhappy pair
He owes his birth, and never will, I fear,
Bloom into youth; for ere that day will Troy
Be overthrown, since thou, its chief defence,
Art dead, the guardian of its walls and all
Its noble matrons and its speechless babes,
Yet to be carried captive far away,
And I among them, in the hollow barks;
And thou, my son, wilt either go with me,
Where thou shalt toil at menial tasks for some

Pitiless master; or perhaps some Greek
Will seize thy little arm, and in his rage
Will hurl thee from a tower and dash thee dead,
Remembering how thy father, Hector, slew
His brother, son, or father; for the hand
Of Hector forced full many a Greek to bite
The dust of earth. Not slow to smite was he
In the fierce conflict; therefore all who dwell
Within the city sorrow for his fall.
Thou bringest an unutterable grief,
O Hector, on thy parents, and on me
The sharpest sorrows. Thou didst not stretch forth
Thy hands to me, in dying, from thy couch,
Nor speak a word to comfort me, which I
Might ever think of night and day with tears."
  So spake the weeping wife: the women all
Mingled their wail with hers, and Hecuba
Took up the passionate lamentation next:—
  "O Hector, thou who wert most fondly loved
Of all my sons! While yet thou wert alive,
Dear wert thou to the gods, who even now,
When death has overtaken thee, bestow
Such care upon thee. All my other sons
Whom swift Achilles took in war he sold

At Samos, Imbrus, by the barren sea,
And Lemnos harborless. But as for thee,
When he had taken with his cruel spear
Thy life, he dragged thee round and round the tomb
Of his young friend, Patroclus, whom thy hand
Had slain, yet raised he not by this the dead;
And now thou liest in the palace here,
Fresh and besprinkled as with early dew,
Like one just slain with silent arrows aimed
By Phœbus, bearer of the silver bow."
  Weeping she spake, and woke in all who heard
Grief without measure. Helen, last of all,
Took up the lamentation, and began:—
  "O Hector, who wert dearest to my heart
Of all my husband's brothers,—for the wife
Am I of godlike Paris, him whose fleet
Brought me to Troy,—would I had sooner died!
And now the twentieth year is past since first
I came a stranger from my native shore,
Yet have I never heard from thee a word
Of anger or reproach. And when the sons
Of Priam, and his daughters, and the wives
Of Priam's sons, in all their fair array,
Taunted me grievously, or Hecuba

Herself,—for Priam ever was to me
A gracious father,—thou didst take my part
With kindly admonitions, and restrain
Their tongues with soft address and gentle words.
Therefore my heart is grieved, and I bewail
Thee and myself at once,—unhappy me!
For now I have no friend in all wide Troy,—
None to be kind to me: they hate me all."

Weeping she spake: the mighty throng again
Answered with wailing. Priam then addressed
The people: "Now bring wood, ye men of Troy,
Into the city. Let there be no fear
Of ambush from the Greeks, for when of late
I left Achilles at the dark-hulled barks,
He gave his promise to molest no more
The men of Troy till the twelfth morn shall rise."

He spake, and speedily they yoked the mules
And oxen to the wains, and came in throngs
Before the city walls. Nine days they toiled
To bring the trunks of trees, and when the tenth
Arose to light the abodes of men, they brought
The corse of valiant Hector from the town
With many tears, and laid it on the wood
High up, and flung the fire to light the pile.

Now when the early rosy-fingered Dawn
Looked forth, the people gathered round the pile
Of glorious Hector. When they all had come
Together, first they quenched the funeral fires,
Wherever they had spread, with dark-red wine,
And then his brothers and companions searched
For the white bones. In sorrow and in tears,
That streaming stained their cheeks, they gathered them,
And placed them in a golden urn. O'er this
They drew a covering of soft purple robes,
And laid it in a hollow grave, and piled
Fragments of rock above it, many and huge.
In haste they reared the tomb, with sentries set
On every side, lest all too soon the Greeks
Should come in armor to renew the war.
When now the tomb was built, the multitude
Returned, and in the halls where Priam dwelt,
Nursling of Jove, were feasted royally.
Such was the mighty Hector's burial rite.

THE END.

Cambridge: Electrotyped and Printed by Welch, Bigelow, & Co.

www.ingramcontent.com/pod-product-compliance
Lightning Source LLC
LaVergne TN
LVHW021146110826
845150LV00005B/1138

* 9 7 8 1 4 2 5 5 4 7 4 1 7 *